Language, Immigration and Naturalization

Full details of all our publications can be found on http://www.multilingual-matters.com, or by writing to Multilingual Matters, St Nicholas House, 31-34 High Street, Bristol BS1 2AW, UK.

Language, Immigration and Naturalization

Legal and Linguistic Issues

Edited by
Ariel Loring and Vaidehi Ramanathan

MULTILINGUAL MATTERS
Bristol • Buffalo • Toronto

Library of Congress Cataloging in Publication Data
A catalog record for this book is available from the Library of Congress.
Names: Loring, Ariel, editor. | Ramanathan, Vaidehi, editor.
Title: Language, Immigration and Naturalization: Legal and Linguistic issues Edited by Ariel Loring and Vaidehi Ramanathan.
Description: Bristol; Buffalo: Multilingual Matters, [2016] | Includes bibliographical references and index.
Identifiers: LCCN 2015044281| ISBN 9781783095155 (hbk : alk. paper) | ISBN 9781783095148 (pbk : alk. paper) | ISBN 9781783095162 (ebook)
Subjects: LCSH: Linguistic minorities--Education--Political aspects. |
 Language and languages--Political aspects. | Language policy. |
 Citizenship. | Nationalism.
Classification: LCC P119.315 .L35 2016 | DDC 306.44/9--dc23 LC record available at http://lccn.loc.gov/2015044281

British Library Cataloguing in Publication Data
A catalogue entry for this book is available from the British Library.

ISBN-13: 978-1-78309-515-5 (hbk)
ISBN-13: 978-1-78309-514-8 (pbk)

Multilingual Matters
UK: St Nicholas House, 31-34 High Street, Bristol BS1 2AW, UK.
USA: UTP, 2250 Military Road, Tonawanda, NY 14150, USA.
Canada: UTP, 5201 Dufferin Street, North York, Ontario M3H 5T8, Canada.

Website: www.multilingual-matters.com
Twitter: Multi_Ling_Mat
Facebook: https://www.facebook.com/multilingualmatters
Blog: www.channelviewpublications.wordpress.com

Copyright © 2016 Ariel Loring, Vaidehi Ramanathan and the authors of individual chapters.

All rights reserved. No part of this work may be reproduced in any form or by any means without permission in writing from the publisher.

Typeset by Deanta Global Publishing Services Limited.

Contents

Contributors vii
Acknowledgements xi

1 Introduction: Language, Immigration and Naturalization: Legal and Linguistic Issues 1
   Ariel Loring and Vaidehi Ramanathan

Part 1: Policies

2 The Value(s) of US Citizenship: An Analysis of the English Writing Test for Naturalization Applicants 27
   Michelle Winn Baptiste

3 The Journey to US Citizenship: Interviews with Iraqi Refugees 56
   Emily Feuerherm and Russul Roumani

Part 2: Pedagogies

4 'The ELD Classes Are … Too Much and We Need to Take Other Classes to Graduate': Arizona's Restrictive Language Policy and the Dis-Citizenship of ELs 79
   Karen E. Lillie

5 Local, Foreign and In-Between: English Teachers and Students Creating Community and Becoming Global 'Citizens' at a Chinese University 101
   Paul McPherron

6 Language and Body in Concert: A Multimodal Analysis of Teacher
   Feedback in an Adult Citizenship Classroom   121
   Olga Griswold

Part 3: Discourses

7 'You Are Part of Where You're From and a Part of Where You're
   Born': Youths' Citizenship and Identity in America   145
   Jasmina Josić

8 Reinforcing Belonging and Difference Through Neighborhood
   Gentrification Projects in Rotterdam, the Netherlands   164
   Jennifer Long

9 Ideologies and Collocations of 'Citizenship' in Media Discourse:
   A Corpus-Based Critical Discourse Analysis   184
   Ariel Loring

   Afterword   207
   Ariel Loring

   Index   210

Contributors

Michelle Winn Baptiste teaches writing and oral communication in the College Writing Programs at the University of California at Berkeley. She specializes in working with multilingual students and appreciates the diversity of cultural identities that her students bring to the classroom. After serving in the US Peace Corps in the Eastern Caribbean, she earned her masters degree in English as a Second Language from the University of Hawai'i at Manoa. She has taught in Hawai'i, Minnesota and Oklahoma, as well as on the Navajo Nation and in Japan and St. Lucia. She is passionate about social justice, photography, language and family.

Emily Feuerherm is an assistant professor of linguistics in the English Department at the University of Michigan, Flint. She holds a PhD in linguistics from the University of California, Davis. Her research integrates language education policy, curriculum design, TESOL pedagogies, discourse analysis and (dis)citizenship in English teaching and learning. She advocates for engaged scholarship and orients her research to community-based participatory action research methods. Her work has appeared in the *CATESOL Journal*, the edited volume *Language Policies and (Dis)Citizenship: Rights, Access, Pedagogies* and she co-edited the volume *Refugee Resettlement in the United States: Language, Policy, Pedagogy*.

Olga Griswold is an associate professor of linguistics at California State Polytechnic University at Pomona, where she has taught since 2007. She holds a doctorate in applied linguistics from UCLA. Her research interests include adult second language (L2) socialization, the analysis of interaction in L2 classrooms, including the roles of gesture and bodily movement, and the development of literacy skills of multilingual writers. She has published articles in *Research on Language and Social Interaction*, *TESOL Quarterly* and *Linguistics & Education*. Her current research project focuses on the academic writing and grammatical skills of Generation 1.5 college students.

Jasmina Josić, PhD is an efficacy analytics and studies manager at the Global Higher Education Line of Business at Pearson. Her research is concerned with examining the internationalization of higher education, the dynamics of educational policies in urban spaces, youth citizenship and identity, student engagement and achievement and the integration of digital resources into teaching and learning. Josić has conducted multiple research studies with youth and managed youth programs in urban US settings.

Karen E. Lillie (PhD, Applied Linguistics) is an assistant professor of TESOL at the State University of New York at Fredonia. Her specialization is in language policy and forensic linguistics. Dr Lillie's research interests specifically relate to language discrimination, immigration, rights for language minorities, dropout rates and ELs, language and the justice system and (restrictive) language policies. She is associate editor of the *Journal of Language, Identity, and Education* and is on the advisory committee for the Language Policy Research Network (LPREN). Dr Lillie was formerly the EL coordinator for the school district in which she taught 9th–12th grade ELs in Arizona.

Jennifer Long is a sessional faculty member at various post-secondary institutions across southwestern Ontario. She holds a doctorate in anthropology from Western University in London, Ontario, Canada, and has held two postdoctoral fellowships at the Western Centre for Research on Migration and Ethnic Relations in London, Ontario. Her research interests include firsthand experiences of immigrant integration and settlement services in Canada and the Netherlands. Her current research interests include newcomer employability and firsthand experiences of diversity in the workplace, across Canada. In addition to her academic work, she is an intercultural competency facilitator.

Ariel Loring holds a PhD in linguistics from the University of California, Davis. She is currently a lecturer in the Anthropology Department of California State University, Sacramento and a writing specialist at UC Davis. Her research interests encompass language policies, citizenship and immigration, language ideologies and discourse analysis. She has published work in *Critical Inquiry in Language Studies*, *Journal of Social Science Education*, the *CATESOL Journal* and two other edited volumes with Multilingual Matters.

Paul McPherron is an assistant professor of English at Hunter College of the City University of New York (CUNY), where he also coordinates the undergraduate ESL program and teaches classes on English linguistics, sociolinguistics, rhetoric, ESL and the structure of English. He is a socio/applied linguist whose research interests involve questions about English language learning in relation to identity, globalization and teaching policies, particularly in China and the United States.

Vaidehi Ramanathan is professor of applied sociolinguistics in the Department of Linguistics at the University of California, Davis. Her research interests include all aspects of language policies, literacy practices and globalization. She is also interested in issues concerning language and health. Her most recent publications include: *Language Policies and (Dis)citizenship: Rights, Access, Pedagogies* (2013) and *Bodies and Language: Health, Ailments, Disabilities* (2011), both of which are published by Multilingual Matters.

Russul Roumani was born in Baghdad, Iraq, which is where she received her AA degree in engineering and worked as a human resources manager for USAID. In 2008, she came to the US as a refugee, via Syria. She resettled in California and began volunteering to help settle other newly arrived Iraqi refugees. She is a current board member of the Mesopotamian Association (since 2010), works as a program coordinator at Opening Doors, Inc. (since 2011) and is a counselor for Arabic speakers at the Muslim American Society Social Services Foundation (since 2012).

Acknowledgements

Our heartfelt appreciation goes to the contributors of this volume for their intellectual rigor, insightful analysis and patience with the process of publication.

We are extremely grateful for the assistance and support from the staff at Multilingual Matters, especially Kim Eggleton and Sarah Williams. Thank you as well to the two anonymous reviewers who gave us such thoughtful feedback.

On behalf of all the authors, we sincerely thank the many unnamed individuals whose participation in our research guided our investigation of the everyday practices of immigration, naturalization and citizenship.

1 Introduction: Language, Immigration and Naturalization: Legal and Linguistic Issues

Ariel Loring and Vaidehi Ramanathan

Purpose of this Volume

This volume aligns the research of scholars from a wide range of specialties who focus on the cutting-edge topics of citizenship, naturalization and immigration while accentuating language. These issues are relevant and important areas of investigation due to their controversial interconnection with governmental policies, naturalization testing, news and public discourse, and pedagogical practices. In all these realms, citizenship and immigration are entrenched in issues of national identity, language status, marginalization of minority and immigrant languages, distribution of community and educational resources, gatekeeping, linguistic discrimination and assessment. The primary objective of this volume is to explore how language and ideologies of naturalization and immigration are reflected and applied in current practice. We are particularly interested in the consequences of such positionings for those seeking naturalization.

While sociopolitical dimensions of contemporary citizenship have been well researched (Extra *et al.*, 2009; Hogan-Brun *et al.*, 2009; Shohamy & McNamara, 2009), less studied are everyday practices, tensions and micro structures that empirically demonstrate how citizenship is practically negotiated (Blackledge, 2005; Joppke, 2007). Using various methodological approaches, each of the chapters raises nuanced issues regarding the complexities of immigration and citizenship for those within the citizenship infrastructure, and one doesn't need training in sociolinguistics to comprehend the extent to which language plays a role in these debates. Many of these concerns involve entry and resettlement in the US or other English-speaking countries and affect people for whom English is a second or third language. These issues often remain unarticulated or masked in the media and non-sociolinguistic circles.

In immigration policy, naturalization refers to the conferment of a legal status on foreign individuals who fulfill legislated requirements. While administrative discourse often frames this process as a symbolic demonstration of attachment and assimilation, there are various reasons why permanent residents choose to become citizens. These reasons are shaped in part by language policies and ideologies, and they not only affect the attitudes of prospective citizens, but also the attitudes of the host country's population.[1] Because these issues are never straightforward or decontextualized, this volume follows a scholarly trajectory of interpreting citizenship more holistically. By shifting away from a discussion of legal documents, this newer orientation to citizenship allows us to ask: What policies keep individuals from participating fully? Where do languages and immigrant groups fall in this framework? The scholars writing in this volume analyze naturalization and immigration concerns in ways that both look at and move beyond legal definitions of 'rights and responsibilities,' raising issues of access, participation, engagement and culture.

What characterizes this volume in particular is both its focus on the everyday legalities of naturalization (such as the process of becoming an American citizen and the language of citizenship tests and classes), as well as a broader consideration of identity and social concerns (the labeling of who is or isn't 'American,' the lived experiences of immigrants in bordered areas and the media's interpretations of this process).[2] For some authors in this volume, this demarcation of 'American' and 'non-American' is based on legal status, in which governmental policies and practices affect native-born citizens and permanent residents differently. But other authors observe that many of the issues that are typically seen as affecting immigrants (language policies, American identities and feelings of belonging) also impact native-born citizens who are seen as or see themselves as outsiders.

Not addressed in this volume is the differentiated treatment of specific populations of migrant people, for instance, undocumented immigrants and refugees. In this vein, resettlement and welfare allotments are also not pursued (but see Feuerherm and Ramanathan [2016] for a detailed discussion of refugeehood and resettlement as they relate to language issues).

The questions this volume explores are:

(1) What does the process of becoming a citizen look like?
(2) In what ways are people excluded from full participation?
(3) How does language position and frame insiders and outsiders?

In addressing these issues, the authors draw from their research in educational policies, naturalization exams and preparation, and community and public discourse.

This introductory chapter provides background information concerning the history of citizenship, scholarly debates in the field and naturalization policies around the world. It outlines key terms which citizenship researchers draw on, especially the authors in this volume. This terrain will foreground a legal discussion of citizenship.

Interpretations of *Citizenship*

The next section of this chapter is a review of evolving legal and scholarly interpretations of the word *citizenship*, punctuated by key quotes, to highlight its nuanced and multidimensional meanings:

> The nature of citizenship, like that of the state, is a question which is often disputed: there is no general agreement on a single definition. (Aristotle, as quoted in Brubaker [1992: ix])

Ancient Greece is usually considered by scholars to be the first society where citizenship was enacted. Aristotle's conception of an ideal citizenship was based on a communitarian model, where all citizens within a city state knew one another. When a state or city became too large for direct citizen participation, Aristotle believed there would be less incentive to be *good citizens*, which he defined as men who demonstrated 'temperance, that is, self-control; the avoidance of extremes; justice; courage, including patriotism; and wisdom, or prudence, including the capacity for judgment' (Heater, 2004: 19).[3] However, as this quote demonstrates, Aristotle himself acknowledged the plural meanings of the word *citizenship*.

Whereas Aristotle perceived citizens as *natural* (and man as a 'political animal'), the Ancient Romans saw citizens as *legal entities* (Heater, 2004). Being a citizen of Rome involved a legal relationship with the state, in which the law guided and protected its citizens. In return, citizens had duties, such as military service and paying taxes, and rights, such as the right to marry and trade. These rights were denied to non-citizens, who could not marry into a citizen-family and were subjected to higher taxes. Roman citizenship included a tiered system compared to Greek citizenship; there were opportunities for slaves and residents of conquered Latin cities to become 'second-class' citizens, without the right to vote or hold office (Heater, 2004).

In the feudal system of Medieval Europe, the relationship between lords and vassals was hierarchical. The vassal's loyalty and allegiance was to the lord, not to a law or nation. Thus, vassals were seen and treated as subjects who passively obeyed, not as equal citizens who participated (Heater, 2004; Jacobson, 1996). Without concepts of *domesticity* and *internationality*, migration was inconsequential (Jacobson, 1996), and during this time period a transition began from subject to citizen (Ullmann, 1967). Unlike a monarchy, the lords in the feudal system were contractually bound to fulfill certain obligations to their vassals, 'giving rise to the idea of the individual and the citizen by implying reciprocity of obligation' (Leca, 1994: 161). In the subsequent Renaissance period, people were no longer seen as subjects, but rather as citizens of a city, and later as citizens of a nation (Leca, 1994). According to Toby Miller (1993: 6), 'at a sociopolitical level, the sovereign state and the citizen of suffrage are perhaps the defining signs of modernity.'

Citizenship and nationhood became linked in the 18th century (Heater, 2004) when nation states replaced city states in Europe (Davidson, 1997). Citizenship was even extended to foreigners, as in France's Constitution of 1791. After a five-year residency requirement and if other conditions were met, French citizenship could apply to those born to foreign parents outside the kingdom, as well as to those born in France to a foreign father (Heater, 2004). Thus, the meaning of *citizenship* grew from a shared network of individuals within the same city, municipality or ethnic region, to a much larger, more abstract *imagined community* (Anderson, 1983). In an imagined community, one way to foster a sense of community is through a shared language.

Summarizing the various directions that scholars have taken in analyzing citizenship, Bloemraad *et al.* (2008) have outlined four trajectories: status, rights, participation and belonging. Research within these domains relates to the topics of national identity and borders, exclusion, multiculturalism and immigrant integration. Still highly influential (as well as critiqued) in this regard is Marshall's (1950) seminal essay 'Citizenship and social class':

> Citizenship is a status bestowed on those who are full members of a community. All who possess the status are equal with respect to the rights and duties with which the status is endowed. (Marshall, 1950: 28)

This view of citizenship reinforces citizenship as a *status* and highlights the *rights and duties* associated with citizenship. From this interpretation, not only do inhabitants have a responsibility to the nation state (duties), but the nation state has an obligation to its inhabitants (rights). Marshall is well known for dissecting three types of citizenship rights, which he describes as evolving chronologically through Britain's history (Marshall, 1950). These rights are *civil* (concerned with individual freedom, such as freedom of speech and the right to own property), *political* (referring to political participation) and *social* (encompassing economic welfare and social security).

This is the interpretation that the US federal governmental office Citizenship and Immigration Services (USCIS) seems to share. Its website includes a document entitled 'Citizenship rights and responsibilities' (2008) that divides the rights the US provides its citizens and the responsibilities of Americans into two columns (reproduced below):

Rights	Responsibilities
• Freedom to express yourself.	• Support and defend the Constitution.
• Freedom to worship as you wish.	• Stay informed of the issues affecting your community.
• Right to a prompt, fair trial by jury.	• *Participate in the democratic process.*
• *Right to vote in elections for public officials.*	• Respect and obey federal, state, and local laws.
• *Right to apply for federal employment requiring US citizenship.*	• Respect the rights, beliefs, and opinions of others.
• *Right to run for elected office.*	• Participate in your local community.
	• Freedom to pursue 'life, liberty, and the pursuit of happiness.'
	• Pay income and other taxes honestly, and on time, to federal, state, and local authorities.
	• *Serve on a jury when called upon.*
	• Defend the country if the need should arise.

While USCIS discourse separates rights from responsibilities, many of the rights and responsibilities listed apply to all American residents, not only citizens (we have italicized those that solely apply to citizens). Additionally, rights and responsibilities are conflated in the US naturalization test questions.[4]

When citizenship is officially granted to naturalized citizens during the swearing-in ceremony, the language of the USCIS field officers reinforces a view of citizenship in this same vein:

> Your Honor, we have (thirty-five) no-shows, I move that they be continued. Your Honor, the remaining (1,694) petitioners are present, each has been certified as having met the requirements for naturalization. Therefore I recommend that the petitions for naturalization be granted. I also recommend that the name changes on order be granted and each petitioner be admitted to citizenship upon taking the oath of allegiance to the United States. (USCIS Officer, Sacramento, 2012)[5]

From the choice of verbs in the above statement (*certified, met the requirements, granted, admitted*), it is clear that the meaning of citizenship in this capacity is a status that is empirically satisfied and subsequently bestowed.

Political theorists define citizenship with the same notion of rights and responsibilities as used in USCIS discourse (Marshall, 1950; Soysal, 1994) but also underscore notions of membership (Castles, 1998; Marshall, 1950; Soysal, 1994), community (Bauböck, 1994; Castles, 1998; Davidson, 2001), participation (Dahrendorf, 1994; Touraine, 1997) and shared values (Cogan & Morris, 2001). Moreover, much has been discussed about two dominant trends of citizenship theory: the liberal assimilationist and civic republican traditions. In the liberal assimilationist theory (see Kymlicka & Patten, 2003) of citizenship, individuals and the nation state participate in a reciprocal relationship of rights and responsibilities. The role of the individual is underscored, with a focus on individual rights. This is because the group (ethnic or minority) is seen as obstructing individuals' cultural and linguistic assimilation (Banks, 2008). Marshall's (1950) triad of the nation state ideals of civic, political and social rights fits into the liberal assimilationist camp. Conversely, in the civic republican tradition, duties and obligations are more crucial than rights, and the community is seen as a necessary bridge between individuals and the state (Bron, 2003; Kuisma, 2008; Yuval-Davis, 2006). This fundamentally Western conception of citizenship that presumes that 'legal' and 'illegal' immigrants can be identified and treats them differently under the law is disputed by Sadiq (2009).[6] Some scholars even believe that citizenship has become devalued, due to the large number of eligible immigrants in the United States and Europe who have permanent resident status but have not undergone naturalization (Jacobson, 1996; Schuck, 1998; but see Loring, 2013a). In this light, research has typically associated citizenship with particular political and national borders:

> Citizenship is meant to be universalistic and above cultural difference, yet it exists only in the context of a nation-state, which is based on cultural specificity – on the belief in being different from other nations. (Castles, 2000: 188)

The oxymoronic relationship between citizenship and nation state, and between cultural difference and cultural specificity, is apparent when comparing countries' national discourse of legal citizenship. The US government defines citizenship as 'shared values of freedom, liberty, and equality' (Citizenship rights and responsibilities, 2008). Similarly, the British Home Office defines a British citizen as someone who 'respect[s] the laws... traditional values of mutual tolerance, respect for equal rights and... allegiance to the state' (as cited in Orgad, 2011: 30). Becoming an Australian citizen means that 'you pledge that you share Australia's democratic beliefs and that you respect the rights and liberties of the people of Australia' (Australian Citizenship, n.d.). The citizenship study material from Citizenship and Immigration Canada professes, '[Canadian citizens] must obey Canada's laws and respect the rights and freedoms of others' (Discover Canada, 2012). While different countries endeavor to present citizenship as a set of unique values and knowledge, the above examples reveal a striking similarity in how citizenship is described. Thus, the above quote from Castles (2000) demonstrates the fundamental link between citizenship and nationhood: legal citizenship is defined as allegiance to the nation state, yet cultural citizenship transcends nationhood.

Recently, scholars have brought attention to other facets of citizenship not traditionally considered, such as gender rights, cultural rights (Castles, 2000) and spatial rights (Yuval-Davis, 2006). Significantly, scholars have argued that globalization has challenged what citizenship traditionally embodies: the role of the nation state (Kuisma, 2008), homogeneous collective identities (Bucholtz & Skapoulli, 2009), and narratives of nationhood (Glick Schiller et al., 1995). In the 21st century, the nation state has a declining influence on citizenship. Globalizing trends and transnational immigration challenge the role of the nation state when constructing one's sociopolitical identity. The concept of *global citizenship*,[7] feasible in a moral sense of the word (if not legal and political), is innovative; for everyone in the world to be equal citizens, there is no hierarchical status of citizens versus non-citizens (Heater, 2002). Naturalization laws and other such post-modern practices worldwide redefine what citizenship means.

Related to what many of the aforementioned scholars call 'full membership' (Bauböck, 2001; Bloemraad et al., 2008; Marshall, 1950) is the term *dis-citizenship*, which implies that citizenship can be just as readily denied as it can be given:

> [Dis-citizenship] raises questions of access and participation, exclusion and inclusion, rights and obligations, legitimate governance and democracy, liberty and equality, public and private, marginalization and belonging, social recognition and redistribution of sources, structure and agency, identity and personhood, and self and other. (Devlin & Pothier, 2006: 2)

Ramanathan (2013a, 2013b) draws on Devlin and Pothier's (2006) term *dis-citizenship*, originally pertaining to people with disabilities, to probe the ways language policies exclude and create *dis-citizens*. This represents a shift in focus by viewing citizenship as an ongoing and dynamic process that emphasizes what citizenship permits, namely access to fuller participation (Heller, 2013; Ramanathan, 2013a; Ricento, 2013; Wiley, 2013; Wodak, 2013). Conceptualizing citizenship in this way includes the everyday living conditions of those seeking naturalization: the languages they bring with them, their native heritages and cultures, the language policies and assimilative ideologies of the host cultures and sources of tensions within the broader community.

Naturalization Policies Around the World

As this volume is largely concerned with naturalization, we will briefly provide an overview of how different countries choose to enact it. Naturalization is one of three ways that citizenship can be bestowed on an individual; the other two are through the principles of *jus soli* (birth within a country's borders) and *jus sanguinis* (blood descent).[8] Countries choose to legislate these three practices in varying combinations and to different extents. For example, in the US and Mexico, anyone born within the country is automatically a citizen, regardless of parental citizenship status (Becerra Ramirez, 2000).[9] However, in India, Malaysia, South Africa and the United Kingdom, the principle of *jus soli* does not apply if the child is born to temporary residents or undocumented parents (Klaaren, 2000; Sadiq, 2009; Weil, 2001). In the Netherlands, *jus soli* citizenship can only be transferred if two generations of the child's ancestors attained Dutch legal residence (Naturalization, n.d.). Countries such as the US, the UK, Australia, Canada and Mexico tend to limit the extent to which citizenship can be transmitted through *jus sanguinis* when no residency ties have been established generationally (Klusmeyer, 2000; Weil, 2001). In South Africa, where *jus soli* citizenship is restricted, *jus sanguinis* citizenship can be transferred indefinitely (Klaaren, 2000). The rigor of naturalization requirements varies greatly among countries, but generally necessitate residency, country-specific knowledge, good moral character, integration and language proficiency.[10]

Beyond national borders, 27 European Union (EU) countries permit 'complementary supracitizenship' (Martiniello, 2000) rights. Those who have citizenship in one EU home country while living in another have rights such as voting in local and European elections (although not in national elections in their home country), unrestricted movement and residence, and conducting business in 1 of the 23 recognized official languages (EU Citizenship, 2012).

While the EU expands citizenship-like rights, it does not do so equally to all residents. By solely supplementing national citizenship, EU citizenship excludes permanent residents, guest workers and asylum seekers from accessing these rights (Martiniello, 2000). Thus, the rules of EU membership still exclude some residents, embodying the assumption that one has to be a 'cultural' European to receive additional rights and benefits.

In contrast to the citizenship-related issues that are raised in the EU, Japan is considering immigration reform based on its aging population[11] and the low numbers of migrants.¹² The UN reported that in order to keep Japan's working population stable, the country would need to accept 600,000 workers a year until 2050 (Morgan, 2001). The problem with increasing the foreign-born population is that Japanese immigration laws have been, and continue to be particularly restrictive. Naturalization requires five years of residency, good moral conduct (assessed through police, tax, employment and neighborhood references), financial independence and renunciation of prior nationalities.¹³ It is seen as exclusive because alternative paths to citizenship are lacking (Kashiwazaki, 2000). Unlike the US, Japan does not have a provision to accept immigrants who aspire to permanent resident status (Morgan, 2001).

China, one of the geographic locations in which data are collected for this volume (McPherron), generally follows the *jus sanguinis* principle for birthright citizenship, but for naturalization no comprehensive statutes exist (Law Library of Congress, 2014). Thus, citizenship by naturalization is less common. Requirements stipulate that applicants must have a near relative who is a Chinese national, live in China or have 'other legitimate reasons' (Hong Kong Immigration Department, 2006) for becoming naturalized. Chinese naturalization is also possible through Hong Kong, where applicants are additionally considered based on their income, good character, knowledge of Chinese and intention to live in Hong Kong (Law Library of Congress, 2014).

In the US, naturalization requirements have expanded throughout the country's history; the first citizenship bill, the 1790 Naturalization Act, mandated that to be a citizen, one had to be free, white, have lived in the US for at least two years, be of good character and take an oath to support the Constitution. In 1917, Congress added a literacy test requirement (Orgad, 2011), but this requirement could be satisfied in any language of the applicant's choosing. It wasn't until 1952, with the passage of the Immigration and Nationality Act (INA), that an ability to speak, read and write *in English* became a component of naturalization, along with a knowledge of US history, government and principles. Importantly, this requirement exists despite the fact that neither English, nor any language, is the official language of the country. Such language tests elevate one language at the expense of others, standardize and promote language correctness, and devalue language diversity (Shohamy, 2006). This is why Shohamy (2001) and McNamara (2000) have called for a critical testing approach that acknowledges that language tests are never neutral, and that their principles, practices and consequences must be considered in light of larger social, educational, political and ideological arenas.

From 2001 to 2007, efforts were made by USCIS to revise the naturalization test, in particular to make it more *fair* to applicants by standardizing its protocol and scoring and more *meaningful* by not testing for memorization, while maintaining the same passage rate (84% on the first attempt) (Kunnan, 2009b). The 'revised' test that applicants see today consists of four parts: speaking, writing and reading in English, and history/civics. The history/civics requirement is met by answering 6 of 10 questions correctly from a pre-published list of 100 questions and their answers. For the reading and writing portions of the test, applicants are given three attempts to both read and write a correct sentence that is given to them.[14] The government provides a vocabulary list for both these sections, which totals 93 terms. To pass the English-speaking requirement, applicants are asked questions from their submitted N-400 naturalization application pertaining to their employment and marital history. The naturalization process culminates with a swearing-in ceremony, in which applicants recite an oath of allegiance in English (see Byrne, 2014).

However, besides standardization, the revised citizenship test of 2008 did not change the content or structure of the test (Kunnan, 2009a, 2009b; Orgad, 2011). Thus, Kunnan (2009a) concludes that the current test is still meaningless and indefensible. This is due to the fact that the test does not meet validity standards as established by the language assessment community and is therefore not an accurate measure of English language ability and US historical knowledge.

Thematic Strands Through the Volume

The US naturalization test follows immigration policy stipulated by the 1952 Immigration and Nationality Act. Analyzing the section of this document regarding naturalization requirements, reproduced below, reveals several key themes that are underscored by the contributors in this volume.

> Requirements as to understanding the English language, history, principles, and form of government of the United States:
>
> (a) No person except as otherwise provided in this title shall hereafter be naturalized as a citizen of the United States upon his own application who cannot demonstrate-
> (1) an understanding of the English language, including an ability to read, write, and speak words in ordinary usage in the English language: Provided, That the requirements of this paragraph relating to ability to read and write shall be met if the applicant can read or write simple words and phrases to the end that a reasonable test of his literacy shall be made and that no extraordinary

or unreasonable conditions shall be imposed upon the applicant; and

(2) a knowledge and understanding of the fundamentals of the history, and of the principles and form of government, of the United States.[15]

(Immigration and Nationality Act, § 312)

Three central themes that this passage evokes are *identity* (and with it, *positionings* and *labels*), *ideologies* (independently, and also specific to *membership* and *belonging*) and *gatekeeping* (along with *access* and *exclusion*).

Identity, positioning and labels

Even within the social sciences, the term *identity* has meant different things in different theoretical paradigms. In the 1960s, the essentialist approach treated identity as fixed and immutable while structuralists saw identity as fluid and adaptable (Sicakkan & Lithman, 2005). Successively, poststructuralists theorize identity in a way that expands the notion of culture (Morgan, 2007) and emphasize that identity is multiple, dynamic and negotiated (Atkinson, 1999; Norton, 2010; Pavlenko & Blackledge, 2004). Applied linguists use the term *identity* in topics such as gender and sexuality (Bucholtz & Hall, 2004; Cameron, 1997), English language teaching (Morgan, 2007; Norton, 2010) and language ideologies (Blackledge, 2005). Key to the work in this volume is the notion that 'individuals create identities by discursively taking up, contesting, or countering the positions that discourses make available' (Kendall, 2007: 125).

The opening sentence of the above INA discourse immediately differentiates between two groups of people: legalized citizens and non-citizens: 'No person except as otherwise provided in this title shall hereafter be naturalized as a citizen of the United States.' Not only does it divide people into these mutually exclusive categories, but it also separates non-citizens into two groups: those who satisfy the requirements stated in the policy and those who do not. The chapters in this volume also demonstrate how identity is constructed through labels, particularly labels such as 'EL' (English learner) and 'non-EL' (Lillie, Chapter 4) and 'foreign' and 'local' (McPherron, Chapter 5).

Many of the authors in this volume highlight poststructuralist aspects of identity. Josić (Chapter 7) uses the phrase 'multiple civic identities' to situate her research; Long (Chapter 8), McPherron, Feuerherm and Roumani (Chapter 3) and Josić all discuss identities as 'imagined,' and the latter two also mention the discursive identity building that their participants construct as new citizens (Feuerherm & Roumani) and as community members (Josić).

Another significant trend found in many chapters is the effect of positioning on one's identity. Positioning is defined by Davies and Harré (1990: 62) as 'the way in which the discursive practices constitute the speakers and hearers in certain ways and yet at the same time is a resource through which speakers and hearers can negotiate new positions.' The consequences of positionings can be varied, including the empowering, silencing or stereotyping of an individual. Positionings can either be inflicted on others ('othering') or on oneself. Josić's interview data with immigrant youth and first-generation Americans show their own self-positionings in society, using a more nuanced distinction than is implied by their nationality. For Long, it is community members whose language choices position Muslim immigrants in a negative light. Widening the analytical lens from positioning to framing, Loring (Chapter 9) observes how national newspaper articles discursively frame citizenship issues.

Positionings are also important to analyze at the methodological level, at which point the term 'positionality' refers to the positioning between researchers and their study. Feuerherm and Roumani point out how the positionality of the researcher affects the co-construction of meaning between interviewer and interviewee. Baptiste, in Chapter 2, further demonstrates how the power and higher status of interviewers (in this case, US adjudications officers) affect the naturalization interview they administer.

Ideologies, membership and belonging

Returning to the analysis of INA section 312, the next phrase stipulates that naturalized citizens must demonstrate 'an understanding of the English language, including an ability to read, write, and speak words in ordinary usage in the English language.'[16] In equating English proficiency with the US nation state, this discourse depicts English speakers as more skilled than non-English speakers. This type of reasoning perpetuates the belief that cultural and linguistic assimilation are necessary for incoming immigrants. Moreover, when the language of the test itself is English, the test becomes a *de facto* policy enforcing English usage in a country that is not *de facto* monolingual (McNamara & Shohamy, 2008).

Due to the fact that US naturalization law includes an English language requirement, the status of English is further elevated over the status of other languages. At the same time, other lesser-known languages spoken in the US are unacknowledged, which leads to their subsequent *erasure* (Irvine & Gal, 2000). Testing English knowledge reinforces the fact that English monolingualism is normative in the US (Silverstein, 1996), while multilingualism becomes less valued. Concurrently, English language ideologies become further encased in ideals of US citizenship. In addition to the ideology that English is crucial for American success, there is a growing belief in English as a global language and in English as necessary for global citizenship (see McPherron). This can be partially attributed to dominant discourses, policy decisions and globalizing trends that treat English as the language of economic, educational and linguistic mobility (Seargeant, 2009; Song, 2010).

The material required to pass the naturalization test is indicative of US ideals and what knowledge is valued in American citizenship. Besides knowledge of English, the content required to become naturalized is described in INA section 312 as 'a knowledge and understanding of the fundamentals of the history, and of the principles and form of government, of the United States.' This manifests itself in history/civics questions that primarily focus on colonial history, how the government functions and the names of current political figures (Loring, 2013b). These dual criteria represent the ideology that belonging and participating in American society as a legalized citizen necessitates a certain type of information and a level of English proficiency.

The other chapters in the volume also call attention to nationalist ideologies and their connection to membership and belonging. Ideological phrases such as 'real Americans' (Griswold, Chapter 6), 'the American dream' (Baptiste) and 'freedom and opportunity' (Feuerherm & Roumani) tie into citizenship instruction, US naturalization test sentences and Iraqi refugee discourse (respectively) in this volume. Elsewhere, these ideologies manifest themselves in the teaching of language and history/civics content (Gordon, 2007; Griswold, 2010; Orgad, 2011), naturalization swearing-in ceremonies (Loring, 2015), bilingual education voter initiatives (Arizona Proposition 203 of 2000; California Proposition 227 of 1998) and the resulting campaign discourse (Wiley & Wright, 2004; Woolard, 1989).

Belonging and membership do not always go hand in hand. To experience a sense of belonging, in this case toward a particular territory, legal membership and geographic vicinity might not necessarily be attained (Sicakkan & Lithman, 2005), as is evidenced by transnational migrants and 'illegal' immigrants (Sadiq, 2009). And conversely, *de facto* membership in a community or nation can occur without a sensation of belonging. As Josić demonstrates in this volume, legal citizenship can help foster belonging, but can also have no bearing on it. The first-generation American youth in her study do not necessarily experience a sense of national belonging to the US, as eloquently voiced by one of her participants:

> As of right now, it is difficult for me to say, 'I'm an American,' because once you say you're an American they just categorize you with what an American is supposed to be... But I can't say it. I mean, I love America, don't take me wrong, like, I take pride in my country but,

I can't. It doesn't spur something in me, I feel like I'm entitled to it, but I can't say it.

Adding further complexity to the notion of belonging and membership is what Sadiq (2009) terms *blurred membership*, in which non-citizens ('illegal' immigrants) experience enduring ties to a host nation, even receiving rights and benefits allocated for citizens. This lived reality for many immigrants around the world reinforces the need to conceptualize citizenship as removed from the legal sphere.

As the phrases 'sense of belonging' and 'notion of belonging' imply, belonging is a subjective feeling that can be evaluated differently by insiders and outsiders. An individual, like an immigrant, may experience a sense of belonging to a new nation state, but others may encounter actions, rituals and linguistic practices that in their eyes impede this identification. Long (this volume) also looks at non-belonging as a perception engendered by observed non-participation.

Those who define citizenship in terms of participation and belonging (Ramanathan, 2013; and Feuerherm & Roumani; Lillie; McPherron, this volume) point out that full citizenship is based on full belonging. Removed from its legal dimension, if an individual feels a sense of community or national belonging and has access to participation in that space, then he or she *is* a citizen of that terrain. McPherron goes the furthest in this volume toward removing *citizenship* from legal status and using it to describe the degree of membership within a university's teaching community and the global English-speaking community.

Gatekeeping, access and exclusion

The INA policy portion analyzed here refers to naturalization applicants in the neutral terms 'person' and 'applicant,' but the use of possessive determiners is consistently masculine: 'a citizen of the United States upon *his* own application' and 'a reasonable test of *his* literacy.' This is a linguistic practice that excludes women from an immediate association with citizenship. Today, the current US naturalization test may not seem as explicitly discriminatory as it once was.[17] But throughout US history, governmental policies have been enacted to restrict certain groups of people (both foreign-born and native-born) from accessing citizenship. These included the 'good moral character' requirement, the 1790 Naturalization Act, the Dred Scott Act in 1857, the 14th Amendment in 1868, the 1882 Chinese Exclusion Act, the Gentleman's Agreement of 1907 between the US and Japan, the Expatriation Act of 1907,[18] the denial of birthright citizenship to Native Americans until 1940 and evolving literacy and language requirements. All of the above are clear instances where specific rules and regulations were created to exclude certain 'undesirable' groups from US citizenship. The same discriminatory practices have also been present around the world and throughout history, with certain groups being restricted from full citizenship: women, foreigners and slaves in Ancient Athens; conquered slaves and city people in Ancient Rome; non-European citizens in the EU; and 'unskilled' foreign workers in Japan.

Thus, we, along with other scholars (Kunnan, 2000; McNamara, 2000; Shohamy, 2001, 2006) argue that naturalization tests and the determination of a passing score are discriminatory and can serve gatekeeping functions. In the last decade, not only have citizenship and immigration testing policies around the world garnered more attention (see Shohamy & McNamara's [2009] special issue of *Language Assessment Quarterly*), but they have also become more rigorous in their language requirements. There has been a shift in the last decade toward stricter citizenship test requirements in many European countries, due to the increased number of immigrants and the perceived threat of immigration to national identity (Hogan-Brun *et al.*, 2009). Even though many European countries are officially multilingual and multicultural themselves, they still require naturalization applicants to acquire high proficiency in the country's national language.

Gatekeeping, as it relates to access, exclusion and power, is a predominant theme that arises in each chapter of this volume. Baptiste's chapter follows the previously mentioned studies in asserting that the subject matter in the US history/civics questions excludes ethnic and racial minorities, as well as women. The power differential between adjudications officers administering the high-stakes naturalization test and prospective citizens is also significant, so much so that when the officers' behavior deviates even slightly from the perceived protocol (such as repeating a question without justification), applicants fear they made a mistake in their answers (Baptiste & Seig, 2007). Baptiste (this volume) also notes that the officers' power to form medical and linguistic determinations is outside their law enforcement training; these decisions can restrict applicants from legal citizenship.

Other instances of unequal power dimensions described in this volume are between newspaper authors and the individuals they portray (Loring, this volume; also see Lambertus, 2003) and between teachers and students in Griswold's chapter. McPherron also notes that teachers are in a position to act as gatekeepers with respect to their students' English access and global citizenship. In Lillie's research, the Structured English Immersion educational policy she analyzes in Arizona schools can also be described as a gatekeeper in that it restricts the opportunities of EL students.

Outside of school settings, Feuerherm and Roumani discuss the struggles inherent in the resettlement system for refugees. They and other scholars note how policies compel refugees to accept menial jobs and hamper access to skilled jobs, resulting in a post-naturalization search for jobs abroad. It is an important point for Feuerherm and Roumani's work and Josić's study that legal paperwork both restricts and expands opportunities for naturalized and native-born citizens. As stated, Long's account of neighborhood gentrification meetings in the Netherlands highlights the theme of belonging as one way that Muslim immigrants are perceived as non-participatory. This depiction in fact arises from the exclusionary nature of these meetings' structure and valued norms: access to this space is problematic for non-Dutch speakers. This is one way in which native-born citizens and speakers of the national language are privileged, and the social structures and policies in place reinforce the discrepancy between immigrants and non-immigrants.

Organization of Volume

Collectively, the chapters in this volume are concerned with the experiences of immigrants/outsiders as they make a life in their adopted/native country. For some authors (Baptiste; Feuerherm and Roumani; Griswold; Long), their focus is on recent border-crossers, who are negotiating shifting identities and additional language hurdles in their process of becoming naturalized citizens. We would consider the issues they tackle to be manifestations of traditional and national conceptions of citizenship. For other authors (Lillie; Josić), the voices that characterize their interview and survey data are not necessarily immigrants, but first-generation native-born Americans who, despite their nationality, struggle with restrictive English language policies and feelings of non-belonging. McPherron's chapter is not concerned with citizenship in its legal sense; for his purposes, citizenship is defined solely in terms of belonging and membership in global communities that don't align with national borders. Loring, in describing how the US media utilizes the word *citizenship*, points out its multifaceted nature: both legal and peripheral interpretations of the word are used. These studies indicate the importance of using a broader and more inclusive definition of citizenship.

The chapters in this volume are organized into three strands: policies (Baptiste; Feuerherm and Roumani), pedagogies (Lillie; McPherron; Griswold) and discourses (Josić; Long; Loring). Opening with Baptiste's chapter provides the reader with an overview of naturalization policy in the US, specifically, the process that applicants undergo and revisions that have been made to the test requirements over time. From recording and observing naturalization interviews, her findings emphasize the institutional values inherent in the naturalization test questions from 1999 to 2000, and she contrasts this with the current test's values since its 2008 revisions. Baptiste concludes that prior to standardization efforts made in 2008, the adjudications officers gave applicants personalized sentences to read and write, the content of which highlighted aspects of the prototypical 'American Dream': working and studying, children and marital status, and ownership of a house or car. The current test has shifted from personalized reading and writing questions to decontextualized questions primarily concerned with history, patriotism and civic involvement.

Feuerherm and Roumani's chapter is centered on the motivations and experiences of Iraqi refugees seeking US citizenship in Northern California. They assert that refugees discursively construct American identities through expressed ideologies of freedom and opportunity. Faced with a lack of opportunities after becoming naturalized, many seek an American passport to gain access to international prospects. The authors pay close attention to the intricate subtleties of interview data, noting how meanings are co-constructed between interviewer and interviewee and advocating for an emic approach to data collection.

The next two chapters (Lillie; McPherron) are organized in the 'pedagogies' strand, but they in fact straddle the divide between policies and pedagogies. Lillie's topic is Arizona's Structured English Immersion (SEI) policy that has been enacted in K-12 schools since 2008 and requires ELs to take four hours of English classes a day, at the expense of other subjects. Her study analyzes EL students' views of this policy, noting that their own awareness of being labeled and segregated on the basis of their English proficiency (as 'EL' and 'non-EL') contributes to their sense of identity and feeling like outsiders. Lillie contextualizes this research within the English-Only movement, anti-immigration discourse, and the theory of dis-citizenship, arguing that the SEI model marginalizes EL students and limits their 'future-selves'' access to opportunities beyond high school.

Turning to a university in southern China, McPherron's research is situated within a policy of increased hiring of foreign English instructors to create a community of 'foreign' and 'local' English teacher collaboration, terms he notes are problematic in and of themselves. He looks at national and university policy documents, efforts by local English teachers to instigate a communicative teaching approach and opportunities for students to participate in the global English-speaking community. McPherron finds that ideologies that foreign teachers and/or native English speakers are the best English teachers persist, which affect the sense of belonging and involvement that these groups feel toward their greater educational community. Students are also affected by competing discourses and ideologies regarding national/linguistic Chinese citizenship and global English 'citizenship.'

Rounding out the pedagogies subsection is Griswold's chapter on multimodal teacher feedback in an adult ESL/citizenship class in Southern California. She analyzes examples of teacher responses where the linguistic, paralinguistic and gestural feedback provided is either harmonious or conflicting. She argues that such conflicting messages do not confuse the students; rather, their purpose is understood as simultaneously validating correct knowledge while suggesting that there are alternate, preferred ways to articulate this knowledge. Such feedback reinforces the type of factual knowledge students need to become naturalized American citizens while ensuring that they demonstrate this knowledge in linguistically and culturally appropriate ways.

In the third and final subsection of 'discourses' are three chapters which focus on discursive representations of citizenship and what it means to be a 'citizen.' Josić's research centers on three New York City high school students who are either first-generation American-born citizens or recent immigrants to the US. Through their discourse, they struggle with self-definition as a citizen; labels of national, racial, ethnic and linguistic identities; and navigating a sense of belonging to and membership of their nations and communities. She highlights the discrepancy between how these youth are seen by others (as 'outsiders,' regardless of their legal citizenship status) and how they view themselves, which is far more complex and contested than their seemingly transparent labels ('immigrant,' 'Black,' 'American') convey.

Long's research is situated against a backdrop of rising Islamophobic political discourse in the Netherlands in the last decade, which permeates the discourse of neighborhood members during community gentrification projects. In reference to the perceived divide between *autochtonen* (native-born Dutch residents) and *allochtonen* (Muslim immigrants), and the absence of Muslim participation in neighborhood meetings, are comments such as 'if *they're* not going to show up to these meetings, then why do *we* have to accommodate *them*?' Long analyzes this type of discourse and its underlying ideologies within the larger social and linguistic structures that unevenly affect public participation. She concludes that those who are perceived as unwilling to integrate in their new country are viewed as unequal members of the ideological Dutch community.

The concluding chapter by Loring investigates the language used to discuss citizenship in *The New York Times* in a three-month span during 2011, combining a corpus and critical discourse analytic approach. Looking at both large-scale trends and specific discursive strategies, Loring finds that when citizenship is discussed in the media, it often refers to its legal dimension and is portrayed as tangible, official and static. However, 'citizenship' can also be used to refer to desirable ethics and values, removed from the realm of immigration. These meanings are important to analyze in that they reflect shared knowledge and assumptions of national identity and belonging between the newspaper body and its general audience.

Notes

(1) We thank an anonymous reviewer for providing the basis for this observation.
(2) The majority of chapters are concerned with US citizenship. We use phrases such as 'American citizen' for convenience sake, but acknowledge that this term should be reconfigured for different countries as needed, e.g. 'who is or isn't *Dutch*' in Long (this volume).
(3) The word 'men' is used here because even at this point in history, citizenship was not universally given. In Ancient Athens, women, slaves, foreigners and the peasantry of rural Athens were excluded from citizenship (Davidson, 1997; Heater, 1990).
(4) In questions (#49) and (#50), voting is regarded as both a right and a responsibility:
(#49) What is one responsibility that is only for US citizens? [serve on a jury; vote in a federal election]
(#50) What is one right only for US citizens? [vote in a federal election; run for federal office]
(5) While this is the recorded language from one swearing-in ceremony, this is a standard address made to the judge presiding over the ceremony.
(6) We place 'illegal' and 'legal' in quotes, for while these are Sadiq's (2009) preferred terms, we acknowledge that many people find the term 'illegal immigrant' offensive and dehumanizing.
(7) See McPherron (this volume) for a further description of what global citizenship entails.
(8) Through marriage and adoption, citizenship can also be acquired. Israel also includes the 'Law of Return' for any and all Jews to immigrate and become citizens (Shachar, 2000).
(9) This has led to current debates in the US about the legal status of 'anchor babies' born to undocumented parents.
(10) The Netherlands has a particularly arduous requirement, which consists of first passing the civic integration examination with a Dutch language requirement prior to entering the Netherlands with a non-visitor visa (Orgad, 2011).
(11) In 2020, it is predicted that more than 25% of the population will be older than 65 (Morgan, 2001).
(12) In the early 1990s, only 1% of the Japanese population was composed of foreigners. In 20 years, the percentage of foreigners has increased only slightly; according to the Organization for Economic Co-operation and Development, in 2010, foreign residents comprised 1.7% of the population (Sanchanta, 2010).
(13) There is also a *de facto* language requirement: the interview is given in Japanese.
(14) See Baptiste (this volume) for a detailed account of how the reading and writing questions changed with this revision.
(15) Subsection (b) that follows describes to whom these requirements do not apply. Applicants who are over the age of 50 and have been in the US for 20 years (or are over the age of 55 and have been in the US for 15 years) are exempt from the policy stated in (a1). As enacted, this means these applicants are exempt from the English reading and writing portion of the test and can take the history/civics portion in the language of their choice by bringing an interpreter. Applicants who are over the age of 65 and have been in the US for 20 years additionally receive special consideration for the (a2) requirement. This means that the (a1) exemptions similarly apply, and in addition these applicants have a reduced set of 20 of the 100 history/civics questions from which their questions are drawn (Department of Homeland Security, 2014). Furthermore, anyone who has a 'physical or developmental disability or mental impairment' does not need to comply with these requirements (this information is collected with

the submission of the N-400 application for naturalization and requires the submission of an additional form).
(16) See Loring (2013a) for an argument that the naturalization test requires above 'ordinary' English proficiency.
(17) But see Loring (2013a) for an argument that certain groups of people are still discouraged from naturalization.
(18) From this act, women automatically acquired the nationality status of their husbands, meaning that US-born women lost their citizenship status when they married foreign men (Volpp, 2005).

References

Anderson, B. (1983) *Imagined Communities*. New York: Verso.
Arizona Proposition 203 of 2000 (2000) English language education for children in public schools. For full text of the proposed law, see http://www.azsos.gov/election/2000/info/pubpamphlet/prop1-I-2000.htm (accessed 15 January 2014).
Atkinson, D. (1999) TESOL and culture. *TESOL Quarterly* 33 (4), 625–654.
Australian citizenship: Why should I become a citizen? (n.d.) Australian Government Department of Immigration and Citizenship. See http://www.citizenship.gov.au (accessed 20 September 2011).
Banks, J. (2008) Diversity, group identity, and citizenship education in a global age. *Educational Researcher* 37 (3), 129–139.
Baptiste, M. and Seig, M. (2007) Training the guardians of America's gate: Discourse-based lessons from naturalization interviews. *Journal of Pragmatics* 39, 1919–1941.
Bauböck, R. (1994) *Transnational Citizenship: Membership and Rights in International Migration*. Brookfield, VT: Elgar.
Bauböck, R. (2001) Cultural citizenship, minority rights, and self-government. In T.A. Aleinikoff and D. Kusmeyer (eds) *Citizenship Today: Global Perspectives and Practices* (pp. 319–348). Washington, DC: Carnegie Endowment for International Peace.
Becerra Ramirez, M. (2000) Nationality in Mexico. In T.A. Aleinikoff and D. Klusmeyer (eds) *From Migrants to Citizens: Membership in a Changing World* (pp. 312–341). Washington, DC: Carnegie Endowment for International Peace.
Blackledge, A. (2005) *Discourse and Power in a Multilingual World*. Philadelphia, PA: John Benjamins.
Bloemraad, I., Korteweg, A. and Yurdakul, G. (2008) Citizenship and immigration: Multiculturalism, assimilation, and challenges to the nation-state. *Annual Review of Sociology* 34, 153–179.
Bron, A. (2003) From an immigrant to a citizen: Language as a hindrance or a key to citizenship. *International Journal of Lifelong Education* 22 (6), 606–619.
Brubaker, R. (1992) *Citizenship and Nationhood in France and Germany*. Cambridge, MA: Harvard University Press.
Bucholtz, M. and Hall, K. (2004) Theorizing identity in language and sexuality research. *Language in Society* 33, 469–515.
Bucholtz, M. and Skapoulli, E. (2009) Introduction: Youth language at the intersection: From migration to globalization. *Pragmatics* 19 (1), 1–16.
Byrne, B. (2014) *Making Citizens: Public Rituals and Personal Journeys to Citizenship*. New York: Palgrave Macmillan.
California Proposition 227 of 1998 (1998) English language in public schools. For full text of the proposed law, see http://primary98.sos.ca.gov/VoterGuide/Propositions/227text.htm (accessed 10 October 2008).
Cameron, D. (1997) Performing gender identity: Young men's talk and the construction of heterosexual masculinity. In S. Johnson and U.H. Meinhof (eds) *Language and Masculinity* (pp. 47–64). Oxford: Basil Blackwell.

Castles, S. (1998) Globalization and the ambiguities of national citizenship. In R. Bauböck and J. Rundell (eds) *Blurred Boundaries: Migration, Ethnicity, and Citizenship*. Brookfield, VT: Ashgate.

Castles, S. (2000) *Ethnicity and Globalization: From Migrant Worker to Transnational Citizen*. Thousand Oaks, CA: Sage.

Citizenship rights and responsibilities. (2008) U.S. Citizenship and Immigration Services. See http://www.uscis.gov/ (accessed 12 July 2015).

Cogan, J. and Morris, P. (2001) The development of civics values: An overview. *International Journal of Education Research* 35 (1), 1–9.

Dahrendorf, R. (1994) The changing quality of citizenship. In B. van Steenbergen (ed.) *The Condition of Citizenship* (pp. 10–19). London: Sage.

Davidson, A. (1997) *From Subject to Citizen: Australian Citizenship in the Twentieth Century*. Cambridge: Cambridge University Press.

Davidson, A. (2001) The state, democracy and citizenship in Australia. In R. Axtmann (ed.) *Balancing Democracy* (pp. 158–175). London: Continuum.

Davies, B. and Harré, R. (1990) Positioning: The discursive production of selves. *Journal for the Theory of Social Behavior* 20 (1), 43–63.

Department of Homeland Security (2014) *USCIS policy manual: Volume 12, Part E, Chapter 2*. See http://www.uscis.gov/policymanual/HTML/PolicyManual-Volume12-PartE-Chapter2.html (accessed 15 January 2014).

Devlin, R. and Pothier, D. (2006) *Critical Disability Theory*. Vancouver: UBC Press.

Discover Canada: The rights and responsibilities of citizenship (2012) Citizenship and Immigration Canada. See http://www.cic.gc.ca/ (accessed 16 August 2014).

EU Citizenship. (2012, September 3) See http://ec.europa.eu/justice/citizen/ (accessed 15 August 2014).

Extra, G., Spotti, M. and Van Avermaet, P. (2009) *Language Testing, Migration and Citizenship: Cross-National Perspectives on Integration Regimes*. New York: Continuum.

Feuerherm, E. and Ramanathan, V. (2016) *Refugee Resettlement in the United States: Language, Policy, Pedagogy*. Bristol: Multilingual Matters.

Glick Schiller, N., Basch, L. and Szanton Blanc, C. (1995) From immigrant to transmigrant: Theorizing transnational migration. *Anthropological Quarterly* 68 (1), 48–63.

Gordon, S. (2007) Integrating immigrants: Morality and loyalty in US naturalization practice. *Citizenship Studies* 11 (4), 367–382.

Griswold, O. (2010) Narrating America: Socializing adult ESL learners into idealized views of the United States during citizenship preparation classes. *TESOL Quarterly* 44 (3), 488–516.

Heater, D. (1990) *Citizenship: The Civic Ideal in World History, Politics, and Education*. New York: Longman Inc.

Heater, D. (2002) *World Citizenship: Cosmopolitan Thinking and Its Opponents*. New York: Continuum.

Heater, D. (2004) *A Brief History of Citizenship*. New York: New York University Press.

Heller, M. (2013) Language and dis-citizenship in Canada. *Journal of Language, Identity, and Education* 12 (3), 189–192.

Hogan-Brun, G., Mar-Molinero, C. and Stevenson, P. (eds) (2009) *Discourses on Language and Integration: Critical Perspectives on Language Testing Regimes in Europe*. Amsterdam: John Benjamins.

Hong Kong Immigration Department (2006) Nationality law of the People's Republic of China: A guide for overseas applicants. See http://www.immd.gov.hk/pdforms/id922ae.pdf (accessed 2 September 2014).

Immigration and Nationality Act, 8 U.S.C. § 312.

Irvine, J. and Gal, S. (2000) Language ideology and linguistic differentiation. In P. Kroskrity (ed.) *Regimes of Language: Ideologies, Polities, and Identities* (pp. 35–84). Santa Fe, NM: School of American Research Press.

Jacobson, D. (1996) *Rights Across Borders: Immigration and the Decline of Citizenship*. Baltimore, MD: The Johns Hopkins University Press.
Joppke, C. (2007) Transformation of citizenship: Status, rights, identity. *Citizenship Studies* 11 (1), 37–48.
Kashiwazaki, C. (2000) Citizenship in Japan: Legal practices and contemporary development. In T.A. Aleinikoff and D. Klusmeyer (eds) *From Migrants to Citizens: Membership in a Changing World* (pp. 434–471). Washington, DC: Carnegie Endowment for International Peace.
Kendall, S. (2007) Father as breadwinner, mother as worker: Gendered positions in feminist and traditional discourses of work and family. In D. Tannen, S. Kendall and C. Gordon (eds) *Family Talk: Discourse and Identity in Four American Families* (pp. 123–164). Oxford: Oxford University Press.
Klaaren, J. (2000) Post-apartheid citizenship in South Africa. In T.A. Aleinikoff and D. Klusmeyer (eds) *From Migrants to Citizens: Membership in a Changing World* (pp. 221–252). Washington, DC: Carnegie Endowment for International Peace.
Klusmeyer, D. (2000) Introduction. In T.A. Aleinikoff and D. Klusmeyer (eds) *From Migrants to Citizens: Membership in a Changing World* (pp. 1–21). Washington, DC: Carnegie Endowment for International Peace.
Kuisma, M. (2008) Rights or privileges? The challenge of globalization to the values of citizenship. *Citizenship Studies* 12 (6), 613–627.
Kunnan, A. (2000) Fairness and justice for all. In A. Kunnan (ed.) *Fairness and Validation in Language Assessment: Selected Papers from the 19th Language Testing Research Colloquium, Orlando, Florida* (pp. 1–14). Cambridge: University of Cambridge Local Examinations Syndicate.
Kunnan, A. (2009a) Politics and legislation in citizenship testing in the United States. *Annual Review of Applied Linguistics* 29, 37–48.
Kunnan, A. (2009b) Testing for citizenship: The U.S. naturalization test. *Language Assessment Quarterly* 6 (1), 89–97.
Kymlicka, W. and Patten, A. (2003) *Language Rights and Political Theory*. Oxford: Oxford University Press.
Lambertus, S. (2003) News discourse of Aboriginal resistance in Canada. In L. Thiesmeyer (ed.) *Discourse and Silencing* (pp. 233–272). Philadelphia, PA: John Benjamins.
Law Library of Congress (U.S.) (2014) *Citizenship Pathways and Border Protection: China*. See http://www.loc.gov/law/help/citizenship-pathways/china.php#_ftnref19 (accessed 20 August 2014).
Leca, J. (1994) Individualism and citizenship. In B. Turner and P. Hamilton (eds) *Citizenship: Critical Concepts* (pp. 148–187). London: Routledge.
Loring, A. (2013a) Language & U.S. Citizenship: Meanings, ideologies, & policies. Doctoral dissertation. ProQuest Dissertations and Theses (Accession Order No. 3596915).
Loring, A. (2013b) The meaning of 'citizenship': Tests, policy, and English proficiency. *The CATESOL Journal* 24 (1), 198–219.
Loring, A. (2015) Citizenship policy from the bottom-up: The linguistic and semiotic landscape of a naturalization field office. *Critical Inquiry in Language Studies* 12 (3), 161–183.
Marshall, T. (1950) *Citizenship and Social Class and Other Essays*. London: Pluto.
Martiniello, M. (2000) Citizenship of the European Union. In T.A. Aleinikoff and D. Klusmeyer (eds) *From Migrants to Citizens: Membership in a Changing World* (pp. 342–380). Washington, DC: Carnegie Endowment for International Peace.
McNamara, T. (2000) *Language Testing*. Oxford: Oxford University Press.

McNamara, T. and Shohamy, E. (2008) Viewpoint: Language tests and human rights. *International Journal of Applied Linguistics* 18 (1), 89–95.
Miller, T. (1993) *The Well-Tempered Self: Citizenship, Culture, and the Postmodern Self.* Baltimore, MD: The Johns Hopkins University Press.
Morgan, C.A. (2001) Demographic crisis in Japan: Why Japan might open its doors to foreign home health-care aides. *Pacific Rim Law & Policy Journal Association* 10 (3), 749–779.
Morgan, B. (2007) Poststructuralism and applied linguistics: Complementary approaches to identity and culture in ELT. In J. Cummins and C. Davison (eds) *International Handbook of English Language Teaching* (pp. 1033–1052). New York: Springer.
Naturalization (n.d.) Immigration and Naturalization Service. See https://ind.nl/EN/individuals/residence-wizard/dutch-citizenship/naturalisation/Pages/default.aspx (accessed 15 August 2014).
Norton, B. (2010) Language and identity. In N. Hornberger and S. McKay (eds) *Sociolinguistics and Language Education*. Bristol: Multilingual Matters.
Orgad, L. (2011) Creating new Americans: The essence of Americanism under the citizenship test. *Houston Law Review* 47 (5), 1–46.
Pavlenko, A. and Blackledge, A. (eds) (2004) *Negotiation of Identities in Multilingual Contexts*. Clevedon: Multilingual Matters.
Ramanathan, V. (2013a) *Language Policy and (Dis)citizenship: Rights, Access, Pedagogies*. Bristol: Multilingual Matters.
Ramanathan, V. (2013b) Special forum: Language policies and (dis)citizenship: Who belongs? Who is a guest? Who is deported? [special issue]. *Journal of Language, Identity, and Education* 12 (3).
Ricento, T. (2013) Dis-citizenship for refugees in Canada: The case of Fernando. *Journal of Language, Identity, and Education* 12 (3), 184–188.
Sadiq, K. (2009) *Paper Citizens: How Illegal Immigrants Acquire Citizenship in Developing Countries*. Oxford: Oxford University Press.
Sanchanta, M. (2010) Group appeals for overhaul of Japanese immigration. *The Wall Street Journal*, 24 November.
Schuck, P. (1998) *Citizens, Strangers, and In-Betweens: Essays on Immigration and Citizenship*. Boulder, CO: Westview Press.
Seargeant, P. (2009) *The Idea of English in Japan: Ideology and the Evolution of a Global Language*. Bristol: Multilingual Matters.
Shachar, A. (2000) Citizenship and membership in the Israeli polity. In T.A. Aleinikoff and D. Klusmeyer (eds) *From Migrants to Citizens: Membership in a Changing World* (pp. 386–433). Washington, DC: Carnegie Endowment for International Peace.
Shohamy, E. (2001) *The Power of Tests: A Critical Perspective on the Uses of Language Tests*. Harlow: Pearson Education Limited.
Shohamy, E. (2006) *Language Policy: Hidden Agendas and New Approaches*. London: Routledge.
Shohamy, E. and McNamara, T. (2009) Language assessment for immigration, citizenship, and asylum [special issue]. *Language Assessment Quarterly* 6 (1).
Sicakkan, H.G. and Lithman, Y. (2005) Politics of identity, modes of belonging and citizenship: An overview of conceptual and theoretical challenges. In H.G. Sicakkan and Y. Lithman (eds) *Changing the Basis of Citizenship in the Modern State: Political Theory and the Politics of Diversity* (pp. 1–36). Lewiston, NY: Edwin Mellen Press.
Silverstein, M. (1996) Monoglot 'standard' in America: Standardization and metaphors of linguistic hegemony. In D. Brenneis and R. Macaulay (eds) *The Matrix of Language: Contemporary Linguistic Anthropology* (pp. 284–306). Boulder, CO: Westview Press.

Song, J. (2010) Language ideology and identity in transnational space: Globalization, migration, and bilingualism among Korean families in the USA. *International Journal of Bilingual Education and Bilingualism* 13 (1), 23–42.

Soysal, Y. (1994) *Limits of Citizenship: Migrants and Postnational Membership in Europe*. Chicago: University of Chicago Press.

Touraine, A. (1997) *What is Democracy?* Boulder, CO: Westview Press.

Ullmann, W. (1967) *The Individual and Society in the Middle Ages*. London: Methuen.

Volpp, L. (2005) Divesting citizenship: On Asian American history and the loss of citizenship through marriage. *UCLA Law Review* 53, 405–483.

Weil, P. (2001) Access to citizenship: A comparison of twenty-five nationality laws. In T.A. Aleinikoff and D. Klusmeyer (eds) *Citizenship Today: Global Perspectives and Practices* (pp. 17–35). Washington, DC: Carnegie Endowment for International Peace.

Wiley, T. (2013) Constructing and deconstructing 'illegal' children. *Journal of Language, Identity, and Education* 12 (3), 167–172.

Wiley, T.G. and Wright, W.E. (2004) Against the undertow: Language-minority education policy and politics in the 'age of accountability'. *Educational Policy* 18 (1), 142–168.

Wodak, R. (2013) Dis-citizenship and migration: A critical discourse-analytical perspective. *Journal of Language, Identity, and Education* 12 (3), 173–178.

Woolard, K. (1989) Sentences in the language prison: The rhetorical structuring of an American language policy. *American Ethnologist* 16 (2), 268–278.

Yuval-Davis, N. (2006) Belonging and the politics of belonging. *Patterns of Prejudice* 40 (3), 197–214.

Part 1
Policies

2 The Value(s) of US Citizenship: An Analysis of the English Writing Test for Naturalization Applicants

Michelle Winn Baptiste

We live in times when Hawai'i-born US President Barack Obama's citizenship has been endlessly questioned by the far right, numerous immigrant families have been separated by a surge in deportations and the Deferred Action for Childhood Arrivals was passed to assist young people, who immigrated undocumented as children, to gain the right to work in the United States. Clearly, citizenship – and the benefits it confers – remains a hotly contested topic in the US.

What is it that Americans value as core to US citizenship? One way to answer this question is to investigate the primary gatekeeping interaction determining whether non-birthright citizenship is granted or denied: the naturalization interview.

My earlier studies on naturalization addressed (1) which factors determine naturalization interview outcomes (Winn, 2000), (2) how to design a citizenship course around task-based language teaching (TBLT) modules (Winn, 2005) and (3) how to design a training course for interviewers on intercultural communication, drawing on successful interactions from interview transcripts (Baptiste & Seig, 2007).

For this chapter, I use transcripts from over 60 observed and recorded naturalization interviews collected at an Immigration and Naturalization Services (INS) office from 1999 to 2000 (Winn, 2000) to investigate the values that eight officers reference during the naturalization interview, specifically in sentences dictated for the English Writing Test that reveal underlying ideologies of what it means to 'be American.'

The following research questions guide the qualitative inquiry presented in this chapter:

(1) What values do the interviewers express during the naturalization interviews (Winn, 2000), especially in the English Writing Test?
(2) How have the expressed values changed since the implementation of the revised test in 2008?

Power in Discourse

In this section, I briefly review the literature on language and power in gatekeeping encounters, as well as the literature on values associated with US citizenship. When conducting a naturalization interview, immigration officers possess the power to frame the discourse, as they belong to what Fairclough (1989: 47) calls 'the societally dominant cultural grouping'; backed by US immigration policy, officers decide whether to recommend approving or denying an immigrant's application for naturalization. Interestingly, Fairclough (1989: 47) himself uses the term 'naturalization,' in describing 'the naturalization of a particular routine as the common-sense way of doing things,' as 'an effect of power, [as] an ideological effect.' Similarly, Bourdieu et al. (1994) argue that often the state's arbitrary practices come to be seen as 'natural.' Often, only through discourse analysis can taken-for-granted norms be uncovered and challenged.

Recognizing the power of values and presuppositions expressed in institutional contexts, Estrada asserts that

> Language [is] permeated with ideas, beliefs, values, and positionings that have been formulated by the dominant majority... Language is ... capable of expressing and shaping our beliefs and values and affecting the way we view others ... giving voice to conceptions of reality held by one group of people and suppressing alternative visions and experiences of other realities. (qtd. in Estrada & McLaren, 1993: 28–29)

The language used in institutions informs thinking processes and excludes alternative perspectives. Gee (1996: 127) defines such language as 'Discourses,' that is 'ways of being in the world ... which integrate words [with] values [and] beliefs.' Referring to Sapir's (1931) work, Erickson and Shultz (1982: 11) maintain that it is possible to make connections between gatekeeping interviews and the processes of 'wider cultural and social-structural patterns of life in society...patterns [that Sapir] says are being creatively reanimated and reaffirmed in the particular communicative acts of individuals face-to-face.' Jupp et al. (1982: 255) report on the significant role that 'interviewers' cultural and professional assumptions' play in the selection of interview questions and interpretations of responses in job interviews. This chapter examines the way that assumptions about citizenship, as well as institutional policies reflective of these assumptions, influence the sentences dictated for the English Writing Test in naturalization interviews. In Winn (2000), underlying values appear to impact interviewing officers' selection of sentences to dictate; later, in the revised English Writing Test (2008) the standardized dictated sentences reveal a valuing of a narrow telling of US history.

Core US citizenship values: Theoretical and historical contextualization

In defining citizenship, Loring (2013a), Abowitz and Harnish (2006) and DeJaeghere (2008) each include the conferring of values. Handbooks written over the years for naturalizing citizens have sought to describe those values ascribed to the ideal US citizen.

Over 100 years ago, in 1914, citizenship programs were first established, emphasizing strict gender roles with men portrayed as 'strong' and women as mothers and homemakers. Orgad (2011) delineates cleanliness, cooking (e.g. how to prepare an egg) and safety (e.g. fire prevention at home) as common themes. Early citizenship handbooks place value on women raising children and maintaining the home.

Twenty-five years later, according to Orgad's (2011) analysis of several citizenship handbooks developed during World War II,

> A good American was described as one who works all day, goes to night school, learns to speak English fast, saves money enough to have a home, learns how to prepare American food, watches baseball, loves to vote, belongs to some clubs, obeys the law, shows loyalty, shares responsibilities, believes in the Constitution, and is familiar with the community. (Orgad, 2011: 1246)

Here, the following themes emerge: (a) working hard; (b) studying; (c) speaking English; (d) owning a home; (e) embracing American culture – both the broader popular culture and the local community culture; (f) voting enthusiastically; (g) being law-abiding and loyal to the US; and (h) believing in the Constitution. The 1940s' emphasis on home ownership and loyalty to the US harks back to the earlier (1914–1920s') citizenship handbooks.

Two decades later, in the 1960s, citizenship handbooks shifted to an emphasis on the US government and history, especially the US Constitution (Orgad, 2011: 1246).

Data

Positioned within this historical context, this chapter examines current images of citizenship, drawing primarily on 67 observed naturalization interviews – 63 of which were audio-recorded. The data were collected across 14 months from 1999 to 2000 during 15 site visits to an INS office. Interviews usually lasted between 10 and 20 minutes. The immigrant applicants interviewed – 43 women and 24 men – came from 16 countries. Applicants from the Philippines, China, South Korea and Vietnam comprised more than half of those observed; the other nations represented included Hong Kong (British nationality), Japan, Taiwan, Brazil, Colombia, Canada, Laos, New Zealand, Pakistan, Panama, Peru and Venezuela (Winn, 2000).

In Winn (2000), the naturalization interviews were conducted by eight district adjudications officers – six women and two men – of various European and Asian ethnic backgrounds; several grew up with parents or grandparents who spoke languages in addition to – or other than – English. Charged with adjudicating numerous legal issues related to immigration and naturalization, the officers do so by conducting inquiries and interviews to issue benefits with accompanying documentation such as visas, green cards (proof of legal permanent residency) and certificates of naturalization.

Naturalization

According to the Office of Immigration Statistics (2013), from 2003 to 2012 an average of three-quarters of a million people applied annually to naturalize. More than two-thirds of those naturalized in the past decade have come from two continents: Asia (including the Middle East and former Soviet republics) and North America (including Latin America and the Caribbean). Immigrants from the top 11 countries accounted for half of those naturalized in 2012: Mexico (102,000), the Philippines (45,000), India (43,000), Dominican Republic (33,500), China (32,000), Cuba (31,000), Colombia (24,000), Vietnam (23,500), Haiti (19,000), El Salvador (16,500) and Jamaica (15,500).

In 2012, the overwhelming majority of those who applied to naturalize were ultimately sworn in as US citizens; that year, only 7% of naturalization applicants' petitions for US citizenship were denied. A hundred years earlier, in 1912, the percentage denied citizenship was similarly low: 10%. Yet, the *number* of applicants has increased 10-fold in this past century (Office of Immigration Statistics, 2013) – with wide divergence in actual numbers in any given year, depending on legal, political, social and economic factors.

To apply for naturalization, applicants must complete an N-400 Application for Naturalization, pay $680 in fees, get fingerprinted for a Federal Bureau of Investigations (FBI) background check and attend a naturalization interview.

The naturalization interview

During the naturalization interview, officers ask questions to confirm and clarify answers on the N-400 Application for Naturalization, which serves three purposes:

(1) to collect personal information, such as name, nationality, employment, education, birth date;
(2) to elicit eligibility for US citizenship, including establishing residency and physical presence in the US, as well as evidence of 'good moral character'; and
(3) to discern attachment to the principles of the US Constitution and commitment to upholding those laws.

In Winn (2000), officers interviewed applicants in cubicle office spaces with the applicant sitting across the desk from the officer. After the applicant entered the cubicle, he or she was asked to remain standing in order to take an oath. Following the oath, the officer would ask for the applicant's green card and begin the interview exchange, with frequent silences as the officer interspersed questioning with examining the applicant's file and typing information into a computer. The order of interview tasks varied from interviewer to interviewer except for the opening oath and concluding signatures on the N-400 and Oath of Allegiance.

The components of the interview in Winn (2000) included (a) asking if the applicant would like to legally change his or her name; (b) having an applicant sign passport photos legibly; (c) verifying information from the N-400 that may have changed since the applicant applied, such as place of employment or study, home address, marital status, number and names of children; (d) confirming the accuracy of the information on the N-400 such as height and birth date; (e) determining the basis for eligibility to naturalize by asking questions such as 'How many times have you been married?' and 'How many times have you traveled outside the US?' followed by specific questions about dates and length of time absent from the US; and finally (f) ascertaining 'good moral character' and loyalty to the US by asking questions about deportation proceedings, arrests, Communist Party affiliation, Selective Service registration (for male applicants), false claims of US citizenship, fraudulent voting in a US election, etc. For the more complex legal questions, many officers provided their own simplified paraphrases – often known as 'foreigner talk,' a communication strategy used by fluent speakers of a language with the intent of improving comprehension for an interlocutor who is a second language learner (Tarone, 2006).

The naturalization test

The United States Citizenship and Immigration Services' (USCIS) current (2012) naturalization requirements specify that a successful applicant with no medical or age/residency exemption[1] must pass four tests:

(1) Navigate the entire interview in English to 'demonstrate an understanding of the English language, including the ability to read, write, and speak words in ordinary usage in the English language' (Title 8 Part 312.1-Code of Federal Regulations).
(2) Answer 6 US History and Government (USHG) test questions accurately (out of 10) to demonstrate 'knowledge and understanding of the fundamentals of the history, and of the principles and form of government, of the United States' (Title 8 Part 312.2-Code of Federal Regulations).
(3) Read aloud one sentence (out of three) 'in a manner suggesting to the USCIS officer that [the applicant] understand[s] the meaning.'
(4) Write one sentence (out of three) 'in a manner that would be understandable to the USCIS officer' (USCIS, 2012).

The evaluation of 'pass' or 'fail' for the English speaking, writing, reading and USHG tests remains solely at the discretion of the interviewing officer, abiding by general USCIS guidelines.

A 'meaningful' and 'standardized' test

The requirement of being able to speak English was introduced in 1906 with the literacy requirement instituted in 1917 – though reading in English was not required until later court decisions mandated it (McKay, 1993). In 1952, the US Congress instigated a USHG requirement. At that time, naturalization was largely handled by the judicial system, leaving USHG questioning up to individual judges who had leeway to engage applicants in lengthy and complex oral examinations (Orgad, 2011).

So, in 1986, when a set of 100 USHG Questions was introduced, it was the first time the content of the USHG test was standardized – for naturalization applicants and adjudications officers alike. These original 100 USHG Questions were written by two INS managers over a weekend in the early 1980s (Ratliff et al., 2004) and became an official component of the naturalization interview in 1986 (Spurlin, 2014).

Eleven years later, the 1997 report to Congress by the US Commission on Immigration Reform (1997: 46) called for further standardization of the naturalization process, pointing to a 'disturbing' lack of consistency in the way the tests were administered across INS officers and offices; the report also criticized the 'current tests' for inadequately 'assess[ing] … understanding or abilities' in English and specified that the administration of the USHG exam should move from an emphasis on 'memorization of discrete facts' to an emphasis on 'substantive understanding of the basic concepts of civic participation.'

Following this critical report by the US Commission on Immigration Reform (1997) and just after the data collection in Winn (2000) was complete, in 2000 the INS began redesigning and standardizing the US naturalization tests. Spurred by the Commission's recommendations, the INS put forward the goals of making the test 'more meaningful' and 'standardized' across all INS offices (Laglagaron & Devani, 2008: 46–47).

Methodology

All 64 sentences dictated for the English Writing Test in Winn (2000) predate the naturalization test revision and were transcribed during and immediately after data collection; for this chapter, I coded the categories that emerged from the data set. Using a keyword analysis process similar to that described by Feuerherm (2013) in her study of refugee accounts, I considered all noun keywords in an initial analysis and deemed the resulting topics significant enough to investigate if at least two officers dictated sentences containing a semantically related keyword. After categorizing sentences based on keyword nouns, I also included relevant adjectives (e.g. 'married…') and verbs (e.g. 'drive…'). Finally, I tabulated the pronouns in the dictated sentences. In keeping with constructivist grounded theory (Engward, 2013; Quimby, 2011), I followed an inductive approach when analyzing the dictated sentences qualitatively and quantitatively – remaining open throughout the process to refining the themes that emerged. The analysis of keywords provided the basis for discovering correlations between the content of the English Writing Test and the values surrounding US citizenship, as expressed in citizenship handbooks and official INS documents.

Findings

Here I describe key findings – presenting each recurring theme with the relevant dictated sentences from the data set and the source material that the eight interviewing officers may have used in composing these sentences. I found that 45% of sentences (29/64) dictated to immigrant applicants for the English Writing Test in Winn (2000) relate to values prevalent in US citizenship handbooks in the first half of the 20th century (Orgad, 2011):

(1) working hard (including studying);
(2) being married (with children);
(3) owning a home (with a modern update: owning a car).

Sentences dictated for the English Writing Test (1999–2000)

For the source material for the English Writing Test in Winn (2000), officers either (1) selected or adapted sentences from the INS/USCIS publication of 100 'Sample Sentences for Written English Testing,' a single page containing two columns of 50 sentences each: 'Civics/History' and 'Everyday Life' (see Appendix A); or (2) composed sentences using the personal information furnished on the N-400 Application for Naturalization or garnered through questioning. Based on keyword semantic analysis, over one-third (or 34%) of the published sample sentences overlap semantically with the sentences dictated in Winn (2000).

Personalized sentences (1999–2000)

In many cases in Winn (2000), an officer would dictate identical sentences to every applicant interviewed that day. In other cases, an officer would focus on a topic for the day yet personalize the sentence for each applicant. Officers sometimes asked applicants questions when formulating a dictated sentence, as revealed in the transcript below. Precursor questions to the English Writing Test thus sometimes included 'How many children do you have?' (information furnished on the N-400) or 'How did you get here today?' (information not requested on the N-400).

In Winn (2000), officers often sought to make the sentence personally relevant to each applicant. In fact, despite the fact that only 14% of the sample sentences contained the pronoun 'I,' 83% (53/64) of the sentences dictated in Winn (2000) contained the personal pronoun 'I' – all but one opening with 'I.'[2] (See Appendix B.) The only sentences that did not contain the personal pronoun 'I' involved the American flag (10 sentences) – or the weather (1 sentence). Although 47% of the sentences (25/53) that contained 'I' pertain to US citizenship, the majority of the sentences containing 'I' – the remaining 53% – contained personal information about an applicant's identity in terms of work, study, family, home, car or other form of transportation (see Appendix C).

For example, in the following excerpt from the English Writing Test, after the applicant had three misspellings in the sentence 'The flag is red, white, and blue,' the officer decided to have the middle-aged Korean woman write a more personalized sentence and thus initiated this unexpected line of questioning (Baptiste & Seig, 2007):

Interviewer:	How did you come today? Do you drive? You drove yourself? How did you come today?
Applicant:	Today and uh today?
Interviewer:	No, how did you come here today?
Applicant:	Uh
Interviewer:	On the bus. You drive?
Applicant:	Yes, drive
Interviewer:	What color is your car?
Applicant:	u::h (0.5 pause) u::h (0.5)
Interviewer:	Your car is what white?
Applicant:	Is my color (0.5) beige color (0.5) ((Laugh)) I'm sorry ((quietly))
Interviewer:	u::h Can you write for me I drive a car? (0.5) Jus- write for me I drive a car

In this case, the interviewer personalizes the sentence in terms of mode of transportation but abandons the idea of including the color of the car when it turns out that the applicant's car is beige, a word the interviewer apparently interprets as too difficult to spell or beyond the vocabulary 'in common usage in the English language.' (Title 8 Part 312.1 – Code of Federal Regulations). Nonetheless, the applicant could not spell the word 'drive' correctly and failed the writing test.

Since officers in Winn (2000) sought to make the dictated sentences meaningful to applicants by personalizing the content, a valuing of the personal emerges in the English Writing Test in use at that time, as revealed by the categorized examples below.

VALUED: Working/studying/speaking English

Employment is often addressed during the N-400 information verification portion of the naturalization interview, but the theme of work appeared frequently in the English Writing Test portion of the interview as well. In fact, working (12 sentences) or studying (2 sentences) emerged as a topic in 22% (14/64) of the sentences, dictated by five officers, in Winn (2000):

I live and work in _____.
I work five days a week.
I am the president of my company.
My husband and I live and work in _____.
I do not work.

I drive my car to work. (6 times)
I ride the bus to work.

The sentence 'I do not work' is particularly interesting in that a 75-year-old applicant is being asked to write a sentence identifying work as a pivotal arena in which she does not participate.

Two sentences similar to those dictated by officers in Winn (2000) are among the 100 Sample Sentences (see Appendix D):

'I drive a blue car to work.'
'I go to work everyday.'

Eight other sentences related to work appear on the list of 100 Sample Sentences:

'You work very hard at your job.'   'It is a good job to start with.'
'They work well together.'   'He wanted to talk to his boss.'
'The man wanted to get a job.'   'His wife is at work right now.'
'He wanted to find a job.'   'His wife worked in the house.'

Of the 100 Sample Sentences, 10% pertain to work. This focus on work clearly emerges in Winn (2000), echoing the earlier citizenship handbooks' emphasis on the hard-working immigrant worthy of naturalizing. Above, the ideas of searching for work and being employed at entry-level positions are emphasized, as well as a male-centric perspective in five sentences; only one sentence explicitly refers to a woman on-the-job, and even then the point of reference is a possessive male pronoun: it's '*his* wife' who is 'at work,' and in another sentence it's 'his wife' who 'work[s] in the house' – harking back to the earliest citizenship handbooks' patriarchal focus on women in the home (Orgad, 2011).

In terms of the expressed value of studying, in Winn (2000) two officers capitalized on applicants' status as students and dictated these sentences, apparently in lieu of a sentence about work:

I am currently enrolled as a student.
I am a student at Rainbow Beauty College.

In the official list of 100 Sample Sentences, two sentences allude to studying:

'The teacher was proud of her class.'
'We are very smart to learn this.'

This theme of studying – and learning English – arose frequently in Winn (2000); when applicants struggled during the USHG test, failed the USHG test or were unable to communicate in English successfully, officers often gave applicants advice about studying. After a 44-year-old Chinese applicant failed the various tests in Winn (2000), the interviewer advised, 'You need a little bit more time to study' and 'You have to study some more English.' Such comments were common in these cases and sometimes included follow-up questions such as 'Did you study a lot or not?' or 'Do you go to school?.' In informal follow-up discussions conducted by the researcher after interviews, officers expressed their belief that those who try hard (i.e. study for the naturalization tests) deserve to become US citizens (Winn, 2000).

At the end of the interview referenced above, when informed that he had failed to pass the tests and advised to study more, the applicant responded that he was 'every day working night time working day time working.' In explaining why he had little time to study and acquire English, he communicated that he worked long hours in a Japanese company and was married to a Korean woman. A native speaker of Mandarin, he was interacting predominantly with speakers of Japanese and Korean; due to his long work hours, he had little time to study and acquire English. Here, two expressed values conflict: working hard and speaking English, as working long hours prevented this applicant from having opportunities to learn English – thus confounding the images of the hard-working (deserving) immigrant and the English-speaking (assimilated) immigrant.[3] After this interview, the interviewing officer explained to me sympathetically that some naturalization applicants 'work so hard they don't have time to study.'

As findings in Winn (2000) reveal, the focal point for applicants preparing for the naturalization interview is often studying for the USHG test with scant attention paid to the English speaking, reading and writing requirements. Yet Winn (2000) showed that among the 10 applicants (out of 67) who failed to be approved to naturalize, no one failed solely the USHG exam. The data in Winn (2000) show that English language proficiency in oral communication, writing and reading was 'the deciding factor in success or failure at the interview' (as reported in Winn, 2005: 293). In Loring's (2013a) recent research, likewise, all four observed citizenship teachers reported that passing the English language requirement is the biggest hurdle for most adult learners in the naturalization process; thus the officers' valuing of studying and learning English represents what *is* essential to success at the naturalization interview.

Two sentences from the 100 Sample Sentences allude to acquiring English:

'I know how to speak English.'
'She can speak English very well.'

Although not contained in any of the 64 sentences that the eight officers dictated in Winn (2000), the topic of learning and speaking English nonetheless clearly emerged during the interviews.

VALUED: Marriage/children

Another theme that emerges in the dictated sentences in Winn (2000) is that of marriage and children – both frequently addressed in the information verification and eligibility portions of the interview. During the English Writing Test, 17% (11/64) of the sentences dictated, by three officers, in Winn (2000) contained information about an applicant's marital status and/or children:

I am married, and I have one child. (3 times)	I have two boys.
I have two beautiful children. (2 times)	I have four sons.
I have three beautiful children.[4]	I am single, and I have no children.
I have three children.	My husband and I live and work in _____.

Interestingly, the applicant who was dictated the sentence 'I am single, and I have no children' was being asked to identify herself by what she lacked: a spouse and children, implicitly referencing a norm of being married with children. With 9 out of 11 sentences in this category dictated to women (who comprised 2/3 of the applicants), a cursory analysis detects at the very least a focus on women as wives/mothers as depicted in the earliest citizenship handbooks (Orgad, 2011). And while there is no explicit reference to marriage in the 100 Sample Sentences, two sentences contain the word 'wife' and present a male reference point, as mentioned above:

'His **wife** is at work right now.'
'His **wife** worked in the house.'

Two sentences on the 100 Sample Sentences similarly relate to one's own children just like the sentences dictated in Winn (2000):

'I have three children.'
'She is my daughter, and he is my son.'

The first sentence 'I have three children' is reproduced exactly in one interview in Winn (2000) with five other similar sentences. Though three other sentences from the 100 Sample Sentences contain the word 'children' and one 'boy,' the terms are used generally – not in relationship to a parent:

'The children bought a newspaper.'	'The children wanted a television.'
'The children play at school.'	'The boy threw a ball.'

Generic sentences like these – about children who are not necessarily one's own – were never dictated in Winn (2000), as the English Writing Test sentences tended to be personalized.

VALUED: Home/car ownership

In Winn (2000), dictated sentences involved not only relationship but also ownership: 16% (10/64) of the sentences, dictated by four officers, contained the word 'house' or 'car':

I live in a big brown house. (2 times)	I drive my car to work. (6 times)
I live in a big house.	I drive a car.

Though the topic of whether an applicant lives in a house or apartment occasionally came up in the information verification portion of the naturalization interview (Winn, 2000) in confirming an address, the dictated sentences above containing the word 'house' do not appear to be personalized, as no officer asked any applicant about the size or color of his or her house. For sentences containing the word 'car,' six out of seven relate to work; some officers sought to personalize such sentences, as shown above, by verifying the mode of transportation an applicant used to come to the interview.

Eight sentences on the official list of 100 Sample Sentences contain the keyword 'house' or 'car' in relation to ownership, like those dictated in Winn (2000):

'She was happy with her house.'	'I bought a blue car today.'
'They live together in a big house.'	'I drive a blue car to work.'
'His wife worked in the house.'	'My car does not work.'
'We have a very clean house.'[5]	'They are very happy with their car.'

Two additional sample sentences: 'The white house has a big tree.' and 'I count the cars as they pass by the office.' refer generically to a 'house' or 'cars,' but the majority – above – refer to one's own house (or car), as in Winn (2000) – echoing the theme of home ownership from the earliest of citizenship handbooks (Orgad, 2011), with the additional expectation of car ownership as a modern component of the American Dream.

A focus on transportation emerges in the sentences dictated in Winn (2000), apparently as a result of officers' attempts to make dictated sentences relevant to applicants' daily lives:

I drive my car to work. (5 times)
I drive a car.
I ride the bus to work.

In fact, 12.5% (8/64) of the sentences, dictated by four officers, contained at least one of these keywords: 'car,' 'drive,' or 'bus.' Interestingly, when dictated the sentence 'I drive my car to work,' one applicant, a native speaker of English, notified the officer that he would write instead 'I ride my bike to work.' – to be accurate, and the officer replied that it was fine: 'You can do that … I just need a writing sample.' Here and elsewhere in Winn (2000), car ownership as the default reveals a bias toward driving one's own car instead of using public transportation. Assumptions about socioeconomic status and a valuing of ownership emerge rather than a valuing of the environment, health and community.

The American Dream

The majority of sample sentences in the 'Everyday Life' category primarily address the following topics: cooking, consumerism, working or seeking work, speaking English, family/children, cars and houses.[6] Similarly, a large number of dictated sentences in Winn (2000) centered on working/studying, marriage/children and home/car ownership. In fact, 44% of the dictated sentences in Winn (2000) encapsulated some aspect of the prototypical American Dream: a nuclear family comprised of husband, wife and children, with a car and a house (maybe even a 'big house') – all made possible by working (or studying) hard. Additionally, the tendency for dictated sentences to begin with 'I' and contain personalized content may reflect the American Dream's focus on the individual rather than the community.

VALUED: US citizenship

Arguably a key component of full access to the ideals of the 'American Dream,' US citizenship – *the* overarching purpose of the interview, appeared as a topic in 39% of the sentences dictated in Winn (2000), by four officers:

I want to be an American citizen. (20 times)
I want to be a United States citizen. (3 times)

There are two sentences on US citizenship found in the 'Civics/History' column of the official list of 100 Sample Sentences – the first one identical to that dictated 20 times (or nearly one-third of the time) in Winn (2000):

'I want to be an American citizen.'
'I want to be a citizen of the United States.'

The INS/USCIS was apparently unsure where to place sentences on US citizenship, since the 'Everyday Life' column of the 100 Sample Sentences also contains this similar sentence – identical to one dictated three times in Winn (2000):

'I want to be a United States citizen.'

It is unclear where US citizenship belongs: it may open up a world of civic involvement (e.g. campaigning and voting), yet it may also affect an individual's everyday life in significant ways (e.g. employment possibilities, travel options and family visa petitions). Regardless of whether the desire to become a US citizen is a matter of civics or everyday life, this theme was the single most prevalent in the dictated sentences in Winn (2000).

VALUED: *The American flag*

Finally, the only USHG topic in the dictated sentences in Winn (2000) is the American flag, a patriotic symbol associated with the American Dream, as well as loyalty to the US, a value promoted in the earliest citizenship handbooks (Orgad, 2011):

The flag is red, white, and blue. (7 times) There are fifty stars.
The flag has fifty stars. The American flag has 13 stripes and fifty stars.

Ten sentences in Winn (2000), dictated by three officers, centered on this theme of the American flag. Sentences identical or nearly identical to those dictated by officers in Winn (2000) from the 100 Sample Sentences include

'The colors of the flag are red, white, and blue.'
'The flag of the United States has 50 stars.'
'The American flag has 13 stripes.'

This focus on the American flag was reiterated as well in the first seven questions of the original 100 USHG Questions (1986), in use at the time of the data collection in Winn (2000):

'What are the colors of our flag?' 'How many stripes are there on the flag?'
'How many stars are there in our flag?' 'What color are the stripes?'
'What color are the stars on our flag?' 'What do the stripes on the flag mean?'
'What do the stars on the flag mean?'

This remarkable emphasis on the American flag persisted in the revised USHG Questions (2008) – though in reduced numbers: three questions, rather than seven.

Up to this point, the analysis has focused on the English Writing Test administered from 1999 to 2000 in one INS office and how the values that emerged in the dictated sentences reinforced the ideology of the American Dream. The remainder of this chapter will investigate how sentences dictated since fall 2008 contain significantly different content but still reinforce a similarly narrow ideological perspective.

Revised Naturalization Tests (October 2008–Present)

Marking the culmination of a decade-long test revision process started by the INS, continued by the Department of Homeland Security and finished by the USCIS,[7] and following widespread pilot tests, the revised English Writing, Reading and USHG tests were first administered on October 1, 2008 (US Embassy, 2008). While some of the test content did change, the testing methods remained the same: demonstrating oral English proficiency by participating in the interview, reading a sentence aloud for the English Reading Test, writing a dictated sentence for the English Writing Test and orally answering USHG Questions. Pursuant to the mandate that sentences selected for the reading and writing exams 'infuse civic knowledge' and 'reinforce civic learning' (USCIS/Office of Citizenship, n.d.), US history, government and civics topics now provide the content for the reading and writing exams. Whereas in the past, as illustrated in Winn (2000), sentences dictated for the English Writing Test were at the discretion of the officer and often taken from the list of 100 Sample Sentences for Written English Testing (last published in 2006) and commonly personalized, since October 2008, a subset of the revised 100 USHG Questions has served as *the sole source of content* for the English Writing Test.

Instead of having a wide array of choices to draw upon when composing a sentence to dictate, officers now receive a randomized set of three USHG questions and answers for each interview and select which pairing to use for the reading and writing tests. The redesigned English Writing Test entails writing the dictated answer to a USHG question the applicant reads aloud for the English Reading Test (Assenyoh, personal communication, May 22, 2014). For the new English Reading Test, 'Who was the first president?' is a sample question. For the new English Writing Test, 'The first president was Washington' is a sample response.

The sentences for the writing test are now composed exclusively of words and phrases from the Writing Vocabulary List published online, with all words on the list derived from a basic subset of the 100 USHG Questions (Kikuta, personal communication, June 3, 2014). The current online vocabulary list serves as a word bank for the sentences used in the English Writing Test; no list of sample sentences is made available to the public. The Writing Vocabulary List contains 75 words or phrases, organized into eight columns: (a) people, (b) civics, (c) places, (d) months, (e) holidays, (f) verbs, (g) other function words and (h) other content words. Words include flag, free, right, Senators, California, Canada, February, Flag Day, Independence Day, Thanksgiving, Columbus Day, can, have, vote, here, in, the, dollar bill, fifty, first, taxes, red and white.

Today, the expressed value of studying that emerged in Winn (2000) is reinforced by the plethora of study materials available to naturalization applicants with computer access and literacy. Although it is unclear whether these materials provide sufficient access to the syntactical, grammatical, and phonological input, knowledge and practice needed to successfully communicate in English and discern the meaning behind some of the complex questions asked during the naturalization interview (see Griswold, 2011), it *is* clear that the study materials make the content of the revised reading and writing tests much more explicit than in the past and that the reading and writing word banks help to scaffold the learning of a finite set of vocabulary terms needed to pass the USHG-focused English Reading and Writing Tests.

Discussion

Because the revised 100 USHG Questions (2008) now play an even larger role in the naturalization process since the questions themselves are the source material (in abridged form), not only for the USHG exam but also for both the English Reading and Writing Tests, this chapter culminates with a brief analysis of what topics were valued enough to be included in the revised 100 USHG Questions – and which ones are absent.

USHG test content

As part of the Naturalization Test Redesign Project from 2001 to 2005, K-12 national and state history standards were examined; in determining the content of the revised USHG exam, input was sought from leaders of community-based organizations, history education experts and pilot participants. The revised USHG Questions (2008) now cover three overarching categories with three subtopics each:

(1) US Government
    Principles of American Government
    System of Government
    Rights and Responsibilities
(2) US History
    Colonial Period and Independence
    The 1800s
    Recent American History and Other Important Historical Information
(3) Integrated Civics
    Geography
    Symbols
    Holidays

Though the 1986 and 2008 versions of the USHG tests share many common topics and both predominantly require factual recall, the 2008 USHG Questions often require more specific and/or complex answers; for example, naturalization applicants can now be asked to name 2 of 16 cabinet-level positions instead of just answering the question, 'What special group advises the President?' (1986). In this way, the revised USHG test can be perceived as more 'meaningful' – albeit still memorization based.

Nonetheless, certain topics are still omitted in the revised 100 USHG Questions, including immigration growth, a topic that emerged in naturalization test redesign focus groups, panels and roundtables, although the founding of the nation, the Civil War and civil rights were the only three topics with unanimous endorsement from the various constituents (Ratliffe et al., 2004).[8] Ultimately, only two ethnic/racial minority groups are named in the revised USHG test, just as in the 1986 version: African Americans and Native Americans. Other ethnic minority groups continue to be glaringly absent from the revised tests (2008). Absent also are any national heroes and heroines of color (Park, 2008: 1025) with the exception of Martin Luther King, Jr. As Park (2008) points out, while Asians and Latinos/Hispanics make up 'the majority of test-takers,' their rich history in the US is completely excluded from the new USHG test that, instead, portrays 'whiteness' as the norm. In fact, the Vocabulary List for the English Writing Test, only names three individuals: Washington, Lincoln and Adams – all white men.

Yet, Laglagaron and Devani (2008) call the revised USHG Questions (2008: 3–4) a 'significant overhaul' and applaud that women are included at all. This inclusion involves merely one question on suffragist Susan B. Anthony and one incidental mention of women's right to vote in one of four potential answers to the question about the four voting-related amendments to the US Constitution: 'Any citizen can vote. (Women and men can vote).' Though women are mentioned in one question and Susan B. Anthony is singled out in another, no woman nor person of color is mentioned by name in the English Writing Test Vocabulary List.[9]

Although the revised USHG Questions do represent some improvements in terms of portraying the diversity of the US by giving voice to the role of African Americans and women in US history and acknowledging the modern-day presence of Native Americans, the revised USHG Questions (2008) maintain a primary focus on constitutional, presidential and war history, presenting a picture of the United States largely through the lens of a hegemonic patriarchal European-American perspective. This particular version of US history, entailing the slightest of nods to non-dominant voices, is now the content of the English Writing Test, as well.

Conclusion

Just as the revised writing test shifts away from personal(ized) topics such as work, family and ownership to a standard history, the new scoring guidelines seek to standardize scoring of the English Writing

Test – allowing applicants to pass even if they make 'some grammatical, spelling, punctuation, or capitalization errors' and 'omit short words' as long as these errors 'do not interfere with meaning', as delineated in the current 'Scoring Guidelines for the US Naturalization Test.' The new scoring rubric is more generous and consistent than the practices observed in Winn (2000); in that study, no officer accepted phonetic spelling, which is now acceptable, and at that time, officers differed in terms of whether they would allow a single spelling error or not.

Even with value placed on standardization, officers can still influence the interview outcome. For instance, they regularly need to make medical and linguistic judgment calls completely outside their areas of expertize – deciding (a) whether a pronunciation error while reading or a spelling error while writing significantly interferes with meaning, (b) whether a medical waiver to excuse an applicant from the English language requirement and/or USHG test should be accepted and (c) whether an interpreter (for those with a waiver of the English language requirement) is adequately and ethically translating. In these ways, the officers have tremendous power in this high-stakes interview well beyond their scope of training in law enforcement.

Fortunately, the officers in Winn (2000) also held fast to a belief in second chances – a legally enforced mandate requiring every applicant who does not pass the first time be scheduled for a second interview within 60–90 days, and several in Winn (2000) did pass on their second attempt. The USCIS has likewise demonstrated its belief in second chances in terms of the restructuring of the naturalization tests. Despite terminating a contract with the National Academy of Sciences in 2005 to aid in test redesign and then shifting emphasis away from creating a more valid assessment of English proficiency as well as a more broadly *meaningful* assessment of USHG knowledge, the USCIS, nonetheless, succeeded in creating a more *standardized* English writing assessment.

The USCIS study materials furnished to support applicants studying for the new English Reading and Writing Tests (2008) along with the less rigorous scoring rubric appear to have resulted in a higher pass rate, as called for by the 1997 Congressional Commission's recommendation to increase naturalization (pass) rates. While initially the number of naturalization applications denied was higher than average: 23% in 2008 and 19% in 2009 – perhaps as applicants, citizenship instructors and officers adjusted to the new tests and the agency handled a backlog of applicants from the 2007 surge spurred by increasing fees and a wariness of the new test, from 2010 to 2012 the number of denials has fallen to a low of 7.5% (Office of Immigration Statistics, 2013).

Clearly, high value is placed on naturalizing immigrants, but to what extent are their stories part of the official history? With the sentence for the writing test now elicited by an answer to a randomly selected question adapted from the revised list of 100 USHG Questions (2008), the values conveyed by the English Writing Test are *less* revealing of underlying ideologies surrounding individual identity and the American Dream as codified in the 100 Sample Sentences and dictated by interviewers in Winn (2000) – and *more* indicative of a particular view of history. Though the emphasis on USHG appears at first glance to be more objective content for the writing test, it is questionable whether an 'official history' can ever be objective, as some voices must be featured at the expense of others (Zinn, 1980), just as the personalized sentences in Winn (2000) focused solely on identities hemmed in by ideological underpinnings of the American Dream. Thus, both the former writing test and current writing test put forward a predetermined ideal of what it means to be American – within the confines of particular identities and understandings of history.

Both the often-personalized sentences in the earlier writing test in Winn (2000) and the answers to the basic USHG questions used in the writing test today fail to encompass the powerful diversity of United States citizens and their history. Park (2008: 1032) laments the exclusion of non-dominant voices and calls for 'expand[ing] notions of citizenship to include notions of otherness' – as we draw on 'democratic principles [to] forge a unified identity.' And Ramanathan (2013: 13) asserts that 'we are products of the tellings and retellings of our national histories.' So we must ask, '*Whose* (hi)stories are told?'

Not only are certain key figures absent from the revised test, but so too are certain values. This chapter reveals that the USHG questions, which inform the new English Reading and Writing Tests, appear not to directly spur a 'transformative' (Banks, 2008, qtd. in Loring, 2013b) nor 'critical' (DeJaeghere, 2007) approach to citizenship (see Kunnan, 2009). And Loring (2013a) argues that community is an essential aspect of citizenship largely neglected by the USCIS materials and tests.

Nonetheless, one question incorporated into the revised 100 USHG Questions does embrace the definition of citizenship that Ramanathan (2013: 1) puts forward: being a US citizen means 'to participate fully' in our democracy:

What are two ways that Americans can participate in their democracy?

- vote
- join a political party
- help with a campaign
- join a civic group
- join a community group
- give an elected official your opinion on an issue
- call Senators and Representatives
- publicly support or oppose an issue or policy
- run for office
- write to a newspaper

Some of the potential answers imply the need for critical thinking as well as portray democracy as citizen activism, as collective enterprise. Above, protest that challenges the power structure is not named but encompassed in Option 8: 'publicly ... oppose an issue or policy.' This question also alludes to the 'we' of community. And 'we' *is* one of the words listed among the 75 lexical items in the new English Writing Test word bank. This 'we' hints at the collective emphasis in the question about how '*Americans* can participate in *their* democracy' (my italics), unlike in the dictated sentences in Winn (2000) that centered almost exclusively on the individual 'I' and never broached the topic of participatory democracy. On a related note, Griswold (2011: 407) argues that the English language requirement for naturalization, though implemented during an era of anti-immigrant sentiment after World War I, could be viewed today as 'prioritizing the participation and identity dimensions of citizenship over those of legal status and individual rights' since proficiency in English may enable political participation and national identification. And valuing political engagement means valuing democracy.

This chapter has divulged the values communicated in the English Writing Test prior to 2008 and then compared these values to those expressed today in the same test. As shown, these expressed values are reflective of official ideologies of what it means to be(come) 'American.' So it must be in the next 'retelling' or revision of the naturalization tests that we strive for a more balanced view of US citizenship, one that empowers individuals *and* communities and includes more of the stories of who we are as a nation – where we have been and where we seek to go.

Notes

(1) Waivers can be sought for medical reasons, physical or mental impairment and a combination of age and legal permanent residency. Applicants over age 50 who have been green card holders for at least 20 years or are over age 55 and have been green card holders for at least 15 years can waive the English language requirement. Applicants over age 65 who have been legal permanent residents for at least 20 years likewise can bring an interpreter and will only be asked questions from an abbreviated list of USHG Questions.
(2) One sentence opened with 'My husband and I...'
(3) In their language ecology model, Kramsch and Whiteside (2007) discuss a complex multilingualism that departs from the idealized (monolingual) native speaker as the model for second language acquisition.
(4) A minor sub-theme that emerges here is that of beauty: three sentences, all dictated by the same officer, refer to 'beautiful children,' though this descriptor is not included in the 100 Sample Sentences.
(5) The value on cleanliness is a carryover from the earliest citizenship handbooks, as is the value on cooking ('You cook very well.') though neither theme emerged in Winn (2000).

(6) A couple of sentences on the list are culturally revealing in *other* ways, including 'You drink too much coffee' and 'I am too busy to talk today.'
(7) In early 2003 in the aftermath of the September 11, 2001 terrorist attacks, the INS was reconfigured into three units within the Department of Homeland Security. The unit titled United States Citizenship and Immigration Services (USCIS) was charged with adjudicating and granting immigration and naturalization benefits.
(8) Only one question – in the geography section – in the revised 100 USHG Questions (2008) is tangentially related to immigration: 'Where is the Statue of Liberty?'
(9) 'American Indians' appears in the Civics column of the English Writing Test Vocabulary List.

References

Abowitz, K.K. and Harnish, J. (Winter 2006) Contemporary discourses of citizenship. *Review of Educational Research* 76 (4), 653–690. See http://www.jstor.org/stable/4124417

Baptiste, M.C. (Winn) and Seig, M.T. (2007) Training the guardians of America's gate: Discourse-based lessons from naturalization interviews. In *High Stakes Gatekeeping Encounters and Their Consequences: Discourses in Cross-Cultural Institutional Settings.* (Special Edition, Guest Editor J. Kerekes). *Journal of Pragmatics* 39, 1919–1941. See http://www.sciencedirect.com

Bourdieu, P., Wadquant, L.J.D. and Farage, S. (1994) Rethinking the state: Genesis and structure of the bureaucratic field. *Sociological Theory* 12 (1), 1–18. See http://www.jstor.org/stable/202032

DeJaeghere, J.G. (2008) Citizenship as privilege and power: Australian educators' lived experiences as citizens. *Comparative Education Review* 52 (3), 357–380.

Department of Homeland Security/United States Citizenship and Immigration Services (2006) Form M-481: Naturalization Study Guide. See http://www.padamati.com/misc/citizen/M-481.pdf

Engward, H. (2013) Understanding grounded theory. *Nursing Standard* 2a 7, 37–41.

Erickson, F. and Schultz, J. (1982) *The Counselor as Gatekeeper: Social Interaction in Interviews.* New York: Academic Press.

Estrada, K. and McLaren, P. (1993) A dialogue on multiculturalism and democratic culture. *Educational Researcher* 22 (3), 27–33.

Fairclough, N. (1989) *Language and Power.* London: Longman.

Feuerherm, E. (2013) Keywords in refugee accounts: Implications for language policies. In V. Ramanathan (ed.) *Language Policies and (Dis)citizenship: Rights, Access, Pedagogies* (pp. 52–72). Bristol: Multilingual Matters.

Gee, J. (1996). *Social Linguistics and Literacies: Ideology in Discourses.* London: Taylor & Francis.

Griswold, O. (2011) The English you need to know: Language ideology in a citizenship classroom. *Linguistics and Education* 22, 406–418.

Jupp, T.C., Roberts, C. and Cook-Gumperz, J. (1982) Language and disadvantage: The hidden process. In J. Gumperz (ed.) *Language and Social Identity* (pp. 232–256). Cambridge: Cambridge University Press.

Kramsch, C. and Whiteside, A. (2007) Three fundamental concepts in second language acquisition and their relevance in multilingual contexts. *The Modern Language Journal* 91, 907–922. See http://www.jstor.org/stable/4626140

Kunnan, A. (2009) Testing for citizenship: The U.S. naturalization test. *Language Assessment Quarterly* 6 (1), 89–97.
Laglagaron, L. and Devani, B. (June 2008) *Immigration Backgrounder 6*. Migration Policy Institute. [online pdf]
Loring, A. (2013a) *Language and US citizenship: Meanings, ideologies, policies*. PhD dissertation, University of California, Davis. Retrieved from Proquest. See http://pqdtopen.proquest.com/pqdtopen/doc/1449818628.html?FMT=ABS
Loring, A. (2013b) Classroom meanings and enactments of US citizenship: An ethnographic study. In V. Ramanathan (ed.) *Language Policies and (Dis)citizenship: Rights, Access, Pedagogies*. (pp. 188–308). Bristol: Multilingual Matters.
McKay, S.L. (1993) *Agendas for Second Language Literacy*. Cambridge: Cambridge University Press.
Office of Immigration Statistics (2013) *2012 Yearbook of Immigration Statistics*. See http://www.dhs.gov/sites/default/files/publications/ois_yb_2012.pdf
Orgad, L. (2011) Creating new Americans: The essence of Americanism under the citizenship test. *Houston Law Review* 47 (5), 1227–1297.
Park, J.W. (August 2008) A more meaningful citizenship test: Unmasking the construction of a universalist, principle-based citizenship ideology. *California Law Review* 96 (4), 999–1047. See http://scholarship.law.berkeley.edu/cgi/viewcontent.cgi?article=1171&context=californialawreview
Quimby, E. (2011) *Doing Qualitative Community Research: Lessons for Faculty, Students and the Community*. [e-book] Beijing: Bentham Science Publishers.
Ramanathan, V. (ed.) (2013) Language policies and (dis)citizenship: Rights, access, pedagogies. In V. Ramanathan (ed.) *Language Policies and (Dis)citizenship: Rights, Access, Pedagogies* (pp. 1–18). Bristol: Multilingual Matters.
Ratliff, L., Baide, A.L., Thai, L., Jarvinen, D. and Ahadi, S. (3 April 2004) The Naturalization Test Redesign. [Conference Presentation and PowerPoint Handout]. Teachers of English to Speakers of Other Languages Convention, Long Beach, CA.
Spurlin, S. (2014) The history of the US citizenship test. On *eHow*. See http://www.ehow.com/about_6375551_history-u_s_-citizenship-test.html
Tarone, E. (1980) Communication strategies, foreigner talk, and repair in interlanguage. *Language Learning* 30 (2), 417–428.
US Commission on Immigration Reform (1977) *1997 Report to Congress: Becoming an American: Immigration and Immigrant Policy*. See http://www.utexas.edu/lbj/uscir/becoming/full-report.pdf
US Embassy (13 February 2008) Revised Naturalization Test. In *IIP Digital*. See http://iipdigital.usembassy.gov/st/english/publication/2008/03/20080307151642ebyessedo0.1677057.html#axzz32CXka0nR
USCIS (2012) *A Guide to Naturalization (Form M-476)*. See http://www.uscis.gov/sites/default/files/files/article/M-476.pdf
USCIS/Office of Citizenship (n.d.) L. Patching (ed.) See Citizenship PowerPoint Presentation https://www.uscis.gov/sites/default/files/USCIS/Resources/Resources%20for%20Congress/Congressional%20Reports/Office%20of%20Citizenship%20Overview.pdf
Winn, M. (2000) Negotiating borders and discourse: A study of interaction in the US naturalization interview. [Scholarly Paper]. Unpublished Manuscript. Department of Second Language Studies, University of Hawai'i at Manoa, Honolulu.
Winn, M. (2005) Collecting target discourse: The case of the US naturalization interview. In M.H. Long (ed.) *Second Language Needs Analysis* (pp. 265–303). Cambridge: Cambridge University Press.
Zinn, H. (1980) *A People's History of the United States*. New York: Harper Collins.

Appendix A
100 Sample Sentences for Written English Testing

CIVICS/HISTORY

A Senator is elected for 6 years.
_____ is the Vice President of the United States.
All people want to be free.
America is the land of freedom.
All United States citizens have the right to vote.
America is the home of the brave.
America is the land of the free.
_____ is the President of the United States.
Citizens have the right to vote.
Congress is part of the American government.
Congress meets in Washington, D.C.
Congress passes laws in the United States.
George Washington was the first president.
I want to be a citizen of the United States.
I want to be an American citizen.
I want to become an American so I can vote.
It is important for all citizens to vote.
Many people come to America for freedom.
Many people have died for freedom.
Martha Washington was the first first lady.
Only Congress can declare war.
Our Government is divided into three branches.
People in America have the right to freedom.
People vote for the President in November.
The American flag has stars and stripes.
The American flag has 13 stripes.
The capital of the United States is Washington, D.C.
The colors of the flag are red, white, and blue.
The Constitution is the supreme law of our land.
The flag of the United States has 50 stars.

EVERYDAY LIFE

He came to live with his brother.
He has a very big dog.
He knows how to ride a bike.
He wanted to find a job.
He wanted to talk to his boss.
He went to the post office.
His wife is at work right now.
His wife worked in the house.
I am too busy to talk today.
I bought a blue car today.
I came to _____ (city) today for my interview.
I count the cars as they pass by the office.
I drive a blue car to work.
I go to work everyday.
I have three children.
I know how to speak English.
I live in the State of _____.
I want to be a United States citizen.
It is a good job to start with.
My car does not work.
She can speak English very well.
She cooks for her friends.
She is my daughter, and he is my son.
She needs to buy some new clothes.
She wanted to live near her brother.
She was happy with her house.
The boy threw a ball.
The children bought a newspaper.

(Continued)

CIVICS/HISTORY	EVERYDAY LIFE
The House and Senate are parts of Congress.	The children play at school.
The people have a voice in Government.	The children wanted a television.
The people in the class took a citizenship test.	The man wanted to get a job.
The President enforces the laws.	The teacher was proud of her class.
The President has the power of veto.	The white house has a big tree.
The President is elected every 4 years.	They are a very happy family.
The President lives in the White House.	They are very happy with their car.
The President lives in Washington, D.C.	They buy many things at the store.
The President must be an American citizen.	They came to live in the United States.
The President must be born in the United States.	They go to the grocery store.
The President signs bills into law.	They have horses on their farm.
The stars of the American flag are white.	They live together in a big house.
The Statue of Liberty was a gift from France.	They work well together.
The stripes of the American flag are red and white.	Today I am going to the store.
	Today is a sunny day.
The White House is in Washington, D.C.	Warm clothing was on sale in the store.
The United States flag is red, white, and blue.	We are very smart to learn this.
The United States of America has 50 states.	We have a very clean house.
There are 50 states in the Union.	You cook very well.
There are three braches of Government.	You drink too much coffee.
	You work very hard at your job.

Form M-481 (Department of Homeland Security/USCIS, 2006)

Appendix B
Complete List of the 64[a] Dictated Sentences for the English Writing Test

(based on unpublished notes from Winn, 2000)

I want to be an American citizen. (22 times)
I want to be a United States citizen. (3 times)

The flag is red, white, and blue. (7 times)
The flag has fifty stars.
There are fifty stars.
The American flag has 13 stripes and fifty stars.

I drive my car to work. (6 times)
I ride the bus to work.
I drive a car.

I am married, and I have one child. (3 times)
I have two beautiful children. (2 times)
I have two boys.
I have three children.
I have three beautiful children.
I have four sons.
I am single, and I have no children.

I live in a big brown house. (2 times)
I live in a big house.

I do not work.
I live and work in _____.
I work five days a week.
I am the president of my company.
My husband and I live and work in _____.

I am currently enrolled as a student.
I am a student at Rainbow Beauty College.

Today is a sunny day.

[a] During 15 of the observed interviews, no sentence was dictated for various reasons (e.g. it was a second interview, and the applicant had already passed the writing exam, or the interviewee was unable to communicate at all in English). At six of the interviews in which the English Writing Test was administered, more than one sentence was dictated because the applicant made at least one mistake. In two of these six cases, a third sentence was dictated.

Appendix C

Table 1 Coded Sentence Dictations for the English Writing Test[a]
(based on unpublished notes from Winn, 2000)

Topic	Keywords	Percent of total sentences	Total number of sentences	Number of unique sentences	Number of interviewers
US Citizen	citizen	39	25	2	4
Working	work company	22	12 (6 double coded for Ownership and 1 for Family)	7	4
Marriage and children	child children husband married	17	11 (1 double coded for Work)	8	3
Ownership	car drive house	16	10 (6 double coded for Work)	4	4
Flag (USHG)	flag stars stripes	16	10	4	3
Studying	student	3	2	2	2

[a] The total adds up to more than 100% because of double coding of six sentences. And since only one officer dictated a sentence related to the weather, one sentence is not included: 'Today is a sunny day.'

Appendix D

Table 2 Relevant Sentences Taken from the '100 Sample Sentences for Written English'

(Parentheses) designate a word form not found in Winn (2000) dictated sentence data[a]

C/H=Civics/History column; EL=Everyday Life column.

Theme	Keywords	Number of sample sentences	Sentences
Citizen	citizen	4 (+4)= 8	I want to be a **citizen** of the United States. C/H I want to be an American **citizen**. C/H I want to be a United States **citizen**. EL The president must be an American **citizen**. C/H
	(citizens)		All United States **citizens** have the right to vote. C/H **Citizens** have the right to vote. C/H It is important for all **citizens** to vote. C/H
	(citizenship)		The people in the class took a **citizenship** test. C/H
Working	work[b]	5 (+5)= 10 *2 also coded for marriage & 1 for ownership	His wife is at **work** right now.* EL I go to **work** everyday. EL I drive a blue car to **work**.* EL They **work** well together. EL You **work** very hard at your **job**. EL
	(worked)		His wife **worked** in the house.* EL
	(job)		He wanted to find a **job**. The man wanted to get a **job**. EL It is a good **job** to start with. EL
	(boss)		He wanted to talk to his **boss**. EL

(Continued)

Marriage and children	children (daughter) (son) (wife)	2 (+2)= 4 *2 also coded for work & 1 for ownership	I have three **children**. EL She is my **daughter**, and he is my son. EL His **wife** is at work right now.* EL His **wife** worked in the house.* EL
Ownership of car/ house	car drive house[c]	7 *2 also coded for work & 1 for marriage	I bought a blue **car** today. EL They are very happy with their **car**. EL My **car** does not work. EL I **drive** a blue car to work.* EL They live together in a big **house**. EL His wife worked in the **house**.* EL She was happy with her **house**. EL
Flag	Flag stars	7	The colors of the **flag** are red, white, and blue. C/H The American **flag** has 13 stripes. C/H The stripes of the American **flag** are red and white. C/H The **flag** of the United States has 50 **stars**. C/H The **flag** of the United States has 50 **stars**. C/H The **stars** of the American **flag** are white. C/H The American **flag** has **stars** and stripes. C/H
Studying	(teacher) (learn) (smart)	(+2) =2	The **teacher** was proud of her class. EL We are very **smart** to **learn** this. EL

[a] The words or word forms 'company,' 'child,' 'boys,' 'sons,' 'husband,' 'married' and 'student' do not appear in the 100 Sample Sentences though they appear in dictated sentences in Winn (2000) coded for either working/studying or marriage/children.
[b] The sample sentence 'My car does not work' was not coded under 'work' due to the lack of connotation with employment, and likewise, the sentence 'I count the cars as they pass by the office' was not included because, though it mentions the word 'office,' the sentence makes no explicit connection to working in 'the office.'
[c] 'The White House' appears in two sample sentences, and 'The House and Senate' in one; none of the three were coded under 'house' due to the lack of connotation with ownership, and likewise, the sentence 'They have horses on their farm' was not coded because a 'farm' was considered categorically different from a 'house.'

3 The Journey to US Citizenship: Interviews with Iraqi Refugees

Emily Feuerherm and Russul Roumani

> *Russul Roumani, soon after getting her US citizenship, was asked if she had an idea for the title of this chapter. She said that the process of reaching her goal to be a US citizen was a journey, and wanted that journey reflected in the title. And so it is.*

The beginning of Monisha Das Gupta's book *Unruly Immigrants* (2006) recalls a day at the Immigration and Naturalization Service[1] (INS) office in ethnographic detail filled with emotional encounters and injustice. She describes the 'rituals of humiliation' where INS officials 'bark,' 'grill' and 'shout' at the immigrants, most of whom are 'immigrants of color.' At the end, Das Gupta (2006: 2) says, 'A deep sense of injustice courses through me. I am ready to explode.' Critical descriptions such as hers are important in uncovering prejudice and inequality in the naturalization process as it occurs in practice, and they help us to identify moments and methods of resistance. Naturalization tests are another contested site of power and control (Gales, 2009), as are tests that determine eligibility for asylum based on folk beliefs of language (Eades, 2009).

And yet, while the journey to citizenship is fraught with moments of inequality, struggle and resistance, gaining citizenship is a celebrated event. Roumani's description of the day she took her citizenship test stands in stark contrast to Das Gupta's experience, though both highlight the emotional nature of citizenship, and the importance of belonging.

> This is my citizenship experience: it was indescribable, I was very happy. Finally after 7 years of feeling of not belonging I can say that I have a home that I belong to. Getting the citizenship allowed me to feel safe and secured. My daughter Aya went with me because she also had to take her citizenship test. At that day, there were 1,236 other people from 94 different countries. You can feel and clearly see the happiness at that place from all the people. Those were the most wonderful moments. (R. Roumani, personal communication, June 30, 2015)

Roumani's feelings of security and belonging upon gaining US citizenship reflect theories of citizenship that highlight connections between citizenship, access to rights, and a sense of belonging (Howe & Covell, 2005; Kymlicka & Norman, 1994). Roumani recognizes that her experience taking the citizenship test is not what all experience; many do not pass the test, and it is especially difficult for those who do not speak English well. Those whose access to rights and participation is limited, experience *dis-citizenship* (Ramanathan, 2013a, 2013b). In fact, Das Gupta's description of the INS office and the demeaning and exclusionary practices she witnessed, are excellent examples of dis-citizenship. Also, the fact that Roumani felt a sense of 'not belonging' for seven years (two after fleeing from Iraq to Syria, and five after resettling in the US as a refugee), demonstrates the power of naturalization and the importance of citizenship. As chief justice Warren argued in *Perez v. Brownell*, a case to revoke US citizenship from someone born in the US, 'Citizenship *is* man's basic right, for it is nothing less than the right to have rights' (*Perez v. Brownell*, 1958: 64).

This chapter focuses on a local study of Iraqi refugees' experiences of naturalization and US citizenship. The research was conducted collaboratively with the founder (Feuerherm) and the program manager (Roumani) of an educational program for Iraqi refugees based in Sacramento, California, the Refugee Health and Employment Attainment Program (RHEAP). This voluntary and community-based program recently developed a citizenship test preparation component, because several of the students (all Iraqi refugees) asked for help with this process. The addition of this new need and component to the program was the motivation for the current chapter.[2] Throughout our work with RHEAP, we have noticed that Iraqi refugees are highly motivated to gain US citizenship, viewed as providing security and access to transnational and global realities through the possession of a US passport. While there are policy-based motivations established to encourage (force?)[3] refugees to seek citizenship, many Iraqi refugees are pursuing the naturalization process as soon as they are allowed. This raises questions about the value of citizenship for refugees, their motivations and experiences in attaining citizenship status and the policies that guide refugees' naturalization process.

The data upon which this chapter is based are semi-structured interviews conducted by an Iraqi refugee community member, Roumani, in the language of the interviewees' choice. Iraqi refugees' accounts of their motivations and experiences in gaining US citizenship in Northern California are analyzed using two methods: research as tool and research as process (Talmy, 2011). The research questions guiding this chapter are (1) to what extent does the process of interview research affect the findings of the research? and (2) at what levels do refugees experience *dis-citizenship* in the process of gaining US citizenship?

Refugees and Citizenship

Citizenship is a term which has been well researched in applied linguistics, particularly regarding the means by which nations construct *citizens* and *non-citizens* (e.g. Bauman & Briggs, 2003), through naturalization tests (e.g. Kunnan, 2009) or through applications for asylum (e.g. Blommaert, 2009). However, these studies are oriented to a teleological definition of citizenship; one where individuals have, seek, gain or reject citizenship and which can be indicated by documents such as passports. Recent theories of *citizenship* promote a more comprehensive view, one which is polycentric (Blommaert, 2013) and focused on full participation (Ramanathan, 2013a, 2013b). Through this reimagining of the term *citizenship* as *dis-citizenship*, instances of exclusion and inequality are highlighted, resulting in a more complex, comprehensive and critical understanding of the in-between spaces and structures which include and exclude. Thus, *full citizenship* is being able to participate in the production and distribution of valued resources, while *dis-citizenship* refuses legitimacy to some (Heller, 2013; Wiley, 2013; Wodak, 2013). This critical and comprehensive view of *dis-citizenship* as the reproduction of power structures and hierarchies does not entirely discount the documents that show 'legitimate' inclusion (such as passports), but rather contextualizes them in both global and local contexts. It is from this theoretical orientation to *citizenship* – or rather *dis-citizenship* – that this chapter begins exploring the issue from the perspective of refugees.

For refugees, issues of citizenship may be fraught with issues of past traumas, alienation and the promise of opportunities in a country of resettlement. Visas and work permits are legal documents which refugees are given upon their arrival in the United States, and becoming a citizen of a country of resettlement, such as the United States, provides the additional document of a passport and the ability to engage in civic matters such as voting and employment in the federal government. These documents are often taken for granted by those who have them as a birthright, but for refugees, these documents are precious and coveted items, bought by their survival of unspeakable persecution and with a promise for a better future in the country of resettlement. Unfortunately, refugees' aspirations for a better quality of life are too often met with the realities of exclusion and *dis-citizenship* based on education and work experience completed in unrecognized institutions (Ricento, 2013) or religious persecution and racism (Blommaert, 2013; Feuerherm, 2013a).

Many refugees experience distinct and perpetual *dis-citizenship* during their resettlement (Camps, 2016; Kanno & Varghese, 2010; Ramanathan, 2013a; Ricento, 2013), because of issues around language, religion, national origin and even gender (Feuerherm, 2013a; Gabrielatos & Baker, 2008). Ironically, similar though more aggressive and traumatic issues were likely the cause of refugees' search for asylum in the first place, as outlined by the definition of *refugee* by the United Nations High Commissioner of Refugees (UNHCR):

The 1951 Refugee Convention spells out that a refugee is someone who 'owing to a well-founded fear of being persecuted for reasons of race, religion, nationality, membership of a particular social group or political opinion, is outside the country of his nationality, and is unable to, or owing to such fear, is unwilling to avail himself of the protection of that country.' (UNHCR, 2014)

As this definition makes clear, refugees were persecuted in their country of origin because of their identities, beliefs and/or nationality, but even when they have resettled they may still face discrimination. Research has shown that even perceived discrimination during and after resettlement can negatively impact refugees' health and well-being (Kira *et al.*, 2010). Nevertheless, the promise of a better life and more opportunities in the United States is seductive, and refugees continue to seek asylum in this country.

Upon arrival to the US, refugees are only offered eight months of cash assistance before they are expected to be self-sufficient. Policies require that they are given access to language and vocational training during these eight months in order to receive their cash assistance. They are encouraged to take the first job available, despite their skills and prior education. Rather than provide the means for them to translate their certificates in order to access jobs with benefits and livable wages, they are pushed into menial or service jobs (Feuerherm, 2013b; Ong, 2003). In fact, refugees arrive with more than trauma and knowledge of another language; they arrive with skills that could be viewed as a resource, but are too often overlooked (Ricento, 2013). Nevertheless, refugees are seeking citizenship in the US, despite their traumatic situations as citizens in their countries of origin and despite the lack of access to jobs in their field, even after citizenship has been attained.

Research shows that the process by which refugees seek asylum and their experiences after being resettled are not just mediated through language, but language ideologies (Blommaert, 2009; Eades, 2009). The process begins when applicants for refugee status narrate their past traumas to officials from the UNHCR in order to prove that they have been persecuted and cannot return to the country from which they fled. To gain access to the US, they must also prove through narratives, letters or other documents that they have not been a member of, or given any support to, terrorist organizations. Those who analyze such narratives are not linguists, and folk understandings about language have influenced asylum seekers in often negative and restrictive ways (Eades, 2009). Once refugees arrive in a country of asylum they must learn the language and find employment. Many refugees view resettlement in the US as an opportunity to experience freedom and opportunity, as the ideologies of the country get exported: 'land of the free' and 'land of opportunity' are ideologies which are reiterated by refugees throughout their narratives of resettlement (Ong, 2003).

Previous research on refugees' motivations for coming to the United States, and their experiences upon arrival has to do with the opportunities they believe will be made available to them. Feuerherm (2013a) shows that Iraqi refugees may not find a safe place in the process of their resettlement because of issues such as discrimination, bullying and lack of opportunities in comparison to what was available in their home country. In Australia, Watkins *et al.* (2012) show that Karen refugees' difficulties are often overlooked because of cultural reluctance to express dissatisfaction and emotional distress. They argue that more cross-cultural training of service providers and educators, as well as translation services are needed. Similarly, Stevenson and Willcott (2007) argue that culturally appropriate, structured resources are also necessary for refugee high school students to be successful in obtaining the level of education they seek. As these studies show, a one-size-fits-all model for education and services is clearly not ideal for refugee populations. Although no research has explored the extent to which refugees might need culturally appropriate resources for the naturalization test, this previous body of research indicates that such a resource may fill an unexpressed need.

Methods

This chapter is part of a larger study that began in 2010 with the founding of RHEAP. RHEAP is a community-based English as a second language (ESL) program developed by Feuerherm and administered by Roumani to help Iraqi refugees develop the skills and networks needed during resettlement. The program consists of an ESL class, health class, potluck dinner and tutoring/conversation practice. In 2013, several participants in the program requested help with the naturalization process, and a citizenship test component was added for those who were planning to take the exam. At this time, Roumani was also planning to take the citizenship test, and was invested in the process personally and professionally.

RHEAP was developed with a participatory action research (PAR) orientation to program and curriculum development, and the program was a collaborative effort between several community members and the Sacramento Immigrant Resource Center,[4] a private non-profit resettlement agency. Although community-based research for action is common in the fields of health (Israel *et al.*, 2005), social work and environmental studies (Wilmsen *et al.*, 2008), it has only rarely been used or theorized in applied linguistics. Notable exceptions include Wallerstein's (1983) curriculum which was developed using PAR principles, and Auerbach's (1992, 1996, 2002) several publications that theorize community-based literacy and English language learning programs. Additionally, Fridland and Dalle (2002) show that PAR is a particularly useful orientation to research and curriculum design when working with refugees, because of their traumatic experiences in their home countries and marginalized status in their country of resettlement.

PAR is research for action and change, and the current chapter takes a PAR orientation to research where every step is oriented to community engagement and participation. PAR is participatory at *every level* of the research process, from identifying research questions, to data gathering and the dissemination of the findings. It is an orientation to research that is more equitable than traditional models of research because it is conducted by and with the target population (Israel *et al.*, 2005), it acknowledges local knowledge systems (Canagarajah, 2005) and it restructures power in the research process to be horizontal across social boundaries. Considering the critical orientation to *dis-citizenship* espoused in this chapter, PAR is a democratizing force in a discipline's knowledge creation. It allows for those who would otherwise be excluded from participating in the research process the rights and resources to participate fully, moving from *dis-citizens* to full participation in the process of knowledge construction and dissemination.

In order to accomplish a greater level of community participation than was possible in the larger study,[5] the research focused on in this chapter is based on the work of Roumani, an Iraqi refugee community member who has been engaged in other community-based research projects as an interviewer and interpreter (Ziegahn *et al.*, 2013). She expressed interest in conducting research on citizenship and the naturalization process in her community to Feuerherm and together they made a list of interview questions (see Appendix A) in English, which Roumani translated into Arabic. After receiving Institutional Review Board approval, Roumani began recording interviews with her social network of friends and acquaintances in the Iraqi refugee community of the Sacramento region. Thus, the research topic, questions and process of gathering data have been largely instigated by the community partner and not the academic partner. After recording the interviews, Roumani passed the recordings, her notes and the signed consent forms to Feuerherm, who transcribed the English audio files. Together they translated (Roumani) and transcribed (Feuerherm) the interviews conducted in Arabic and English. Roumani gathered a total of 16 interviews between February and May 2014. The next section will discuss the interview process and the construction of US citizens through the interviews, contextualizing the research process and findings.

The Construction of 'Citizens' Through the Interview Process

Qualitative interviews, particularly those conducted from a PAR orientation, have not been adequately theorized in the applied linguistics literature. However, the 2011 special issue of *Applied Linguistics* covers a range of issues around qualitative interviews. The theories focused on are especially those regarding the positionality hypothesized by interviewers whose identity is outside of, and potentially counter to, the group of interviewees. Miller (2011) explicitly discusses researcher-influenced bias by advocating positioning analysis. Talmy (2011) and Mann (2011) both advocate for theories that focus on the co-construction of the interview as a social event through which interviewer and interviewee together create meaning. Talmy in particular demonstrates that findings from research can be altered by taking such a different approach. These are all excellent points, especially Talmy's discussion of the interview research as a *process*, but no article in this special issue addresses using members of the community as interviewers – they do not question the standard format of researcher–interviewer–academic interviewing a community of which they are not a member. However, if modernist traditions of research are going to be challenged, then so too ought the *processes* of modernist research be contested and alternatives be theorized. It is from this orientation to research, one which is participatory and challenges traditional notions of research and knowledge, that the interviews will be presented.

For each interview, Roumani informed the interviewee why he or she would be interviewed, explained our research and asked if the interviewee would prefer to conduct the interview in English or Arabic. Despite the fact that under any other circumstance they would be speaking in Arabic, all but one chose to conduct the interview in English. They all said that it would be good practice for them to speak in English, and many of them were preparing for their citizenship test, which would be administered in English. After every interview, Roumani played the interviews back to the participants. Not only was this an opportunity for them to correct any information they provided (none did), but also it was a chance for the interviewees to listen to their voices speaking English.

The interviewees discursively constructed themselves as new citizens in the interviews, but these constructions were not the production of the interviewee alone. Rather, they were co-constructed between Roumani and the interviewee. As Talmy (2011) shows, viewing an interview as a co-constructed event between the interviewer and interviewee allows for a deeper understanding of the interview as a process, beyond just a means of gathering information. Because Roumani, as the interviewer, is a member of the community and a friend of the interviewees, the co-construction of the interview is particularly evident in her interviews. For example, in the following excerpt, Roumani provides a prompt to the interviewee's answers, as they co-construct the discourse of the good citizen in the interview (see Appendix B for transcript notations):

15. **R**: what did you think so far about your experience here in the United
16.   States.
17. **A**: my experience about, uh, uh, here it's, THE LIFE here it's, because
18.   you know the democracy my children they go to school they take
19.   the good education here for them and for us for me for my wife and
20.   we work we you know 'cause=
21. **R**: =(whisper)The good life=
22. **A**: =and uh we have a good life\.
23. **R**: okay good. So did you take the citizenship test?
24. **A**: yes.
25. **R**: did you pass?
26. **A**: YES

In Line 21, Roumani whispers *the good life* during the interview and this phrase is taken up by Ahmed directly afterward to signal his acceptance of Roumani's intervention and evaluation of his meaning. When listening to the interview later, Roumani commented that she knew what he meant and was offering an analysis. Later in this same interview, a similar co-constructed segment occurs.

71. **R**: why do you want to become a citizenship?
72. **A**: .. ah.
73. **R**: (whisper) passport
74. **A**: (laugh) .. we get a pass[port it's] the important things. [And] the
75.   other things is we
76. **R**:   [okay] (smiling)   [okay]
77. **A**: feel like citizen here=
78. **R**: =uhuh=
79. **A**: =and we feel happy because my children become a citizen and they
80.   take a good education and they live here and they like to take a
81.   citizen

Again, Roumani in Line 73 is co-constructing the interview by providing answers to her questions. Because of the pause before Ahmed answers, it appears that he is searching for the words he wants to use, and Roumani supplies *passport*. This is the first mention of the passport as a reason for wanting to gain citizenship, and although Ahmed agrees, with a laugh, that the passport is important, he continues the thought by saying that he and his children identify with the US and the family *feel[s] happy* to be citizens. Here, again, the element of *belonging* is a key component of citizenship.

Roumani's positionality, identity and goals are influencing the interviews, making the co-construction of the interview process salient.

One of her main reasons for wanting US citizenship was for the benefits of international travel and opportunity. In Line 73, where Roumani whispers to the interviewee *passport* as one of the reasons he wants to become a citizen, she is co-constructing the interview and her identity and motivations for citizenship become salient through this process. In fact, this is not the only time when she whispers suggestions during the interviews, nor is it the only time she suggests that a passport may be a motivation for citizenship, though many interviewees indicated they wanted a passport without a prompt from Roumani.

In traditional interview relationships, where the researcher is outside the community, providing answers to your own interview questions would be an egregious flaw in the interview process, perhaps even invalidating the data. We argue that this phenomenon is not invalid in this case. Because Roumani is a member of the community and knows all of the interviewees personally, she has a good sense of their motivations for applying for citizenship. As Ballard and Sarathy (2008) show, local community members' knowledge can significantly benefit the research, even if the process of gathering data appears superficially less rigorous. Furthermore, in every case where Roumani interjects an answer to one of her own questions, the interviewees agree with her analysis, repeating the word she proffers. In the previous transcript with Ahmed, Roumani offers an analysis of his meaning, which he agrees with by repeating what she says. In the example below, it is evident that the interviewee, Sara, is struggling to understand and respond to the questions in English. Here, Roumani helps her by supplying words or rephrasing questions based on her knowledge of the interviewee.

26. **R**: did you choose to come here to the United States?
27. **S**: yes
28. **R**: okay. and why\. why did you choose to come here
29. **S**: my daughter need many things to make to her face
30. **R**: uhuh
31. **S**: and uh..
32. **R**: you mean surgery
33. **S**: surgery yes and …. I come with her=
34. **R**: =to be with her to help [her]
35. **S**:   [to] help her, yeah
36. **R**: what do you think of your experience here in the United States
37. **S**: … I still until I take a citizen and return. to my country
38. **R**: I mean your experience. Is it easy or is it hard
39. **S**: no. here it's very hard

As this transcript makes evident, Sara struggles with what she wants to say in English, but Roumani helps by supplying her with *surgery* in Line 32, finishing her sentence in Line 34 and rephrasing the question from Line 36 in Line 38. Sara chose to do the interview in English, to practice speaking English, but doing so required her to rely on Roumani's knowledge of the intimate details of her life. After each interview, Roumani and the interviewees listened to the recording together, and in each case the interviewees agreed that they said what they wanted and made no changes to their answers. It is common in Iraqi culture for help to be offered in even the smallest circumstances, such as when someone is searching for a word in a language that he or she does not speak fluently. Such is the case with Roumani; she offers help and guidance through the process, as is expected in her culture. Rather than invalidating the research, her knowledge of her interviewees and the rapport they have built make the research findings valid.

In each interview a discursive construction of citizenship is performed through an expressed attachment to the US. This attachment is articulated in reference to discussions of 'home' and the place where children are educated. Despite the troubles that many experienced in the first years of resettlement, all but one of the Iraqi refugees interviewed indicated that they felt their experiences were overwhelmingly positive. No one complained of unfair treatment, bullying or specific difficulties with any part of the resettlement or naturalization process. Only Sara, who had been in the US for only 15 months, complained that her life was very hard and that she did not plan to stay in the US. However, she was the only interviewee who did not construct positive associations with living in the US and an identity tied directly to becoming a citizen. Her goal was to get citizenship to acquire a passport, then return to her son who was living in Yemen.[6] Despite the fact that the interviewer was a trusted member of their community, not an outside researcher, and has herself endured difficulties throughout the process of resettlement, only this one of the 16 interviewees did not construct an identity that was aligned with positive ideologies of US citizenship. It is likely that in their responses, interviewees were constructing their answers to not only reflect their imagined identities as US citizens, but also based on their awareness of the purpose of these interviews as a larger study regarding their naturalization process.

Other research that has used community members as interviewers has not theorized the potential for an awareness of the larger audience or the co-construction of an interview event. For example, Christopher et al. (2005) discuss the importance of developing culturally sensitive interview tools for the Native American communities. Focusing on the Apsáalooke community, Christopher et al. (2005: 133) showed that the traditional interview process where the interview is 'neutral, distant and businesslike' would not be effective with this community and instead encouraged rapport building and interview processes that were aligned with the community's values and linguistic resources. However, they do not theorize the process of the interview as a co-constructed event, only as a means for gathering data. As evidenced by the transcript excerpts above, the community member is a key player in the interview process, as much as any other interview researcher might be. It is clear that even when attempting to adjust interview practices to a PAR approach, doing so without critically examining the co-construction of the event could result in a one-dimensional view of the results.

Motivations for Citizenship: A Passport to the World

As Talmy (2011) argues, analyzing an interview as a process of co-construction of meanings is important. However, one particular trend in the interviews in the current chapter requires the integration of the interview as research instrument. This refers to an orientation to interviews as a method for exploring an individual's attitudes and beliefs, in this case, in regard to his or her motivations for gaining citizenship. Although the process of interviews as co-constructed meaning is important, it is also important to address some of the findings from the interviews. Instead of having a singular focus on interview as process, we argue that interviews should be analyzed according to methods that are appropriate for their context and content. As such, this section will focus on Iraqi refugees' responses to the question of why they wanted to become US citizens.

All of the Iraqi refugees interviewed applied for citizenship as soon as they were able, or planned to as soon as they would become eligible, after about five years of residency. The most prevalent reason why refugees wanted to get citizenship (in 13 out of 16 interviews) was to get a US passport. The three outliers were a woman who focused on her need for medical treatment, a man who expressed an alliance with the United States as his home, and a woman who mentioned protection and that it would allow her to 'do anything.' This last case could, in fact, be a reference to being able to travel internationally, and it was Roumani's impression from informal discussions with the participant that she did want citizenship to be able to travel.

Getting citizenship for a passport is a motivation not unique to this group: Loring (2013: 196) shows that both students and teachers in citizenship classes identify 'the economic, global and familial benefits' they will receive as their motivation for gaining citizenship. The global benefits in particular – international opportunities and travel – are a primary motivation for the Iraqi refugees in this study. Roumani herself became a citizen in part to get a passport so that she could travel and (possibly) work abroad. Although she is employed in Sacramento, she has not been able to find a full-time job that pays enough for her to support her three children, all who are or will soon be attending college. If she cannot find a full-time job here with a living wage, she will seek employment abroad, especially looking for openings in the Middle East. Her US passport can help her find a job with the United Nations or other international organizations that provide humanitarian support in that part of the world. Access to a global economy is a benefit that many immigrants and refugees must turn to, particularly because of exclusionary certification policies (Ricento, 2013) and language barriers which limit access to the best jobs. Such exclusionary measures are instances of *dis-citizenship* (Devlin & Pothier, 2006; Ramanathan, 2013a, 2013b), resulting in transnationality and flexible citizenship (Glick Schiller *et al.*, 1995; Ong, 1999).

Several participants, like Sara in the transcript above, indicate that they want to get the passport not only for travel, but also to live outside of the United States. The following transcript with Muhammad explains that having a passport from the US allows one to access international employment, and this is a key component of his motivation to be naturalized:

26. **R**: and can you tell us WHY do you want to become a citizen.
27. **M**: to get the passport=
28. **R**: =okay=
29. **M**: =actually the United States passport it's your passport to a:ll over
30.   the world
31. **R**: uh-huh
32. **M**: it's VERY important especially for someone like me came from
33.   Middle East and he DENIED EVERYWHERE he want to get visa
34.   or trying to get work. So if I get United States citizenship I think
35.   all the world will be open for me with my professional. I get a
36.   better opportunity for a better job. in the world.

Muhammad is one of the few Iraqi refugees who was able to transfer his career as a project manager in construction from Iraq to the US. He had his BA in civil engineering from Iraq transferred to a certificate in the US and found a job in construction. However, despite the fact that he has access to a job in his field, he views the passport as an opportunity for travel and better employment outside of the US. He is not alone in this view. Many Iraqi refugees want the US passport so that they can return to Middle Eastern, Arabic-speaking countries such as Qatar and the United Arab Emirates where having a US passport will increase their salary compared to what it would be if they only had Iraqi passports, and compared to what they can find domestically. Thus, families utilize their resources across political and economic borders in order to defend against their subordination (Glick Schiller *et al.*, 1995). The US passport has the power to transform a transnational individual into a global citizen with access to global opportunities. This pragmatic view of naturalization arises from the *dis-citizenship* experienced by Iraqis in their search for a living wage in the field of their choice.

Despite the fact that a passport is not the only reason participants wanted to attain citizenship (several mentioned safety and security, educational and employment opportunities for themselves and their children and a sense of belonging to the country), it was the most widely referenced reason for seeking naturalization. The fact that the passport is more than a travel document, but a means for gaining international employment for these Iraqi refugees, raises questions regarding the policies of resettlement and naturalization. Resettlement policies' focus on early economic self-sufficiency, in many cases above the health and well-being of the refugees, may be one part of the reason. Another may be the types of opportunities available (or lack thereof) in the United States.

Discussion

Despite being interviewed by a member of the community, nearly all of the Iraqi refugees in this study aligned themselves with the US, and only one mentioned the negative aspects of her experiences. Fifteen out of sixteen interviewees actively constructed themselves and their children as Americans. There was no mention of any prejudice they or their children have experienced because of their religion, nationality, primary language or other aspect of their identity during these interviews, despite the fact that the authors know of instances of bullying and exclusion in these participants' lives. Rather, they were discursively constructing themselves and imagining themselves as primarily American. 'The modern nation-state ... grows less out of natural facts – such as language, blood, soil, and race – and more out of a quintessential cultural product, a product of the collective imagination' (Appadurai, 1996: 161). All but one of the Iraqis interviewed had reimagined themselves as American during these interviews, and identified with ideologies of freedom and opportunity found here.

This raises the question posed at the beginning of the chapter: to what extent does the process of interview research affect the findings of the research? This chapter has shown that research conducted with community members increases the validity of the findings. As one who was etic to the community of Iraqi refugees, Feuerherm assumed that there would be more specialized training wanted/needed to prepare applicants for the naturalization test, as was indicated by other research about refugee services (e.g. Stevenson & Willcott, 2007; Watkins *et al.*, 2012). Furthermore, by being a US citizen since birth, Feuerherm's identity may have influenced the Iraqi refugee immigrants away from claiming ownership of their budding American identity (see Feuerherm, 2013a). Instead, because a trusted member of their community was conducting these interviews (Roumani), participants were comfortable in claiming knowledge about the naturalization process and were open about their feelings of belonging to the US. Additionally, between when the interviews were conducted in February 2014, and the writing of this chapter in July 2015, all of the interviewees who took the naturalization test passed and are now citizens.

What was especially salient in the process of the interviews was the extent to which they were co-constructed. Roumani's knowledge of her community and the cultural expectations of the interview process resulted in surprising findings about the community's identity and motivations for becoming naturalized US citizens. Clearly, more theorizing of community-internal co-construction of the interview is necessary. Hypothesizing about the positionality of the researcher in relation to the co-construction of an interview has been discussed at great length when the researcher is etic to the community, and this chapter begins to address an emic perspective in the co-construction of interviews.

In addition to aligning with the US and constructing an identity of belonging, the interviews showed that participants were motivated by the global opportunities naturalization would provide. This was particularly evident in reference to passports, international travel and international job opportunities. Ricento (2013) provides a striking example of the *dis-citizenship* experienced by refugees when they are resettled in regard to their employment options. For many of the refugees in this study, the lack of opportunities for full participation domestically – or the *dis-citizenship* they have experienced – is leading them to seek better opportunities, with a US passport, abroad. Refugees are resourceful, and many view a US passport as a resource to build transnational identities. Policymakers should critically reflect on the process of naturalization and reorient resettlement and naturalization policies to be more supportive, especially recognizing the capacities and resources/resourcefulness with which refugees arrive. This would require a paradigm shift where refugees would be viewed as resources themselves, not a drain on resources. Too often, refugees are portrayed as victims who drain supportive resources, even by the agencies responsible for supporting them (Tyeklar, 2016). And finally, it would entail providing more access to jobs that provide living wages in the refugees' fields.

What can be done to combat such far-reaching policies and ideologies regarding the abilities and resourcefulness of refugees? One step toward more equitable engagement would be to have refugees participate in the resettlement policies and practices they are experiencing. This requires recognizing the resources and capacities of our own students, research participants and community partners, and involving them as equitable partners through all stages of research. Research in the medical and environmental fields has theorized and used participatory research to great effect (see Israel et al., 2005; Wilmsen et al., 2008) while applied linguistic research lacks theorization of this process. It remains under-researched and under-theorized despite the recognition that interviews are context-bound instances of social processes, where meaning is co-constructed by the participants (Mann, 2011; Talmy, 2011; Talmy & Richards, 2011). As Feuerherm (2013b) shows, the more ownership refugees have in the services that are available to them, the more successful those services are. The same can be said of research that focuses on refugees, or any minority or underprivileged group: the more the ownership of research is shared with the participants, the more invested participants will be, and the more valid the findings will be. Finally, through this democratizing process of participatory research, the effects of *dis-citizenship* in research will be challenged and those who had been excluded will instead be empowered through capacity building and knowledge creation.

Notes

(1) INS became the US Citizenship and Immigration Services (USCIS) in 2003 when it became part of the Department for Homeland Security.
(2) We initially planned to assess the needs of Iraqi refugees in order to build a curriculum that matched their perceived needs as closely as possible, but found that none of the refugees were struggling to access and use naturalization test preparation resources.
(3) Refugees are eligible to apply for citizenship after four years and nine months of residence. However, if the refugees are receiving cash assistance for dependents or through supplemental security income, it is terminated after seven years of residence if citizenship has not been attained. In other words, policies are in place to encourage/force refugees into applying for and attaining US citizenship through access to cash assistance. In none of the interviews was cash assistance mentioned as one of the reasons why the refugees chose to apply for citizenship.
(4) The organization's name as well as all participants' names are pseudonyms to protect the identities of the participants.
(5) The larger study was a dissertation, and because of this it was necessarily limited to more traditional means of gathering and analyzing data.
(6) Sara did not choose to come to the US for herself, but for her daughter's medical needs. Part of her interview transcript is included in Motivations for Citizenship: A Passport to the World.

References

Appadurai, A. (1996) *Modernity at Large: Cultural Dimensions of Globalization*. Minneapolis, MN: University of Minnesota Press.
Auerbach, E. (1992) *Making Meaning Making Change: Participatory Curriculum Development for Adult ESL Literacy*. McHenry, IL: Center for Applied Linguistics and Delta Systems, Inc.
Auerbach, E. (ed.) (2002) *Community Partnerships*. Case Studies in TESOL Practice series. Alexandria, VA: TESOL.
Auerbach, E., Barahona, B., Midy, J., Vaquierano, F., Zambrano, A. and Arnaud, J. (1996) *Adult ESL/Literacy: From the Community to the Community: A Guidebook for Participatory Literacy Training*. Mahwah, NJ: Lawrence Erlbaum Associates.

Ballard, H. and Sarathy, B. (2008) Inclusion and exclusion: Immigrant forest workers and participation in natural resource management. In C. Wilmsen, W. Elmendorf, L. Fisher, J. Ross, B. Sarathy and G. Wells (eds) *Partnerships for Empowerment: Participatory Research for Community-Based Natural Resource Management* (pp. 167–181). London: Earthscan.

Bauman, R. and Briggs, C. (2003) *Voices of Modernity: Language Ideologies and the Politics of Inequality.* Cambridge: Cambridge University Press.

Blommaert, J. (2009) Language, asylum, and the national order. *Current Anthropology* 50 (4), 415–441.

Blommaert, J. (2013) Citizenship, language and superdiversity: Towards complexity. *Journal of Language, Identity and Education* 12 (3), 193–196.

Camps, D. (2016) Restraining English instruction for refugee adults in the United States. In E. Feuerherm and V. Ramanathan (eds) *Refugee Resettlement: Language, Policies, Pedagogies* (pp. 54–72). Bristol: Multilingual Matters.

Canagarajah, S. (2005) Introduction. In S. Canagarajah (ed.) *Reclaiming the Local in Language Policy and Practice* (pp. xiii–xxix). Mahwah, NJ: Lawrence Erlbaum Associates.

Christopher, S., Burhansstipanov, L. and Knows His Gun-McCormick, A. (2005) Using a CBPR approach to develop an interviewer training manual with members of the Apsáalooke nation. In B.A. Israel, E. Eng, A.J. Schulz and E.A. Parker (eds) *Methods in Community-Based Participatory Research for Health* (pp. 128–145). San Francisco, CA: Jossey-Bass.

Das Gupta, M. (2006) *Unruly Immigrants: Rights, Activism, and Transnational South Asian Politics in the United States.* Durham, NC: Duke University Press.

Devlin, R. and Pothier, D. (2006) *Critical Disability Theory.* Vancouver: UBC Press.

Eades, D. (2009) Testing the claims of asylum seekers: The role of language analysis. *Language Assessment Quarterly* 6 (1), 30–40.

Feuerherm, E. (2013a) Keywords in refugee accounts: Implications for language policies. In V. Ramanathan (ed.) *Language Policies and (Dis)Citizenship; Rights, Access, Pedagogies* (pp. 52–72). Bristol: Multilingual Matters.

Feuerherm, E. (2013b) *Language Policies, Identities and Education in Refugee Resettlement,* doctoral dissertation. Retrieved from ProQuest, UMI Dissertations Publishing (3602059).

Fridland, G. and Dalle, T. (2002) Start with what they know; build with what they have: Survival skills for refugee women. In E. Auerbach (ed.) *Community Partnerships* (pp. 27–40). Alexandria, VA: TESOL.

Gabrielatos, C. and Baker, P. (2008) Fleeing, sneaking, flooding: A corpus analysis of discursive constructions of refugees and asylum seekers in the UK press, 1996–2005. *Journal of English Linguistics* 36 (1), 5–38.

Gales, T. (2009) The language barrier between immigration and citizenship in the United States. In G. Extra, M. Spotti and P. Van Avermaet (eds) *Language Testing, Migration and Citizenship* (pp. 189–210). New York: Continuum International Publishing Group.

Glick-Schiller, N., Basch, L. and Szanton Blanc, C. (1995) From immigrant to transmigrant: Theorizing transnational migration. *Anthropological Quarterly* 68 (1), 48–63.

Heller, M. (2013) Language and dis-citizenship in Canada. *Journal of Language, Identity, & Education* 12 (3), 189–192.

Howe, R.B. and Covell, K. (2005) *Empowering Children: Children's Rights Education as a Pathway to Citizenship.* Toronto, ON: University of Toronto Press.

Israel, B.A., Eng, E., Schulz, A.J. and Parker, E.A. (eds) (2005) *Methods in Community-Based Participatory Research for Health.* San Francisco, CA: Jossey-Bass.

Kanno, Y. and Varghese, M.M. (2010) Immigrant and refugee ESL students' challenges to accessing four-year college education: From language policy to educational policy. *Journal of Language, Identity & Education* 9 (5), 310–328.

Kira, I.A., Lewandowski, L., Templin, T., Ramaswamy, V., Ozkan, B. and Mohanesh, J. (2010) The effects of perceived discrimination and backlash on Iraqi refugees' mental and physical health. *Journal of Muslim Mental Health* 5 (1), 59–81.

Kunnan, A.J. (2009) Politics and legislation in citizenship testing in the United States. *Annual Review of Applied Linguistics* 29, 37–48.

Kymlicka, W. and Norman, W. (1994) Return of the citizen: A survey of recent work on citizenship theory. *Ethics* 104 (2), 352–381.

Loring, A. (2013) Classroom meanings and enactments of citizenship: An ethnographic study. In V. Ramanathan (ed.) *Language Policies and (Dis)Citizenship; Rights, Access, Pedagogies* (pp. 188–208). Bristol: Multilingual Matters.

Mann, S. (2011) A critical review of qualitative interviews in applied linguistics. *Applied Linguistics* 32 (1), 6–24.

Miller, E. (2011) Indeterminacy and interview research: Co-constructing ambiguity and clarity in interviews with an adult immigrant learner of English. *Applied Linguistics* 32 (1), 43–59.

Ong, A. (1999) *Flexible Citizenship: The Cultural Logics of Transnationality*. London: Duke University Press.

Ong, A. (2003) *Buddha is Hiding: Refugees, Citizenship, the New America*. Berkeley, CA: University of California Press.

Perez v. Brownell, 235 F2d 364 (356 U.S. 44 1958). See https://www.law.cornell.edu/supremecourt/text/356/44#writing-ZS (accessed 6 July 2015).

Ramanathan, V. (2013a) Language policies and (dis)citizenship: Rights, access, pedagogies. In V. Ramanathan (ed.) *Language Policies and (Dis)Citizenship; Rights, Access, Pedagogies* (pp. 1–16). Bristol: Multilingual Matters.

Ramanathan, V. (2013b) Language policies and (dis)citizenship: Who belongs? who is a guest? who is made to leave? *Language, Identity and Education* 12 (3), 162–166.

Ricento, T. (2013) Dis-citizenship for refugees in Canada: The case of Fernando. *Journal of Language, Identity, & Education* 12 (3), 184–188.

Stevenson, J. and Willott, J. (2007) The aspiration and access to higher education of teenage refugees in the UK. *Compare: A Journal of Comparative Education* 37 (5), 671–687.

Talmy, S. (2011) The interview as collaborative achievement: Interaction, identity, and ideology in a speech event. *Applied Linguistics* 32 (1), 25–42.

Talmy, S. and Richards, K. (2011) Theorizing qualitative research interviews in applied linguistics. *Applied Linguistics* 32 (1), 1–5.

Tyeklar, N. (2016) The U.S. refugee resettlement process: A path to self-sufficiency or marginalization? In E. Feuerherm and V. Ramanathan (eds) *Refugee Resettlement: Language, Policies, Pedagogies* (pp. 152–171). Bristol: Multilingual Matters.

UNHCR (2014) 'Flowing Across Borders.' See http://www.unhcr.org/pages/49c3646c125.html (accessed 2 June 2014).

Wallerstein, N. (1983) *Language and Culture in Conflict: Problem-Posing in the ESL Classroom*. Menlo Park, CA: Addison-Wesley Publishing Company.

Watkins, P.G., Razee, H. and Richters, J. (2012) 'I'm telling you...the language barrier is the most, the biggest challenge': Barriers to education among Karen refugee women in Australia. *Australian Journal of Education* 56 (2), 126–141.

Wiley, T. (2013) Constructing and deconstructing 'illegal' children. *Journal of Language, Identity, & Education* 12 (3), 167–172.

Wilmsen, C., Elmendorf, W., Fisher, L., Ross, J., Sarathy, B. and Wells, G. (eds) (2008) *Partnerships for Empowerment: Participatory Research for Community-Based Natural Resource Management* (pp. 217–238). London: Earthscan.

Wodak, R. (2013) Dis-citizenship and migration: A critical discourse-analytical perspective. *Journal of Language, Identity & Education* 12 (3), 173–178.
Ziegahn, L., Ibrahim, S., Al-Ansari, B., Mahmood, M., Tawffeq, R., Mughir, M., Hassan, N., Debondt, D., Mendez, L., Maynes, E., Aguilar-Gaxiola, S. and Xiong, G. (2013) *The Mental and Physical Health of Recent Iraqi Refugees in Sacramento, CA.* Sacramento, CA: UC Davis Clinical and Translational Science Center.

Appendix A

Interview details
Interviewer: _____
Interviewee(s): _____
Date of interview: _____
Location of interview: _____
Start and stop time of interview: _____

Background on interviewee:
Age: _____
Marital status: _____ Number of children: _____
Ethnic identity: _____ Gender: _____
Highest level of education: _____
Career experience: _____
_____
How long in the US: _____
Visa status (SIV, Refugee, Family reunion, etc.): _____
Primary resettlement area: _____

Interview questions
1. Did you go to a secondary resettlement country before coming here?
2. Did you choose to come to the United States? Why?
3. What do you think of your experience in the US so far?
4. Did you take the citizenship test?
    a. If no: Do you plan to take the citizenship test? Why or why not? Have you started to prepare for it? Why or why not? Why do you want to become a citizen OR why do you not want to become a citizen?
    b. If yes: Did you pass? What did you think about it? What did you do to prepare for it? How long did you prepare for it? Did you feel prepared for it? Did you know in advance about all that was required for citizenship? Did you fill out the forms yourself or did someone help you? If someone helped you, who were they? Did you find the test difficult or easy? Why? How long did it take you? Why do you want to become a citizen?

Appendix B

Transcription key

Numbering of lines comes from the original transcription
Speaker represented by their initial (R for Roumani, A for Ahmed, S for Sara and M for Muhammad)

CAPS	Loud speech
:::	Word said longer than other words
=	Linked speech
[ ]	Overlapped speech
( )	Additional information such as laughing or whispered speech
.	Each '.' marks a 1 second pause

Part 2
Pedagogies

4 'The ELD Classes Are ... Too Much and We Need to Take Other Classes to Graduate': Arizona's Restrictive Language Policy and the Dis-Citizenship of ELs

Karen E. Lillie

A fear of the 'Other,' often directed toward non-English-speaking immigrants, is prevalent in many parts of the United States. One only has to turn on the news to see headlines including terms such as 'illegal aliens' or 'illegal immigrant,' labels which perpetuate negative stereotypes and often are targeting those who do not speak English. False ideological beliefs about how best to help non-English-speaking immigrants 'assimilate' into US society may be present in education policies which inform districts how to educate immigrant children or the children of immigrants – or, more broadly, English language learners (ELs).[1]

The state of Arizona has taken a particularly harsh stance against immigrants (e.g. SB 1070) while simultaneously implementing a highly restrictive language policy in schools for ELs. Many recent works are documenting the negative implications this may have on various levels (Arias & Faltis, 2012; Moore, 2014; Rios-Aguilar & Gándara, 2012a, 2012b[2]); however, no known prior studies have queried students – the ones who are impacted most directly – about their own perceptions of Arizona's language policy as practiced in school and the impact of this on their future.

In this chapter, I will discuss the concept of *citizenship* in the United States and how this shifts when analyzing the term in relation to certain institutions such as schools. This is significant when English-Only sentiments have steadily increased to a point where educational instruction is now infringed upon and has subsequently limited certain students' access to full 'citizenship' in the state of Arizona. I will then describe Arizona's policy and the instructional model in place today for ELs, including a synthesis of recent scholarly work regarding the negative implications that Arizona's policy has on ELs and their education. Finally, I will share data from a survey administered to over 2000 students in Arizona schools: the students who are/were subjected to the policy as practiced. The implications of Arizona's policy will be discussed as it relates to (a) students' ability to access content and graduate, (b) students' perceived treatment at school, and (c) whether the policy thus impacts their ability to become 'citizens,' students' awareness of this invisible border and what this means for the future inclusion of Arizona's ELs in America.

Redefining Citizenship

Citizenship as a construct in a traditional sense is often bestowed on native-born persons or those who have legal documentation to signify allegiance with a nation. Immigrants coming to the US may or may not have this paperwork or the benefit of a birthright status in order to claim this definition of citizenship. Recently, scholars have been advancing the notion that *citizenship* is more fluid and must account for the political, economic and social constructs that identify one as being a 'citizen' or not (see Ramanathan, 2013a, 2013b). As Chang and Aoki (1997: 311) state, the term *immigrant* implies that one has crossed a specific, fixed border; however, the 'immigrant may learn after crossing...that she has not left it behind, that the border is not just a peripheral phenomenon. She may learn, through the juridical and extrajuridical policing of the border, that she carries the border with her' because the borders are based on societal constructs. Ramanathan's (2013a, 2013b) definition of *citizenship* as one's belonging to a community and his or her ability to participate fully in the larger society is a way to expand the prior limiting and exclusionary paradigm and reconsider what it means to be a 'citizen.' To Ramanathan and others,[3] citizenship is a *process* which can be impeded by local conditions including politics, teacher pedagogies, actual borders, and, importantly for this chapter, policies which may or may not establish equitable conditions for the participants involved.

Pushing past the confines of labeling people as citizens based solely on the traditional definition of citizenship therefore means examining those areas (such as educational institutions) which are often wrongly thought to be beyond any of the ideological constraints embedded within the broader society. Under *Plyer v. Doe* (1982), all children, regardless of their immigrant status, have the right to an education in the US (see Olivas, 2012; Wiley, 2013b). However, policies of schools – especially restrictive language policies – which are established and largely affect those who are often seen as the 'Other', whether because of their racial/ethnic background or because of their linguistic diversity from mainstream society (in this case, English learners, or ELs), can be what creates false borders and determines who will be able to fully participate and access all that society has to offer. So how is it that these ideologies about who belongs, who has access, and who is a rightful 'citizen' continue and multiply, particularly in schools?

Critical race theory (CRT) in education examines how majoritarian stories are used to maintain the status quo of the dominant (White, upper-middle class) society at large while challenging the more traditional ideologies embedded in educational institutions for teaching minority populations, such as *equal opportunity* and *color-blindness* (Solórzano & Yasso, 2009). These types of ideological stances mask and thus maintain the privilege of dominant groups. Since majoritarian stories perpetuate the dominant society's beliefs, they are often taken as truth, are viewed as the norm and are seen as natural, as 'common sense.' CRT theorists posit that through majoritarian stories we are informed that

> limited or Spanish-accented English and Spanish surnames equal bad schools and poor academic performance. It also reminds us that people who may not have the legal documents to 'belong' in the United States may be identified by their skin color, hair texture, eye shape, accent, and/or surname. (Solórzano & Yosso, 2009: 136)

It is through these deficit stories that academic failure is seen as the fault of the student, largely due to their cultural difference. The implication then is that the students must be culturally assimilated and that this can occur by learning English (see Solórzano & Yasso, 2009: 138). LatCrit[4] theorists further include issues of ethnicity and importantly, immigration status and language, with race (Chang & Aoki, 1997; Marx, 2009; Monzó & Rueda, 2009; Revilla & Asato, 2002). ELs with Spanish-accented English, for example, are often seen by teachers as having lower intelligence or as unsuccessful because of the focus on what they believe these students are 'lacking' – the English language (Marx, 2009; Monzó & Rueda, 2009). Applying CRT and LatCrit to education, it can become more apparent how often non-English speakers are considered 'second-class citizens' (Monzó & Rueda, 2009: 38) through the reinforcement of deficit ideologies around ELs and ELs' abilities and the devaluing of what these emergent bilinguals actually bring to society. This is especially the case in states with enacted English-only policies. Language policies in schools which exclude the native languages of students maintain the myth that knowing English means one can be a full 'citizen'; in the case of Arizona, particularly with the restrictive language policy in place, the state may be impeding these students from becoming full members of society as studies are beginning to document since the implementation of the English-only model (Arias & Faltis, 2012; Moore, 2014).

Ramanathan (2013a: 3) calls us to 're-cognize' our thinking of citizenship and 'take account of how language policies...serve to draw borders and exclude.' The studies and data presented in this chapter are testament to just how the policy in Arizona marginalizes and 'draws borders' around ELs. A dichotomy is created of 'us' and 'them,' of 'EL' and 'non-EL.' I argue in this chapter that the state of Arizona is attempting to culturally and linguistically assimilate ELs under the ideological guise of helping children reach the 'American Dream'[5] through its highly restrictive language policy known as Structured English Immersion (SEI), and that this has coincided with anti-immigrant discourse in the state. The restrictive language policy in Arizona is asking ELs to assimilate to the 'American' culture and language, at the expense of their own histories and identities, thus promoting and creating environments of *dis-citizenship* (Ramanathan, 2013a). The policy in Arizona schools precludes ELs from an equal education, which in turn impedes their ability to be full members of society in the future. This is true for all of Arizona's ELs, but is perhaps more true for immigrant children (both first and second generation) who have the added barrier of physical borders and paperwork on top of the burden of learning English in order to 'fit in' and 'be American.' To understand how this policy came to be, one must first examine the historical trend in the United States toward the use of English, toward immigrants and toward ELs.

English-Only in America

A largely held myth in America is that English is the official language of the country. English-only ideologies have been present throughout America's history and these sentiments tend to increase in times wherein tension exists regarding politics or within the economy, and during periods of high immigration (Crawford, 2004; Gándara *et al.*, 2010). As Wiley (2004: 322) notes, language diversity is often seen as something which is 'imported' via immigration even though, historically, linguistic diversity has been derived from the 'incorporation of indigenous peoples through conquest and annexation and the involuntary immigration of enslaved Africans' thus continuing a dominant ideological misconception that knowing English means one is a citizen. Linguistic assimilation has been a 'universal mandate' for ELs because the dominant discourse assumption is that these minority groups will benefit from taking on American culture and the 'American' language (i.e. English) (Wiley, 2004: 324; Wiley & Lukes, 1996).

Leniency existed toward other groups (e.g. White, European immigrants) and their languages throughout the early days of America's existence

(Wiley, 2004, 2013a; Wright, 2011). From about 1880 onward, immigrant populations from Europe were increasing and thus tolerance toward (non-English-speaking) immigrants began to wane; this only intensified with the advent of World War I (Tiersma, 2012; Wiley, 2013a). America's past century especially has seen a call for immigrant assimilation, with many English-only proponents articulating that immigrants 'need' to know English in order to be a 'good American' (Gándara et al., 2010; also Crawford, 2000a, 2000b; Wiley & Lukes, 1996). Again, one of the ways to assimilate people is to focus on the teaching of English in schools.

Regardless of the diverse linguistic makeup of the US, the idea of having multiple languages and teaching in languages other than English in US schools has been contentious, and bilingual education has never been a countrywide requirement (Crawford, 2004; Wright, 2011). A few court cases have dealt with language rights, with some involving language education; however, most courts leave the decisions of how to educate ELs up to the individual state.[6] One of the earlier cases[7] on language rights and schooling was *Meyer v. Nebraska* (1923). With the beginning of World War I, school districts started to limit the languages which could be used when educating children. In *Meyer*, a school teacher was convicted of using German and thus violating Nebraska's English-only law. The law stated that no language other than English could be used for instruction purposes, and that children could only learn another language once they were through the eighth grade (Tiersma, 2012). Ultimately, the Supreme Court decided in favor of Meyer, noting that parents had the right to choose how their children were educated, even if that meant doing so in another language. Fast-forward 100 years and we find that today while parents may have the right to choose how to educate their children, in some instances, such as those states with highly restrictive, English-only language policies, this 'choice' is via difficult-to-come-by parental waivers, assuming parents are even aware that this option exists (see Wiley & Wright, 2004).

The concept of being a 'good' American was a message readily promoted by a more recent English-Only Movement which began in the 1980s and saw the founding of a group known as US English.[8] This group's main impetus was for English to become the official language of the States (Crawford, 2000a, 2004; Del Valle, 2003). US English promoted many false ideological messages to the public, many of which stemmed from anti-immigrant sentiments and a fear of an 'encroachment of other tongues' (Crawford, 2004: 133). Some of the falsehoods derived from this English-Only Movement, and which have influenced the initiative that changed the language policy of Arizona, included that immigrants were not learning English, that language diversity would lead to political separatism and that bilingual education would divide the country (Crawford, 2004; Lillie & Moore, 2014). An attempt was made to pass the

English Language Empowerment Act which Senator Hayakawa (a founder of US English) claimed was necessary because it would '"send a message" to immigrants that English-speaking ability is an obligation of American citizenship' (Crawford, 2004: 134). While the Act did not pass the Senate, messages like this have continued and have set the stage for the more recent initiatives known as English for the Children.

English for the Children

While proponents of the earlier English-Only Movement were not always directly attacking the language of schools (Lillie & Moore, 2014), the more recent initiatives have worked toward ensuring that English is the sole medium of instruction for all ELs, a population which often includes immigrant children and the children of immigrant parents (Baker, 2011; Gándara & Hopkins, 2010). Under the guise of the majoritarian ideology of helping all children 'succeed' in the 'American Dream' by ensuring their 'right to learn English' (Wiley & Wright, 2004: 150), the English for the Children initiatives began the assault on bilingual education in California in the 1990s. Similar to Wodak's (2013) discussion of election campaigns, English for the Children was adept at using catchy slogans (e.g. 'Let's Teach English to All of America's Children' on the group's webpage[9]) and effectively used the media (i.e. newspapers, advertisements) to help secure the public vote by making it seem as if the push for English-only schooling was beneficial to *all* students and not just focused on immigrant or non-native English-speaking children. Johnson (2006: 17) notes this organization 'used the American dream metaphor as a tool to convince language minority communities that their children needed English to succeed' while promoting a method of learning English in an immersion setting. During their campaign, the idea of needing English to achieve the 'American Dream' was replicated in newspapers throughout the state by targeting bilingual education as the problem. Johnson (2005, 2006: 22) shares types of media discourse present at that time, such as 'these children need to learn English...so that they can enjoy the American dream that all others are enjoying except them.' Ultimately, this impetus for English-only instruction led to the dismantling of and almost virtual eradication of bilingual education in three states: California (Proposition 227), Massachusetts[10] (Question 2) and Arizona (Proposition 203).

Proposition 203 decrees that immigrant children could become 'more productive members of society' by learning English since English is 'the language of opportunity' and this will 'thereby [allow] them to fully participate in the American Dream of economic and social advancement.'[11] The Proposition, which ultimately became Arizona Revised Statutes (A.R.S.) §15-751 through §15-757, stipulates that English immersion is the means to achieve this end. Further, this needs to be done as 'rapidly... as possible' because the belief is that young immigrants can become fluent if 'heavily exposed' to English (Section 1.5 & 1.6). Although it was not specified what the actual instructional model should look like, other than it be English immersion, Proposition 203 set the stage for the SEI model as it stands today.

Arizona's SEI model

Arizona has arguably the most restrictive language policy for educating ELs in the US, a policy which resulted in the creation of the model known as Structured English Immersion (SEI) used statewide since 2008. Much has been written on the history leading up to the enactment of the policy in place today (Arias & Faltis, 2012; Combs, 2012; Lillie & Moore, 2014). What is important to remember here, however, is that all of Arizona's current policy was debated and determined during a time of heated disputes around immigration. From 2006 on, two years after a group known as Protect Arizona Now (PAN) was established,[12] multiple state initiatives were passed which dealt directly with undocumented immigrants (Magaña, 2013; Santos *et al.*, 2013; Wiley 2013b). This time period was capped with the anti-immigrant bill SB 1070 in April 2010, two years after the SEI model had been in full implementation mode. Under this law, immigrants were 'criminalized for their mere presence in Arizona' (Magana, 2013: 24). Santos *et al.* (2013: 88) examined the effects of SB 1070 on children and found that there was a significant negative association with awareness of the law and a child's 'sense of being American' especially for first- and second-generation immigrant youth. In other words, a greater awareness of SB 1070 was associated with having a weaker sense of being American.

This is compounded by additional, more recent anti-immigrant media discourse prevalent statewide. A quick search on Arizona's AZCentral (a major news source via Arizona's channel 12 News and the *Arizona Republic*) of the term 'immigration' pulls up over 700 entries, most often having 'immigrant' linked with 'illegal.' Fitzsimmons-Doolan (2009) conducted an extensive corpus analysis on Arizona's newspapers and found that 'illegal' was the most frequent collocate for the terms 'immigration' and 'immigrant,' both in a language policy and an immigration corpora (see also Loring, this volume). Further, within the language policy corpora, she found 'a trend of linking a language policy to perception of immigration. For example "Something has to be done, and even though official English admittedly won't stem illegal immigration, it's a symbolic move"' (Fitzsimmons-Doolan, 2009: 393–394). Fitzsimmons-Doolan's work shows an often negative semantic preference when Arizona's newspapers reference immigrants, and that language policy is usually seen as a necessary means to control an increase (real or perceived) in immigration. Arizona's SEI model is founded on an ideology of English being the means to better preparing ELs to reach the 'Dream.' However, research is showing that this model is precluding ELs from various possibilities and equal opportunities afforded to native-English-speaking children. Therefore, during this period of anti-immigrant sentiment, many ELs in Arizona are not only marginalized in society (and perhaps internalizing these destructive narratives) by initiatives and laws such as SB 1070 and negative media metaphors, but they may also be restrained from reaching their full future potential thanks to the restrictive policy in place, as will be presented here.

When students begin school in Arizona, the families are required to complete a home language survey known as the PHLOTE. The PHLOTE asks three questions to determine what language(s) the student speaks at home. If a student is identified as speaking another language, even if in addition to English, they are given a state language proficiency test. This test is the Arizona English Language Learner Assessment (AZELLA) and there are validity concerns regarding its use (Florez, 2012). Should a student take the AZELLA and not meet a certain cutoff score, they are labeled one of four proficiency categories: pre-emergent, emergent, basic and intermediate. Any of these labels means that the student will be enrolled in the SEI model, which requires four hours of prescribed English language development (ELD) classes *every day*. Arizona's SEI has been critiqued for its lack of sound second language acquisition theory and its disregard for best practices within this model's design (Combs, 2012; Krashen *et al.*, 2012; Lillie & Moore, 2014; Long & Adamson, 2012). Ideally for the Arizona Department of Education (ADE[13]), each hour is devoted to a specific topic including an hour each of reading, writing, conversational English/academic vocabulary and, finally, of grammar. This varies somewhat based on both grade level (e.g. elementary, middle or high) and proficiency level as students are grouped first by proficiency within grade levels and then across grades should there not be enough students of one proficiency level to constitute a fully enrolled classroom (Lillie & Markos, 2014). To exit the program, students must prove they have reached a level of English proficiency, again as measured by the AZELLA. At that point, the ELs become reclassified fluent English proficient (RFEP, sometimes referred to simply as RC). Once reclassified, these students are monitored for two years during which time they are reassessed on the AZELLA to see if they are maintaining their 'fluent' proficiency level. Should a student not pass the AZELLA during this monitoring period, they are sent back into the ELD classrooms and are labeled ELLARs (EL after reclassification).

In addition to the numerous issues identified with this model's design, particularly because of its contradiction to sound pedagogy for ELs (August *et al.*, 2010; Krashen *et al.*, 2012; Lillie & Moore, 2014; Long & Adamson, 2012), scholars are documenting the many negative implications since SEI's large-scale implementation in 2008 (Arias &

Faltis, 2012; Moore, 2014; Rios-Aguilar & Gándara, 2012a, 2012b). In looking specifically at the ways in which SEI precludes ELs from full access and participation in not just the school but also the larger society (and thus the policy promotes dis-citizenship), there are three significant concerns which result from the SEI model design. One of the first is that students are grouped by proficiency levels in this model. This means that not only are ELs segregated because of their physical classroom status (e.g. 'mainstream' versus EL classroom), but they are also segregated linguistically (Gándara & Orfield, 2012). The linguistic segregation is exacerbated by the fact that they are separated from their native-English-speaking peers. The issue of segregation was one of the most repeated concerns by ELD coordinators across the state of Arizona in regard to not only the physical and social delineation of students but also because of how problematic this segregation is in relation to the ELs' missing academic content (Rios-Aguilar et al., 2012b). Segregating ELs from non-ELs is detrimental to not only ELs' language acquisition but also to their social development, as students have been documented to notice the 'difference' between the ELs and non-ELs, making ELs further stigmatized and marginalized (Gándara & Orfield, 2012; Lillie & Markos, 2014; Lillie et al., 2010, 2012; Rios-Aguilar et al., 2012a, 2012b).

The other two concerns are related: the lack of content instruction and the amount of time devoted to the SEI model and the implications of that. The ELD classrooms under SEI are not to focus on content area instruction (e.g. math, science or social studies), rather the emphasis is supposed to be on the English language by using the 'Language Star' and Discrete Skills Inventory (Combs, 2012; Krashen et al., 2012; Lillie et al., 2010, 2012; Lillie & Moore, 2014). Further, one study found that any content that ELs might receive was not comparable in amount, scope, or quality to that of their non-EL peers (Lillie et al., 2010). This is problematic because it means that the students are most likely not getting the access to content knowledge that they will need when they are finally able to exit the SEI model. In other words, they are not getting the same exposure to content that non-EL students are getting. Since studies have documented that ELs are not exiting the model in the ADE's goal of one year (Krashen et al., 2012; Lillie et al., 2010, 2012; Martinez-Wenzl et al., 2012), this suggests that the longer that students are in SEI, the more the achievement gap will widen.[14] In addition to this, the fact that the SEI model requires a minimum of four hours every day reduces the number of courses that ELs can take when they are not in their ELD classrooms. They are literally prevented from taking other courses. This is especially significant when talking about high school ELs who need to meet certain requirements in order to graduate. Studies are showing that secondary-level ELs are having a difficult time meeting their graduation requirements and therefore do not graduate, if at all, within a typical four-year time frame (Lillie & Markos, 2014; Lillie et al., 2010, 2012; Rios-Aguilar et al., 2012a, 2012b). Therefore, by virtue of involvement in SEI, ELs are not getting an equal education as compared to their non-EL peers because of their limited exposure to academic content and age/grade appropriate curricula, and they are also more limited in their ability to meet a typical four-year timeline for graduation (again, as their non-EL peers are able to do) because of their lack of content credits which prevents this from occurring.

Students' Awareness of Dis-citizenship?

While prior studies all examined the policy, none looked at what student-level data might illustrate. In the spring of 2011, I surveyed 2165 EL and RC students in 6th–12th grade using an 85-item demographic and Likert-scale survey[15] to capture not only a portrait of who these students are but also their perspective toward SEI (Lillie, 2011), ultimately to examine their overall attachment to school (and whether the language policy in place was an influencing factor on this attachment). The survey was given in English and Spanish and it asked students about their background, their schooling experiences, their attitudes toward the SEI model and their future aspirations. The data I present here share some of the findings in relation to accessing content, graduation and segregation. While predominantly a quantitative survey, I share student responses elicited from an open-ended question as these provide more evidence of how students have an awareness of how the SEI model may be preventing them from achieving full participation in their school (which I then argue inhibits them from being full members of society at large). In short, if students are aware of the larger issues inherent in the SEI model, and relate this to their own opportunities and future aspirations, then they may be aware of their dis-citizenship even if they cannot word this in quite the same way.

Two large, urban districts completed the survey, both districts being eligible for Title I funds and serving a large population of students receiving free/reduced lunches. Both districts also have high concentrations of ELs. The Ashton District[16] serves students in 5th–8th grade, but only 6th–8th graders were surveyed. Uniondale was a K-12 district but I only surveyed those ELs and RC students who were in the middle schools (6th–8th) and high schools (9th–12th). The return rate was very high (76%), with a total of 1637 students completing the survey (see Table 4.1).

An effort will be made here to share the data from these students as it pertains to the theme of (dis)citizenship. Much of the data support earlier scholarship which shows that ELs are segregated, they are hindered in graduating within a typical four-year time frame and they are missing out on academic content. Further, students are aware of this. Again, while

Table 4.1 Survey distribution

District (grades surveyed)	Surveys delivered	Surveys returned	Response rate (%)
Ashton (6th–8th)	1542	1322	86
Uniondale (6th–12th)	623	315	51
Totals	2165	1637	76

primarily a quantitative survey, a few questions were open-ended; the very last question asked students if they would like to tell me anything else about their school and English language classes. While the younger students in the Ashton District did not usually write as much (only 8% wrote something, $n=118$), in the Uniondale District the students were very vocal in their thoughts, with a third of them sharing extra information with me ($n=104$). This will also be shared here, as they wrote it, in an effort to add support to the quantitative findings.

Since SEI was implemented statewide in school year (SY) 2008–2009, all of my participants most likely were involved in the SEI model at some point. My survey was administered in the SY 2010–2011, so RC students who responded could have been involved when SEI was first implemented and could have tested out of the program at the end of SY 2008–2009. Those students would have been in their second year of monitoring as an RC student at the time of the survey. Demographic information of the students can be seen in Tables 4.2 and 4.3.

There was an equal distribution of males and females. Spanish was the primary language for most of the students, and many listed they were bilingual in both Spanish and English. There were other languages reported in Ashton (e.g. Vietnamese, Burmese) but those numbers were low in relation to the population surveyed (i.e. fewer than 5). In Uniondale there was a more diverse linguistic landscape with students reporting that they spoke other languages, most including Arabic, Nepalese and Somali.

When asked about their language abilities, students largely seemed to value their bilingualism while acknowledging how important they felt it was to know English. Just over two-thirds (69.5%) of the students

Table 4.2 Frequency breakdown of grade by district and classification

	6th	7th	8th	9th	10th	11th	12th	Total
Ashton								
ELs	217	78	75	–	–	–	–	374
RCs	370	355	218	–	–	–	–	948
Uniondale								
ELs	31	38	30	30	36	17	26	213
RCs	18	26	15	16	6	6	13	102

Table 4.3 Frequency breakdown of reported L1 by district and classification

L1	Ashton (6th–8th)		Uniondale (6th–12th)		Totals
	EL	RC	EL	RC	
English	25	59	4	9	97
Spanish	218	488	57	49	812
English and Spanish	119	388	–	–	507
Other	11	5	143	43	202

in Ashton felt that you should know English and 62.2% felt this way in Uniondale. A great deal of student commentary included thanking teachers for helping them learn English. Two prime examples of this were from an EL who wrote 'thank for my teacher and my school. they give me new life and they help me to become a grade person in this world. I give thank for my teacher and school' and another who said 'I am so fortunate that I get this occasion to read and learn more about English.' The RC students did, at times, thank the teachers, but more of the statements regarding learning English revolved around the recognition that English was a tool for graduating and moving on. One RC student wrote 'everyone should pass High School english get to it get to work. We need to know english more to guacate High School and ELd. We need more help on english then our own language we need to get to learn english more.' Another RC student even suggested 'why Learn english? I know were in America but most of the student know Spanish the english' showing, perhaps, an awareness that Spanish is valuable and yet not considered as such in Arizona.

In the Uniondale district, just over a third (36.7%) of RC and EL students reported that they had always gone to school in Arizona. Perhaps even more disturbing is that in the Ashton district, 78.6% ($n=1025$) of the EL and RC students stated that they had *always gone to school in Arizona*, with 764 RC and 261 ELs reporting this. Of those ELs, just over half of them (53.8%) stated they had been in the SEI model for three years, and another 26% said two years. All of this is alarming for two reasons. Remembering that this district was only middle-school respondents, for those students who have always lived in Arizona, the ones who were 11 years old when this survey was administered would have been born when Proposition 203 was passed or shortly thereafter. If these students have only been schooled in Arizona, this means that (1) they have always lived in a state which upholds an English-only ideology and (2) that a number of them are still classified as ELs in a state where bilingual education was essentially eradicated in place of a restrictive policy which stressed a goal of making ELs proficient in English quickly (and touted the SEI model as the means to do so). This supports other findings that there are major concerns regarding the model (e.g. not exiting the model in one year or less and thus being labeled as EL for a longer time period) and/or the identification process (e.g. issues with the PHLOTE and AZELLA). I turn now to students' responses about how the model might be impacting their schooling and future aspirations, and their awareness of the policy's (as practiced) implications.

Access to core content/missing content and graduating concerns

All of the schools were typically in session from 8am to 3pm, with a variation of about 30 minutes depending on grade level, for a total of seven hours a day. At Ashton, the curriculum for a non-EL student consists of math, language arts, science, and social studies, with art, music and physical education as an 'exploratory' (e.g. either by rotating the schedule, such as gym, or by enrollment, such as choir). The same can be said for the middle schools in Uniondale. Considering the schools provide lunch for 30 minutes, this leaves only about 6.5 hours of actual class instruction, not including time for going between classes, and four of those are devoted to SEI for ELs. The majority of the ELs (77.1%) in Ashton reported that they were taking four hours of ELD every day. This means that they had about two hours a day remaining for other content area courses and suggests that they are not getting an equal distribution of content classes outside of the four hours devoted to ELD. Most said their school day consisted of reading, writing, an elective and math. At the high schools in Uniondale, the schedules all incorporated only six classes a day. Again, most students (76.7%) reported they took four hours of SEI when an EL, meaning there were only two other free course slots for the rest of the day in order to take either content or electives.

Within the data from Uniondale, students responded in such a way that I was able to determine whether or not students were taking math, science and social studies (see Table 4.4).

It is apparent that while most ELs and RC students are getting math, the number of ELs who reported taking science or social studies drops dramatically. Only half of the ELs are getting science and less than a quarter of the ELs surveyed are getting social studies, and yet these

Table 4.4 Core content courses students reported taking in Uniondale

	EL (n=213)		RC (n=102)	
	f	%	f	%
Math	205	96.2	96	94.1
Science	126	59.2	89	87.3
Social studies	31	14.6	74	72.5

Note: All percentages were rounded to the tenth.

are core requirements for graduation. Looking more closely at just the high school students (both RC and EL), while 94.6% reported they were taking a math class, only 60.8% said they were taking a science class and, worse, only 26.5% said they were taking social studies. Considering these are all required credit-bearing classes for graduating high school, it is disquieting that all the numbers are not closer to 100%. Therefore, the longer that these students stay in SEI, they are not only literally being limited from taking the other content area classes, but the further behind they will be in the academic content needed for when they exit the program.

A big issue with the lack of content area classes is that the ELD classes do not count as four credits toward school (graduation) requirements (Lillie *et al.*, 2010). Students at the high school were very aware of this and remarked on how they wished the ELD classes would count because it was preventing them from graduating. One RC student stated 'It's unfair that they dont count the ELLs English classes as regular classes.'[17] ELs were also very much aware of the fact that the four hours of SEI were limiting their chances of graduating in a timely fashion, whether it be because they were missing required content credits or because they would literally age out of the school:

- 'It's very hard to hard to graduate when we have 4 houre of English… So if it's was not the the 4 English class I just gen graduate this year but now I will graduate next year.'
- 'The ELD classes are good and I can learn english but they too much and we need to take other classes to graduated.'
- '…ELD is bad for us becaues some people is old than the cant graduate from high school.'
- 'I think ELD class is too many It is difficult to graduate from high school.'

Graduating and Future Selves

Of the ELs and RC students in both districts, almost all recognized how important college was and expressed a desire to go. Almost all of the students in Uniondale expect to finish high school (98.4%), and another 96.4% plan on going to college. However, almost half of the respondents[18] in Uniondale acknowledged that they worried they would be unable to do so and move on. Part of this stems from the fact they felt too much time was devoted to the ELD classes, such as one EL who wrote 'students can't even take other classes beside that at the end of the year they can't even graduate from school because all the classes you have to take. is better if we can't take lese class to be ready for collage.'

In the Ashton middle schools, with most participants only in 6th grade, they were already thinking about graduating from high school. Of all the respondents, 80.7% agreed that graduating from high school was a priority. For the students in Uniondale, 95.7% agreed. Student comments included statements like 'I want finish high school to go next step to my life' (an EL) and 'So I just hope I do graduate from High School and college!!' (an RC student). The top choices for future professions included careers in medicine and law. For example, one student stated 'Well my goal is to become a surgeon because I promssed my great grandpa that I would so I can make him proud and if I graduate from collage I'm going to be the first in my famalie.' On the other hand, one RC student did ask 'would imigrant's get to go to college?' suggesting that perhaps the anti-immigrant initiatives and the surrounding discourse in the state were making their way into the schools.[19] Students were ultimately aware that their involvement in SEI was impeding them from meeting graduation requirements and some stressed this was because of the amount of time spent in ELD classes at the expense of other required class credits. Unfortunately, if the students are prevented from graduating, this directly impacts their ability to go on to college and meet their dreams of becoming certain desired professions (i.e. their future selves).

Segregation and bullying

In both districts, students were asked questions revolving around how they felt they were treated in school and how they were grouped for their classes. Some of the questions asked if they felt discriminated against while they were ELs, and whether or not ELs were always grouped with one another for their classes (see Table 4.5).

Even though students largely felt that cultures were respected at school and they disagreed that ELs were discriminated against in school, the comments students shared did not support the survey responses. For example, students remarked that because they were segregated, they were

Table 4.5 Responses around the theme of segregation or discrimination

	Ashton		Uniondale	
Survey Item	f	M (SD)	f	M (SD)
All cultures are respected at school.	1298	3.60 (1.13)	305	3.73 (1.25)
Students who speak a language other than English are not treated fairly.	1310	2.49 (1.16)	299	2.83 (1.19)
ELs grouped together in all other classes.	1292	3.57 (1.17)	203	3.99 (1.01)
Kids treat/ed me differently (because of EL status).	1298	2.23 (1.20)	202	2.89 (1.33)

missing the (linguistic) interaction with their non-EL peers. As one EL stated, 'I think to have some class with kids that speak only english at lest we can learen english from them.' Of greater concern, students in both districts (but more at the middle schools) brought up issues of bullying toward ELs and a lack of respect. Some examples of statements include the following:

ELs:
- I am always bullyed in my school.
- Everybody should be treated nicely no matter what language they speak.
- Does in you school kids treat you faer because you are in English classes?
- Sometime's other kid's mak fun of me.
- yes, is that sometime's I feel bulided.

RC students:
- yes i do want to tell you that other students bully sudetns that are in ell classes and call them retared!
- Other students make fun of the students who dont English and they tells us that we are dumb. They bully us!
- Have you ever gotten bully?
- Teachers should respect us students.
- Teachers should respect kids more often.

Students' unsolicited responses about bullying toward ELs suggest that segregation in schools is furthering the *othering* of students. In short, the policy's stipulation that students be grouped by language ability is further cementing the idea of 'EL' and 'non-EL' and perhaps creating a hierarchy of students within a school system with ELs being reduced to second-class persons because of their lack of English (via a deficit perspective). Were ELs allowed to mix more often with native-English-speaking peers, it might be that this separation between the two groups would not be as stark. As evidenced in other studies, the distinction between the ELs and non-ELs is noticed as early as kindergarten (see e.g. Lillie *et al.*, 2010; Lillie & Markos, 2014) and the identifying feature children noticed was the ability to speak English. Separating students on the basis of linguistic ability not only hinders ELs' acquisition of English but it continues to foster what some scholars have termed *ESL Ghettos* (Gándara & Orfield, 2012; Gifford & Valdés, 2006). The SEI model requires this linguistic segregation, but it thus ensures that a line is drawn between those who are native-English-speakers and those who are not, and perhaps enhances a sense of identity among the children based on which classes they took and which labels were ascribed to them (e.g. EL or non-EL) during school. The borders created around/by linguistic ability are evident in the comments of the students who were bullied simply for being or having been identified as an EL. If ELs and RC students are feeling this way as a result of how policy constraints segregate them, this suggests some awareness that they are not being provided the opportunity to be full members of their larger school community. They are excluded from being citizens of their own school.

The Dis-Citizenship of ELs

If citizenship is to be reconceptualized as 'what it allows one to do' (Ramanathan, 2013a: 1), then the policy in Arizona is precluding these ELs from becoming full citizens of not only the school, but also of the wider society in which they live. This is compounded by the anti-immigrant discourse in the state. The SEI policy of Arizona is evidence of what Menken (2013: 209) meant when she stated 'restrictive English-only policies marginalize emergent bilingual students... (and) bar these students from reaping the benefits of their bilingualism and limit their future opportunities.' Further, Menken's (2013: 227) study showed that many ELs were entering secondary schools and would 'struggle to acquire the necessary academic language and literacy skills' and would therefore 'face limited chances for success.' The students I surveyed are at a distinct disadvantage because they are all in secondary schools already and are still missing out on content. Regardless of their desire to move on to college, their lack of content instruction and limited access to content credit may signal that they will struggle to graduate and thus be further obstructed in reaching their dream of going to college. In short, a ripple effect occurs because of the policy. It starts at the possibility of students not graduating or graduating at a disadvantage. If that happens, their future selves will be hindered from that which other students (who were not limited by restrictive language policies) have more access – that is, a college education and certain types of jobs which might require such advanced schooling. This in turn can consequently influence future generations. The policy may therefore perpetuate a stratified society of (formerly) EL versus non-EL.

Monzó and Rueda's (2009) study documented that students were aware of how knowing English signified that they were (or were not) American. Again, while many of the students in my study felt it was important to know English, there was some evidence that the students were aware that learning English was a tool to promote their advancement through school. Monzó and Rueda (2009: 32) also remark that if students become aware of citizenship as being not simply related to residency status but rather as 'a symbol of full participation as a person,' it is likely that these children will grow up becoming acutely aware of their marginalized status in society resulting from the policy's stratification of being labeled as 'EL' versus non-EL. Once labeled as such, these labels become embedded in one's identity and can be carried with these children for life. Santos *et al.* (2013: 91) further note that 'perceptions of exclusion of not fully belonging, even when they are US citizens, are amplified by pieces of legislation like SB 1070.' The students were very cognizant of the bullying that went on toward ELs, which was one of the biggest themes from the comments they freely provided. The outward stigmatization (i.e. bullying), in addition to any internalized majoritarian stories from an English-only state, may only hurt ELs' identities and sense of future selves. Anti-immigrant discourse, coupled with a restrictive English-only language policy, continues the marginalization of ELs in the state of Arizona and can only further these children's dis-citizenship in America. This is also compounded by the current immigration debates at the national level and the discourse which thus ensues. Unless the policy is modified, ELs will continue to be precluded from accessing an equal education as compared to their non-EL peers. The policy must change in order to support these students in fully realizing their potential and sense of belonging in a diversified US as situated in a globalizing world.

Notes

(1) It is important to note not all ELs are immigrants, nor are all immigrants automatically ELs.
(2) Rios-Aguilar and Gándara (2012a, 2012b) are the introduction articles to two special issues dealing with Arizona policy.
(3) Ramanathan's (2013a, 2013b) work includes discussion from many scholars on a way to bring a new understanding to the term *(dis)citizenship* as it connects to language policy, ideology and citizenship.
(4) LatCrit (Latino/a Critical Race Theory) is an extension of CRT.
(5) Section 1.2 of Proposition 203 uses this term in the law itself (see http://www.azed.gov/wp-content/uploads/PDF/PROPOSITION203.pdf)
(6) See Wiley (2013a, 2013b) for a discussion on state rights.
(7) See Del Valle (2003), Lillie (2014) and Wiley (2013a) for more in-depth discussions of court cases which have dealt with language rights and schooling in the US, including *Lau v. Nichols* (1974), *Castañeda v. Pickard* (1981) and others.
(8) See Crawford (2000a, 2000b, 2004) for a deeper discussion and critique of the English-Only Movement and US English.
(9) See http://www.onenation.org/home.html
(10) Question 2 did not eliminate two-way bilingual programs (Smith *et al.*, 2008).
(11) See Sections 1.1, 1.2, 1.3 and 1.6 in Proposition 203: http://www.azed.gov/wp-content/uploads/PDF/PROPOSITION203.pdf
(12) This group introduced a ballot initiative in 2004 which began the stream of anti-immigrant ballots for the next six years. This ballot required proof of citizenship for voting with identification cards and more strict policing regarding undocumented employees, among other things (Magaña, 2013).
(13) One can refer to the ADE's description of SEI here: http://www.azed.gov/wp-content/uploads/PDF/SEIModels05-14-08.pdf

(14) García *et al.* (2012) have shown that Arizona has not made progress in closing the achievement gap between ELs and non-ELs under the SEI model.
(15) The survey was coded from *strongly agree* (5) to *strongly disagree* (1) and included an option of *neutral/not sure*.
(16) All names are pseudonyms.
(17) Again, all quotes from students are directly transcribed from the paper surveys, thus errors and misspellings are included to maintain integrity to the data and show students' handwritten responses.
(18) The surveys given to high schoolers included the item *I worry that I will not graduate from high school*. Since Ashton was only a middle school district, their survey did not include this item.
(19) Arizona does not allow in-state college tuition or financial aid for undocumented students and does not allow undocumented persons to take adult education classes under Proposition 300 (see Campbell, 2011).

References

Arias, M.B. and Faltis, C. (eds) (2012) *Implementing Educational Language Policy in Arizona: Legal, Historical, and Current Practices in SEI*. Bristol: Multilingual Matters.

Arizona Revised Statutes (2000) Article 3.1 §15-751 to 15-757: English Language Education for the Children in Public Schools. See http://www.azleg.state.az.us/ArizonaRevisedStatutes.asp?Title=15 (accessed 21 December 2015).

August, D., Goldenberg, C. and Rueda, R. (2010) Restrictive state language policies: Are they scientifically based? In P. Gándara and M. Hopkins (eds) *Forbidden Languages: English Learners and Restrictive Language Policies* (pp. 139–158). New York: Teachers College.

Baker, C. (2011) *Foundations of Bilingual Education and Bilingualism* (5th edn). Bristol: Multilingual Matters.

Campbell, K.M. (2011, Spring) The road to S.B. 1070: How Arizona became ground zero for the immigrants' rights movement and the continuing struggle for Latino civil rights in America. *Harvard Latino Law Review* 14, 1–21.

Chang, R.S. and Aoki, K. (1997) Centering the immigrant in the inter/national imagination. *California Law Review* 85 (5), 309–361.

Combs, M.C. (2012) Everything on its head. In M.B. Arias and C. Faltis (eds) *Implementing Educational Language Policy in Arizona* (pp. 59–85). Bristol: Multilingual Matters.

Crawford, J.W. (2000a) *Anatomy of the English-only movement*. See http://ourworld.compuserve.com/homepages/JWCRAWFORD/anatomy.htm (accessed 15 December 2006).

Crawford, J.W. (2000b) *At War with Diversity: US Language Policy in an Age of Anxiety*. Clevedon: Multilingual Matters.

Crawford, J.W. (2004) *Educating English Learners: Language Diversity in the Classroom* (5th edn). Los Angeles, CA: Bilingual Education Services.

Del Valle, S. (2003) *Language Rights and the Law in the United States: Finding Our Voices*. Clevedon: Multilingual Matters.

Fitzsimmons-Doolan, S. (2009) Is public discourse about language policy really public discourse about immigration? A corpus-based study. *Language Policy* 8 (4), 377–402. doi: 10.1007/s10993-009-9147-6.

Florez, I.R. (2012) Examining the validity of the Arizona English language learners assessment cut scores. *Language Policy* 11 (1), 33–45. doi: 10.1007/s10993-011-9225-4.

Gándara, P.C. and Hopkins, M. (eds) (2010) *Forbidden Language: English Learners and Restrictive Language Policies*. New York: Teachers College Press.

Gándara, P., Losen, D., August, D., Uriarte, M., Gómez, M.C. and Hopkins, M. (2010) Forbidden language: A brief history of U.S. language policy. In P. Gándara and M. Hopkins (eds) *Forbidden Language: English Learners and Restrictive Language Policies* (pp. 20–33). New York: Teachers College Press.

Gándara, P. and Orfield, G. (2012) Segregating Arizona's English learners: A return to the 'Mexican room.' *Teachers College Record* 114 (9), 1–27.

García, E.E., Lawton, K. and Diniz de Figueiredo, E.H. (2012) The education of English language learners in Arizona: A history of underachievement. *Teachers College Record* 114 (9), 1–18.

Gifford, B.R. and Valdés, G. (2006) The linguistic isolation of Hispanic students in California's public schools: The challenge of reintegration. *Yearbook of the National Society for the Study of Education* 105 (2), 125–154.

Johnson, E.J. (2005) WAR in the media: Metaphors, ideology, and the formation of language policy. *Bilingual Research Journal* 29 (3), 621–729.

Johnson, E.J. (2006) Dreams of (under)achievement: A critical metaphor analysis of the American dream and the formation of language policy in Arizona. *Journal of Borderland Education* 1 (1), 11–28.

Krashen, S., MacSwan, J. and Rolstad, K. (2012) Review of 'research summary and bibliography for structured English immersion programs' of the Arizona English language learners task force. In M.B. Arias and C. Faltis (eds) *Implementing Educational Policy in Arizona: Legal, Historical and Current Practices in SEI* (pp. 107–118). Bristol: Multilingual Matters.

Lillie, K.E. (2011) Giving the students a voice: Surveying students about Arizona's structured English immersion restrictive language policy (doctoral dissertation). Retrieved from ASU Electronic Dissertations and Theses.

Lillie, K.E. (2014) Making an example of Arizona: Analyzing a case of restrictive language policy for minority rights. In E. Stracke (ed.) *Intersections: Applied Linguistics as a Meeting Place* (pp. 294–312). Newcastle Upon Tyne: Cambridge Scholars Publishing.

Lillie, K.E., Markos, A., Estrella, A., Nguyen, T., Peer, K., Perez, K., Trifiro, A., Arias, M.B. and Wiley, T.G. (2010) *Policy in Practice: The Implementation of Structured English Immersion in Arizona*. Los Angeles, CA: Civil Rights Project: University of California, Los Angeles.

Lillie, K.E., Markos, A., Arias, M.B. and Wiley, T.G. (2012) Separate and not equal: The implementation of structured English immersion in Arizona's classrooms. *Teachers College Record* 114 (9), 1–33.

Lillie, K.E. and Markos, A. (2014) The four-hour block: SEI in classrooms. In S.C.K. Moore (ed.) *Language Policy Processes and Consequences: Arizona Case Studies* (pp. 133–155). Bristol: Multilingual Matters.

Lillie, K.E. and Moore, S.C.K. (2014) SEI in Arizona: Bastion for states' rights. In S.C.K. Moore (ed.) *Language Policy Processes and Consequences: Arizona Case Studies* (pp. 1–27). Bristol: Multilingual Matters.

Long, M.H. and Adamson, H.D. (2012) SLA research and Arizona's structured English immersion policies. In M.B. Arias and C. Faltis (eds) *Implementing Educational Language Policy in Arizona: Legal, Historical, and Current Practices in SEI* (pp. 39–55). Bristol: Multilingual Matters.

Magaña, L. (2013) Arizona's immigration policies and SB 1070. In L. Magaña and E. Leed (eds) *Latino Politics and Arizona's Immigration Law SB 1070* (pp. 19–26). New York: Springer.

Martinez-Wenzl, M., Pérez, K.C. and Gándara, P. (2012) Is Arizona's approach to educating its ELs superior to other forms of instruction? *Teachers College Record* 114 (9), 1–32.

Marx, S. (2009) 'It's not them; It's not their fault': Manifestations of racism in the schooling of Latinas/os and ELLs. In R. Kubota and A. Lin (eds) *Race, Culture, and Identities in Second Language Education: Exploring Critically Engaged Practice* (pp. 81–97). New York: Routledge.

Menken, K. (2013) (Dis)citizenship or opportunity?: The importance of language education policy for access and full participation of emergent bilinguals in the United States. In V. Ramanathan (ed.) *Language Policies and (Dis)citizenship: Rights, Access Pedagogies* (pp. 209–230). Bristol: Multilingual Matters.

Meyer v. Nebraska, 262 U.S. 390; 43 S. Ct. 625; 67 L. Ed. 1042; 1923 U.S. LEXIS 2655; 29 A.L.R. 1446.

Monzó, L.D. and Rueda, R. (2009) Passing for English fluent: Latino immigrant children masking language proficiency. *Anthropology & Education Quarterly* 40 (1), 20–40. doi: 10.1111/j.1548-1492.2009.01026.x

Moore, S.C.K. (ed.) (2014) *Language Policy Processes and Consequences: Arizona Case Studies.* Bristol: Multilingual Matters.

Olivas, M.A. (2012) *No Undocumented Child Left Behind: Plyle v. Doe and the Education of Uundocumented Schoolchildren.* New York: New York University Press.

Ramanathan, V. (2013a) Language policies and (dis)citizenship: Rights, access, pedagogies. In V. Ramanathan (ed.) *Language Policies and (Dis)citizenship: Rights, Access, Pedagogies* (pp. 1–16). Bristol: Multilingual Matters.

Ramantahan, V. (2013b) Language policies and (dis)citizenship: Who belongs? Who is a guest? Who is deported? [Special forum]. *Journal of Language, Identity, and Education* 12 (3), 162–166.

Revilla, A.T. and Asato, J. (2002) The implementation of proposition 227 in California schools: A critical analysis of the effect on teacher beliefs and classroom practices. *Equity & Excellence in Education* 35 (2), 108–118. doi: 10.1008/10665680290175130

Rios-Aguilar, C. and Gándara, P. (eds) (2012a) Horne v. Flores and the future of language policy [Special issue]. *Teachers College Record* 114 (9) pp. 1–5.

Rios-Aguilar, C. and Gándara, P. (eds) (2012b) (Re)conceptualizing and (re)evaluating language policies for English language learners: The case of Arizona [Special issue]. *Language Policy* 11 (1).

Rios-Aguilar, C., González-Canche, M.S. and Moll, L.C. (2012a) A study of Arizona's teachers of English language learners. *Teachers College Record* 114 (9), 1–33.

Rios-Aguilar, C., González-Canche, M.S. and Moll, L.C. (2012b) Implementing structured English immersion in Arizona: Benefits, challenges, and opportunities. *Teachers College Record* 114 (9), 1–18.

Santos, C., Menjívar, C. and Godfrey, E. (2013) Effects of SB 1070 on children. In L. Magaña and E. Leed (ed.) *Latino Politics and Arizona's Immigration Law SB 1070* (pp. 79–92). New York: Springer.

Smith, J.M., Coggins, C. and Cardoso, J.M. (2008) Best practices for English language learners in Massachusetts: Five years after the question 2 mandate. *Equity & Excellence in Education* 41 (3), 293–310. doi: 10.1080/10665680802179485

Solórzano, D.G. and Yosso, T.J. (2009) Critical race methodology: Counter-storytelling as an analytical framework for educational research. In E. Taylor, D. Gillborn and G. Ladson-Billings (eds) *Foundations of Critical Race Theory in Education* (pp. 131–147). New York: Routledge.

Tiersma, P. (2012) Language policy in the United States. In P. Tiersma and L. Solan (eds) *The Oxford Handbook of Language and Law* (pp. 249–260). New York: Oxford University Press.

Wiley, T.G. (2004) Language planning, language policy, and the English-only movement. In E. Finegan and J.R. Rickford (eds) *Language in the USA: Themes for the Twenty-First Century* (pp. 319–338). Cambridge: Cambridge University Press.

Wiley, T.G. (2013a) A brief history and assessment of language rights in the United States. In J.W. Tollefson (ed.) *Language Policies in Education: Critical Issues* (2nd edn). New York: Routledge.

Wiley, T.G. (2013b) Constructing and deconstructing 'illegal' children. *Journal of Language, Identity, and Education* 12 (3), 167–172. doi: 10.1080/15348458.2013.797255

Wiley, T.G. and Lukes, M. (1996) English-only and standard ideologies in the U.S. *TESOL Quarterly* 30 (3), 511–535.

Wiley, T.G. and Wright, W.E. (2004) Against the undertow: Language-minority education policy and politics in the 'age of accountability.' *Educational Policy* 18 (1), 142–168. doi:10.1177/0895904803260030

Wodak, R. (2013) Dis-citizenship and migration: A critical discourse-analytical perspective. *Journal of Language, Identity, and Education* 12 (3), 173–178. doi: 10.1080/15348458.2013.797258

Wright, W.E. (2011) Historical introduction to bilingual education: The United States. In C. Baker (ed.) *Foundations of Bilingual Education and Bilingualism* (5th edn, pp. 182–205). Bristol: Multilingual Matters.

5 Local, Foreign and In-Between: English Teachers and Students Creating Community and Becoming Global 'Citizens' at a Chinese University

Paul McPherron

Moving from entrenched political and legal debates around immigration, naturalization, language testing and integration toward a polycentric, processual and global view in which a wider definition of citizenship as 'the right to participate fully' is theorized (Blommaert, 2013; Ramanathan, 2013a, 2013b), this chapter examines the tensions inherent in national and local English teaching policies in China and the simultaneous local and global influences and orientations of university teachers, students and administrators at a university in south China, named here China Southern University (CSU). More specifically, based on data collected at CSU over a 10-year period, this chapter investigates the history of national policies that define English teachers at universities in China and how these definitions of 'foreign' and 'local' have affected professional identities, teaching activities, relationships and access to local and global citizenship at CSU.

English has been taught in mainland China (henceforward China) for over 500 years (Adamson, 2004; Gil & Adamson, 2011), but since the early 1980s and the opening of the Chinese economy, English learning and teaching have been central in Chinese educational policy in order to meet the needs of the 'four modernizations' in agriculture, industry, national defense, and science and technology (Mao & Min, 2004). Accordingly, over the past decades, more and more Chinese citizens have begun learning English, particularly K-12 and university students. For example, Wen and Hu (2007) estimated that the majority of Chinese students in kindergarten through university study English (over 120,000,000 students in 2007), and they estimated that there were over 850,000 teachers of

English in 2007. At the university level, in 2001, the Ministry of Education (MOE) issued a directive that 5–10% of all university courses should be taught in English or other foreign languages, with the eventual goal of 20% of all university classes conducted in English (Feng, 2009). With an increase in English teaching at all educational levels in China, many schools, particularly Chinese universities, have sought to hire 'foreign experts'[1] to teach or co-teach English language and culture classes, and many universities have attempted to replace traditional grammar-based teaching activities with curriculums based on communicative language teaching (CLT) and task-based language learning (TBLT) principles (Hu, 2005; Hu & McKay, 2012).

Similar to other universities in China, since its inception in 1983, CSU has sought to hire more and more foreign English teachers, employing some of the first foreign English teachers in China in the 1980s. After many years of hosting one or two foreign teachers in the English department, in 2002, the university created the English Language Center (ELC) to coordinate all English language teaching instructors and programs at CSU, and through the ELC, the university strategically focused on hiring more foreign English teachers, in particular striving to create a balance between an even number of local and foreign teachers of English on campus. As Liu and Xiao (2011: 42) report:

> We realize the importance of creating a supportive language learning environment which is particularly beneficial to students in an EFL setting, so we have recruited many international teachers and Chinese teachers with overseas experience. Currently, out of the 50 instructors at the ELC, 23 are international teachers, and this is unique in higher education in general English teaching in China.

Thus, with the creation of the ELC, CSU administrators sought to create a community in which local and foreign teachers equally belong and collaborate on all aspects of language instruction, both inside and outside the classroom. This explicit goal of not only hiring foreign teachers but also creating a community in which local and foreign teachers work together and collaborate on teaching projects was somewhat rare in China in the early 2000s. As Liu and Xiao (2011: 44) report, 'Because of the composition of the ELC faculty, we have been dedicated to building a community in which teachers from both China and abroad can work together collaboratively, collegially, and comfortably.' Indeed, one of the main reasons that I chose to teach at CSU as an MA-TESOL graduate from the United States was the emphasis on building community and collaboration between local and foreign teachers. However, I still vividly recall the first words by the then director of the ELC in 2004 to the foreign teachers at a welcome dinner after we had arrived at CSU on complimentary air tickets, 'Welcome to China, you have come to reform English language teaching.'

Thus, in this chapter, I move the discussion of citizenship from legal and policy aspects to a global view in which the data, examples and discussion presented reveal the multiple orientations and integrations of CSU teachers and administrators, including myself, to local and global citizenships. In this way, the chapter reveals the new spaces created at CSU for teachers and students to 'fully participate' or not as local and foreign citizens in the CSU and global English-speaking communities. The chapter draws on data from over 10 years of ethnographic fieldwork that I have collected at CSU as a classroom teacher and researcher, including classroom observations and teacher interviews, and it is centered on the following research question:

> In an era of globalization, how do negotiations and tensions over teaching methods and the expansion of English affect relationships, citizenship practices and the ability of students, teachers and administrators to fully participate in local CSU and global English-speaking communities?

In this chapter, I address this question by drawing on the following three entry points: (1) a brief review of national and CSU policies and documents; (2) a description of local teacher interpretations of CLT reforms and the benefits of foreign teachers; and (3) an analysis of the production of the musical *Fiddler on the Roof* as part of extracurricular English language activities at CSU. Throughout the chapter, I contextualize the data with personal reflections from my own experiences teaching at CSU.

The chapter is rooted in qualitative ethnographic and case study research methods in TESOL and applied linguistics (Creswell, 2013; Heigham & Croker, 2009; Richards, 2003; Watson-Gegeo, 1988). I drew on a grounded theory approach in collecting, coding and analyzing the various data sources (Charmaz, 2006). As I placed myself and my colleagues' processes of identity formation and discovery as central to the chapter, I also drew on what Phan (2008) describes as 'auto-ethnography,' an approach that uses personal data, including memories, journals and reflections, in order to open a space between individual and collective accounts of learning and identity processes. This space offers a more nuanced view of identity as neither pre-given (essentialist) nor completely mobile and unfixed (postmodern). The data were drawn from over a 10-year period from 2004 to 2014 in which I was teaching and researching at CSU and include: (1) observations of foreign and local teachers classrooms in 2004, 2007, 2010 and 2013 ($n=62$); (2) interviews with foreign and local teachers in 2007, 2010 and 2013 ($n=32$); (3) interviews with two different ELC directors in 2007 and 2013 ($n=2$); (4) one interview and collected correspondences with the vice-chancellor of CSU in 2010; and (5) collected national and CSU teaching policies and documents from 2004 to 2014.[2,3]

'To Meet the Needs of China's Social Development and International Exchanges': English Language Teaching and Learning in China and CSU

Founded outside a coastal city in Guangdong Province in 1981, CSU has been tied from its inception to economic and educational reforms at the national level in China. CSU was the first university to be built in the region, and its creation coincided with the nearby city being named a Special Economic Zone (SEZ) in 1983. Accordingly, CSU's position from the start was to link the region with international business communities outside of China as well as increase the reputation and visibility of the local region within China. In fact, the initial funds for the university came from a prominent Hong Kong businessperson and his philanthropic foundation, and for many years the foundation has had a strong influence on shaping the university through continued monetary investment in many university projects and the overall university budget. In addition, foundation employees have served in a variety of upper administration positions at CSU and on the university's board of directors, and the foundation has implemented many curricular and cultural changes at the university including a change to a credit system in which students take classes with other students outside of their major classes, a requirement for students in all majors to achieve a high proficiency in English, an increase in extracurricular programs for practicing English, and the creation and funding for multiple international conferences and professional development opportunities for CSU teachers (Liu & Xiao, 2011).

Perhaps most significant in terms of English teaching pedagogy, since 2002, the foundation and ELC directors have emphasized student-centered, communicative and self-learning teaching and curriculum approaches as advocated by various Chinese MOE policy statements in the 2000s (Feng, 2009). It is important to note that none of the recommended approaches, be it CLT or TBLT, were a specific method or set of activities, but in terms of learning language, the guidelines generally focused on teaching a language by using it instead of teaching about it. Grammar rules and vocabulary are typically discussed after pair and group work activities in which students negotiate meaning and produce language (Nunan, 2005; Savignon, 2001). At CSU, a 2007 report on internationalization stated that the move to student-centered teaching had been completed, noting that 'the University has rid itself of the obsolete spoon-feed teaching methodology and renewed...to train elite students with a broader vision and international knowledge and raise their level of creativity' (Internationalization Committee, 2007).

At the same time, it is important to note that student-centered approaches to teaching have not been universally accepted by all teachers, students and scholars in China. In fact, Hu (2005) writes that the Chinese education system has neither the resources nor the culture of learning[4] for adopting student-centered approaches to teaching. Further, Adamson (2004) points out that reforms in Chinese education have always been tied to political trends and negotiations of the amount of outside influence on the Chinese school system, and 'traditional Chinese' teaching methods that place an emphasis on group memorization/recitation tasks, grammar study, memorization of vocabulary and education for national not personal goals are still common. As an illustration of the new student-centered teaching goals as well as echoes of a more 'traditional' Chinese culture of learning, the 2007 *College English Curriculum Requirements* noted:

> The objective of College English is to develop students' ability to use English in an all-around way, especially in listening and speaking, so that in their future work and social interactions they will be able to exchange information effectively through both spoken and written channels, and at the same time they will be able to enhance their ability to study independently and improve their cultural quality so as to meet the needs of China's social development and international exchanges. (Ministry of Education, 2007: 5)

Although praising communicative and 'all-around' English activities that promote individual learning styles, the report focused on using these methods for 'China's social development and international exchanges.' What is interesting here is the split between, on the one hand, a nationalist discourse that encourages English learning to benefit the group/nation (almost as a family) and, on the other hand, a self-improvement discourse that encourages English learning through self-learning and process-oriented methods.

At CSU, these competing discourses and cultures of education have mirrored the development of teaching practices. For example, over the course of my work at CSU, Vice-Chancellor Tsing – an executive at the Hong Kong Foundation with experience as an administrator in the United States – often recounted a story when she first came to CSU in 2002: the desks in all of the rooms were bolted to the floor, making it impossible to rearrange the students into groups with desks facing each other instead of the teacher. Eventually, Vice-Chancellor Tsing convinced the university to buy new desks without bolts for most classrooms (see Figure 5.1), and she often remarked that the unbolting of the desks was the first step toward widespread curricular changes at CSU and illustrated the perseverance needed to reform Chinese education. Walking through the teaching

Figure 5.1 CSU classroom with desks 'unbolted' (Personal photo, 2013)

buildings at CSU and observing classes in different departments over the last 10 years, however, it often appeared that many classrooms were still set up with rows facing a teacher who was lecturing, perhaps revealing the limits of a simple structural change of desks for banks of tables as a sign of global citizenship in CSU classrooms.

By advocating student-centered approaches, communicative teaching methods and extracurricular activities often associated with the global West, CSU and the MOE were clearly aligning with 'imagined communities' (Anderson, 1983) and international teaching norms, and the sketch of the university and ELC program presented above provides the overall context of the key cultural tensions and native speaker ideologies that frame the reform teaching agenda, the positioning of foreign and local teachers and the citizenship practices of teachers and students at CSU.

'Raise Your Hand. I Just Want You to Open Your Mouth': Local Teacher Conceptions of CLT and Foreign Teachers

Moving from a discussion of national Chinese and local CSU policies and practices that delineate teaching methods and learning goals, in this section, I focus on interpretations of CLT and student-centered learning by local teachers as well as their views on the role of foreign teachers. To start, consider the following examples from a local teacher's classroom. Sue came to CSU in 2002 and holds an MA-TESOL degree from a UK university. Sue had allowed me to participate in her classroom as an observer and participant during the spring 2007 semester, and we often discussed her teaching activities, the characteristics of Chinese learners and how she was changing her position in the classroom from one of 'knowledge provider' to one of 'skills facilitator.' As she readily accepted the national teaching reforms through a focus on 'all around skills,' she would often ask me, 'Is my classroom communicative?' or 'Do my students speak enough?' In one recorded interview, she discussed how she was changing the way students view teachers in China:

Su: So that in Chinese culture in student's mind teachers should be resourceful, knowledgeable just like a living dictionary. If you are not sure of the meaning of the word, the teacher will be very embarrassed.
P: Do you think that is changing in China?
Su: For me, I think that I change. If the students ask me some questions, I will turn to the dictionary or turn to other foreign teachers and often share my frustration with the students. And, it seems that they respect me more than before. (Personal interview, April 4, 2007)

In addition, Sue felt that CSU students were 'too passive' and worried about being correct when they speak, and she worked to create activities where students would feel comfortable to make mistakes. An example of Sue's desire to force her students to be more active came during the first weeks of her class in the spring of 2007. On the first day of class, Sue presented the following three PowerPoint slides:

Slide 1: 'Why English is very important'
1. English has become an international language for communication around the world.
2. Over 1 billion people use English in the world today.
3. Many companies around the world require English for job positions.
4. Find a better job with good English.

Slides 2: What is a successful learner?
- Having their short and long-term goals.
- Grasping every opportunity to practice with native speaker or other people both in and outside of class.
- Think critically and positively.
- Not afraid to make mistakes in public.
- Reflecting on their learning frequently.

Slide 3: What is a successful learner?
- Assuming the responsibilities for their own learning.
- Never rely on the teacher all the time.
- Self-confidence and willingness to take risk.

(Classroom observation, March 8, 2007)

The slides echoed many points that Sue told me she had read in the TESOL literature from Savignon (2001), Ellis (2003) and Nunan (2005).

In order to reinforce these points, during the second day of her class, Sue asked the students to remember the main points from the first day with a clear emphasis on getting students 'to open their mouths':[5]

1	**Su**:	((at front of the room addressing entire class)) Why is English important (?)
2	**Sts**:	((Heads looking at desks or at windows)) (3.0)
3	**Su**:	((Opens PPT slide that was shown last class; 1st slide lists four reasons for learning English))
4	**Sts**:	((reading slide)) (4.0)
5	**Su**:	((Moves to 2nd slide which lists aspects of a 'successful learner')
6	**Sts**:	((reading slide)) (4.0)
7	**Su**:	((Moves to 3rd slide with further aspects of a 'successful learner'))
8	**Sts**:	((reading slide)) (4.0)
9	**Su**:	((closes the slide show)) This is a possible answer to a test that you will take, such as the CET 4 or CET 6 [College English Test].[6] Will you be able to respond? ...Why is English important (?) (3.0)
10	**S1**:	English is use around the world
11	**S2**:	English is an important tool
12	**S3**:	English as an international language and with English many things are possible.
13	**Su**:	I feel a little...maybe you can say a little disappointed at your reaction. Because last time I remember very clearly that everybody hold these ideas clearly in your minds...But not Friday Saturday Sunday Monday...four days have passed and you forget them. So you don't remember them well... I'm a little disappointed... The next question what is a successful learner (?) There are eight points. You came up with how many (?) O.K. one point is O.K. raise your hand...I just want you to open your mouth.
14	**S4**:	Have short and long term goals
15	**Su**:	YES having short and long term goals
16	**S5**:	think critically
17	**Su**:	think critically (?)
18	**S6**:	and positively
19	**Su**:	YES think critically and positively

(Classroom observation, March 13, 2007)

The above classroom activity was similar to many teacher-initiated activities in Sue's classroom, and it follows a traditional initiation-response-feedback (IRF) sequence in which positive feedback includes a positive response from the teacher followed by repetition of key phrases in the student' response (see Griswold, this volume). The activity also offers an interesting example of how local teachers at CSU are interpreting a communicative approach to teaching. The recitation of previously learned texts may not have been truly communicative according to some scholars, but students were still using English to communicate in these knowledge display exercises, and in our conversations, they noted the comfort and fun they have in her class. Thus, it was difficult for me to tell Sue that her activities looked more like traditional memorization exercises than the 'meaning making' exercises associated with CLT classrooms, and I wrote in my journal, 'Can I define what communicative teaching is?' (Personal journal, April 1, 2007). At the time, I was very concerned that my opinions or critiques of Sue's classroom could alter our friendship, and I often asked myself, 'What is my responsibility as someone who is supposedly here to "reform" teaching and help teachers learn about CLT methods?'

By focusing on 'opening your mouth,' Sue was preparing her students for her view of global citizenship and working through a version of CLT in which confidence is just as important as displaying correct English grammar, and as I noted in my journal, she herself felt confident through these teaching techniques, particularly when calling on students by name to participate, speaking about her classroom to foreign teachers and even when being evaluated negatively by local teachers. In fact, Sue narrated a story about a colleague who had evaluated her classroom and told her that she had not criticized and corrected her students enough and instead had let them talk too freely. She felt that this was the opposite of her teaching goals, and she demanded that a foreign teacher observe her classroom, revealing her sense of agency as a reform teacher as well as her privileging foreign over local teacher opinions. Eventually, a visiting professor from Canada viewed her classroom and praised her use of PowerPoint slides and group seating arrangement to the entire faculty, even suggesting that other teachers should replicate her PowerPoint slides on successful learning. In the end, I did something similar in response to her question, 'Is my classroom communicative?' I complimented the way her students participated in class, and I told her how I used her slides and recitation exercises in my classroom as well, and we both agreed that 'communicative' was in 'the eye of the beholder' and perhaps there was a 'CLT with Chinese characteristics.'

Empowerment through adoption of CLT teaching methods reveals what Blommaert and Backus (2012) would call the 'perpetual reshufflings of norms in a polycentric environment' in which Sue orients her classroom to both global English teaching practices and her students' needs, abilities and cultural backgrounds, perhaps not fully integrating into either the local or global community. At the same time, her desire for approval from me and other foreign teachers and administrators, as representatives of the global teaching community, reveal a continued linguistic insecurity among many local teachers at CSU who still typically considered foreign teachers as better teachers of English. For example, Ma, a local teacher with over 20 years of experience teaching at CSU, states:

> I encourage them [her students] to take foreign teachers class. It's not only because their language is better but it's part of their culture. I think that it's one of the benefits of coming to ELC. You can have exposure to the culture that comes here... [Students say] 'Teacher, why you don't like us.' I say 'just go to the foreigner's classes.' If they are good person, I'm sure that they are all qualified as a teacher. If they are open, friendly, responsible, they could give more than Chinese teacher give. (Personal interview, May 18, 2007)

Pam, another local teacher with over 20 years of teaching experience, echoed Ma's position, 'If the foreign teacher really pays attention to the methods, then they really are good [better] than local teachers' (Personal interview, 2007). And, similarly, Angie, a local teacher of English in her first year of teaching after completing an MA in England, did not directly state that native speakers are better teachers, but she points out that she does not have the 'personality' to teach in the open and student-centered style associated with foreign teachers.

> Chinese teachers are changed a lot, here. Some local teachers try to change the traditional methods. It's up to individual likes and dislikes. I try to be easy-going and communicate with my students. For body language I can't use it well because of my personality. I can draw them into different groups and do the activities together. For this point I cannot do it like foreign teachers. (Personal interview, June 6, 2007)

Angie and Ma's attribution of a privileged status to foreign teachers is perhaps not surprising as from the first day I arrived at CSU, native speakers were at least outwardly considered experts and better teachers than local Chinese teachers of English, and even Sue appeared to seek confirmation from foreign teachers about her classroom activities.

Ma, Angie, Sue and other teachers at CSU do not, at least outwardly, resist the position of foreign teachers in the ELC, and in fact, they openly support and state the inherent worth of foreign teachers as being better than local teachers, a form of linguistic insecurity in which the teachers validate a prescriptive and native speaker ideology toward language use. Thus, an effect of the education reform in CSU teaching policy and the 'foreign' label is to empower teachers such as Sue to participate as citizens in international English teaching communities, but at the same time, local teachers ultimately connect good teaching with foreign teachers, placing an ideological and at times social barrier between foreign and local teachers as collaborators who can each participate equally as local citizens in the CSU teaching community. Put in another way, the discourse and practice of education reform at CSU both expands and limits the imaginations of CSU English teachers, both foreign and local, in terms of what quality education is and who can provide it.

'I Can Proudly Say That We Made a Miracle': Musicals as Signs of Global Citizenship

In examining the performance of the English musical *Fiddler on the Roof* as part of the 2010 English Festival program, this section picks up the polycentric process of becoming a citizen in both local and foreign English-speaking communities and the role of foreign and local teachers in extracurricular English-learning activities, a key aspect of the English learning curriculum at CSU. The university and ELC had successfully produced the musical *Pippin* in 2006, and in 2010, according to Vice-Chancellor Tsing, the university and its sponsoring foundation wanted to produce another musical in order to bring back 'that whole co-curricular environment aspect of large-scale productions' (Personal interview, June 1, 2010). In an interview, she noted that:

> It's not just classroom English. We want to show students that English is a everyday language. If you work in a certain environment, you use it. So students from different disciplines need to learn how to use every day English. Productions like this where you have a director who can speak English then everyone has to step up to the plate because that becomes the language of function. Using it in singing, using it in language makes it more real so it's not just in hopes that someday they will use it. (Personal interview, June 1, 2010)

Earlier in the same interview, the vice-chancellor stated an additional purpose of musicals and arts education in general as providing more than just language education:

> I'm hoping that students will align their moral compass in that direction that will be beneficial to society...To develop your own character and be a well-rounded person you need exposure to the Arts. We are not in

Shanghai or Beijing. You can't just expect students to go to concerts, ever. We have to artificially create their own environment. (Personal interview, June 1, 2010)

The audition invitation for participating in *Fiddler on the Roof* that was sent to students further illustrates the musical as not just a language learning activity but connected to internationalization and cultural efforts at CSU:

> I'd like to recommend you to audition for next year's English musical project—'Fiddler on the Roof.' This is a very popular musical drama that has been staged on New York's Broadway every year for the past 45 years. It is a story of a Jewish family during the Russian revolution and how traditions are made and broken in their culture...This will be a big step in promoting and developing global arts and culture at [CSU]. Won't you consider joining us?

And, the students who auditioned and eventually performed the roles in the play clearly picked up on the musical as not simply a language learning activity, but a connection to 'global arts and culture' and perhaps a means to travel and connect with international audiences. For example, one student wrote in an email to the director of the play about his decision to try out for the play:

> I still remember that it was Ming...who recommended me going for the audition before the summer vacation. I was just so excited when hearing that there might be possibilities of going to Hong Kong, Israel, and Germany if the show went well. So I went for the audition without hesitation. (Personal communication, December, 2010)

In promoting the tryouts, there was no mention or promise that the musical would be performed in other countries, but the earlier production of *Pippin* had been performed in the nearby major city of Guangzhou, and the students clearly saw participation in the musical as a way to travel and gain experiences outside of CSU. In fact, travel, new experiences and the confidence that comes from completing a difficult task may have been the lasting effects of this musical production, as many students wrote to Dan, the foreign teacher assigned to direct *Fiddler on the Roof*, about their joy in finishing the play, not necessarily their participation in an English-speaking environment. To sample just a few of the comments, one student who performed as Chava wrote:

> I can proudly say that we made a miracle. For me, it's a most crazy happiness. It make me have got the most touching and sweetest

memory. I am fortunate enough to meet all of you. (Personal communication, December 2010)

And the student who played the character of Tevye in the play wrote:

> When the show finished, the audience didn't want to leave because they said they hadn't watched enough. Two foreign teachers tearfully told our director, 'This is a musical! Fantastic! Perfect! Amazing!' Several foreign teachers came to hug me and said, 'The musical is the best and the most successful performance in the English Festivals in [CSU]. You did a wonderful job! You sang extremely well!' I felt so grateful and touched that I really wanted to cry out loud. (Personal communication, December 2010)

Similarly, the student who played the role of Lazar Wolf described his apprehension with singing and acting and his sincere appreciation and sense of accomplishment in an email to Dan.

> I still remember that in the first rehearsal, I wanted to give up. I was concerned that the performance would influence my studies, and I was worried that I couldn't handle the all-English instructions as well as memorizing so many English songs. However, one day, I didn't know where the energy came from, it told me, 'Just do it! Do something you like!' If I believed in Christianity, I would have worshiped God; if I believed in Buddhism, I would have worshiped the Buddha; if I believed in communism, I would have . . . Now I really want to thank the whole team and myself. Without their help during the whole time, I wouldn't have overcome the difficulties. No, it shouldn't be only me who faces difficulties; the whole team had different problems but we all sustained and conquered the difficulties. (Personal communication, December 2010)

In their comments, the student responses here reveal the continued ways that foreign audiences and teachers act as gatekeepers to students' citizenship in global English communities, but just as importantly, the students clearly gained confidence to 'open their mouths' in ways similar to the students in Sue's classroom. Further, in small ways, the students took the opportunity of participating in a Western musical to reappropriate and style the musical according to their own tastes, interests and sense of humor. For example, the dancers, who had no speaking part in the play, decided to break from the somewhat kitschy, Horah-inspired circle dancing found in many of the play's scenes to add individual breakdancing routines, including the grasshopper and moonwalk (see Figure 5.2). Further, no copy of the Torah could be found at CSU, and the rabbi in the

Figure 5.2 Dancers practice their performance of 'To Life' (Playbill photo, 2010)

wedding scene used an *Oxford English Dictionary* as a replacement as he spontaneously mumbled random English numbers as a way of mimicking an official proclamation of marriage at a wedding ceremony. Grimshaw (2010) points out that these stylings of Western genres (in this case the placement of hip-hop dance moves into a neo-Eastern European, Jewish dance number) challenge a dominant discourse that constructs Chinese learners as passive recipients of English language and culture, but more importantly in terms of citizenship, they reveal again the individual repertoires and local interpretations of citizenship in global English communities as in Sue's classroom.

Although the production of *Fiddler on the Roof* was clearly beneficial for the students on multiple levels, the director – Dan – who had worked at CSU since 2004 and had participated as musical director in the production of *Pippin*, commented to me after the play was over:

> I was reluctant from the start to take on the project, because of the underlying politics of being a foreign teacher with a role that demanded (pseudo-) voluntary cooperation with local teachers. Giving someone from the 'Public English' department the role of music director was not likely to sit well with the music department, which was also expected to be a major player in the project. Of course, the rationale was that the show was all-English and I did have a music background. Closer to the truth was perhaps that the Arts Education College (music & dance) already had their own agenda for the year (i.e. regional competitions) and did not want the extra burden of a show that would be jointly sponsored by another department (ELC— of which I was the sole representative). Both departments, though,

were under the umbrella of the [Foundation] and obligated to the Foundation's request. (Personal communication, April 2011)

As described here, the production of a musical with direction and input from multiple departments across the university was complicated by differences in language, motivation and a sense of ownership of the musical. Dan was assigned the role of full-time director mainly because no other department or local teacher wanted to take an active role in the musical. Thus, a project and production that was designed to be a collaborative task where students from a variety of departments would communicate in English with local and foreign teachers across campus became the sole responsibility of a hesitant foreign teacher, further reinforcing foreign teachers as model teachers and gatekeepers of English.

Further, Dan became very disillusioned during much of the production process, writing in his teaching diary about the 'ulcer-inducing' stress of attending meetings that 'amounted to zero' in which 'the Arts Ed college director would smile and nod to [Vice-Chancellor Tsing] and then, outside of her presence, tell me to handle everything' (Personal communication, 2011). Furthermore, Dan predicated tensions between his position as musical director and his colleagues and friends in the music department. He noted:

> I predicted a loss of friendship over this project, and sadly, the prediction seems to hold true. Five years prior to this project, when we had our first attempt at Broadway on the [CSU] stage, I played in the pit band under the musical direction of one of the local music teachers who had become a good friend—in fact my only close friend outside of my own department [ELC]. When I was asked to be musical director of this project, my first question was why my friend wasn't being asked, and how he would react. [Vice-Chancellor Tsing's] pitch was about the English language needs of the show, but perhaps there were other reasons. At some point, my friend was asked to help, and to be the rehearsal pianist. He politely declined and we have not had a conversation since. (Personal communication, April 2011)

Dan did, however, work very closely with another local ELC staff member who was able to translate Dan's directions when needed and help coordinate the 100+ performers. Further, the show itself was a surprize success, and Dan wrote me that the show was 'the result of what <u>can</u> be done at [CSU] (ulcers unnecessary with proper cooperation)' (Personal communication, April 2011, original emphasis).

Discussion

> Some signs, consequently, will inevitably be seen as signs of citizenship as well as dis-citizenship, and it is likely that the political dynamics of citizenship in superdiverse societies will hinge on the degrees to which people – experts, legislators, opinion makers – are capable of imagining the levels of complexity that characterize the real social environments in which people 'integrate.' (Blommaert, 2013: 196)

In response to the earlier research question, it is clear from the above examples that the structural and discursive framing of foreign and local teachers significantly affected the ability of teachers and students at CSU to fully become citizens and feel as if they belonged to the CSU teaching community, but at the same time, there are many important discussions, dialogues, interpretations and collaborations occurring at CSU that do not simply re-instantiate a foreign/local dichotomy in which foreign teachers are automatically privileged. Menard-Warwick (2013: 89) defines citizenship as about belonging and 'the capacity to define and promote one's own interests and values,' and it appears that moments and spaces existed at CSU for teachers and students to promote their values and interests. For example, Sue was able to apply her own interpretation of the official 'foreign' teaching methods, and students who participated in *Fiddler on the Roof* were able to gain confidence in their speaking abilities and a sense that their participation and interpretation of a famous musical mattered. Dan was not able to connect as much with his local counterparts in the above example, but he was able to connect with students and ELC staff members in ways that he never would have been able to in the classroom.

At the same time, Sue's insistence on interpreting CLT as primarily about confidence and opening your mouth would not be interpreted as 'correct' by all foreign teachers, and it simultaneously distanced her in some ways from local teachers who may view her as not 'local' or Chinese enough in her teaching, what Blommaert (2013) would call a sign of 'dis-citizenship' at worst or at least an in-between sense of identity that is not authentically local or foreign. Further, there remain important questions about whether participation in extracurricular activities such as musical performances offers students access to authentic citizenship in global English and whether the money spent on such productions would be better spent on Mandarin, Cantonese and local dialect musical and cultural productions. In other words, as some of my students have remarked to me over the past 10 years, is CSU promoting the students' citizenship in global English at the expense of their Chinese citizenship and language identity? Which citizenship will be more important and integral to Sue's and her students' futures?

What seems an important response to these questions is the promotion of spaces to engage in the types of discussions of teaching and identity that Sue and I had about CLT with Chinese characteristics. Not mentioned above, one innovation that the ELC has implemented in recent years, as part of its initiative to encourage individual learning, is the creation of a Center for Independent Language Learning (CILL). Importantly, the programs at the CILL not only focus on English learning, but they also offer both group classes and units for self-study for teachers and students to learn many different languages. Many of the units were created by CSU teachers and students, and many of the classes, in particular the Mandarin Chinese classes, are taught by ELC teachers. Further encouraging teachers to use the CILL, in 2012, the ELC director allowed Mandarin or Cantonese Chinese language teaching and learning at the CILL to count toward fulfillment of an ELC requirement in which all teachers needed to work on extracurricular activities at CSU (in the past only foreign teachers were required to participate in extracurricular activities). This added a social and collaborative aspect to the quantitative evaluation process, and it helped to reframe the privileged status of foreign, English-speaking teachers. As the ELC director stated in 2013, 'I want more teachers who are able to talk about teaching from a student's perspective. How can I help you to learn more effectively rather than how am I going to teach you this content and test you on it?' (Personal interview, October 11, 2013).

Although this chapter noted the many inequalities, ideologies and discourses that create a form of dis-citizenship and prevent foreign and local teachers from fully and equally participating in the CSU community, the data presented hinted at activities and dialogues in which teachers, students and administrators side-stepped dominant discourses and built relationships and community, working in collaboration and coordination as well as promoting personal confidence and choice. In a context in which English has become so powerful that some commentators compare it to an 'ideology' or 'a force strong enough to remake your resume, attract a spouse, or catapult you out of a village' (Osnos, 2008), it is not surprising that tensions and misunderstandings exist between foreign teachers who are often told that they are the reformers of English teaching and local teachers and students who draw on a variety of motivations and desires in teaching and learning English. What appears to be an important aspect that will allow students and teachers to move away from a simplistic foreign/local dichotomy is the creation of spaces outside of the traditional classroom setting in which there is less pressure to perform solely as a foreign or local teacher. CSU and the ELC are still working and striving to create an international community, an important and worthwhile goal for many CSU students. However, in imagining the realities and possibilities of where people actually feel they 'belong,' CSU and other internationalizing universities should focus as much on the classroom as on extracurricular programs that create spaces for teacher and students to interact as equal members and citizens of local, global and in-between communities.

Acknowledgments

I would like to thank all of the dedicated teacher and student participants at CSU who have assisted me throughout my work on this project and many others. In particular, Sue and Dan have opened their classrooms and connected me to many other students and teachers. Without these vital connections, longitudinal ethnographic projects such as this are simply impossible.

Notes

(1) At CSU, a 'local' teacher is a teacher who is a citizen of the People's Republic of China (PRC), Macau or Hong Kong, and 'foreign' teachers are everyone else. The terms 'foreign' and 'local' are in quotes here to highlight their contested and problematic meaning. Outside of citizenship status, it is difficult to define who is 'foreign' at CSU as many of the Chinese teachers of English come from other provinces of China and speak dialects and languages very different than Chaoshanhua and Cantonese which are used by many CSU students. Further, teachers from Chinese communities abroad such as Singapore, Malaysia, Canada and elsewhere often share cultural and linguistic backgrounds with CSU students. Henceforward, the terms will not be in quotes but refer to their meaning in the CSU context.
(2) All names of students, teachers and administrators in the chapter are pseudonyms.
(3) See McPherron (2008, 2009, 2011) for a further description of the data collection methods and sources used when collecting data at CSU.
(4) Jin and Cortazzi (2002: 55) define culture of learning as the 'interpretative frameworks through which classroom events, other participants and their educational identities are evaluated.'
(5) The transcript uses the following notion symbols:
    (( )) = Description or summary of participant/s action
    (?) = Question/Rising tone
    CAPS = Emphasis/falling tone
    … = Short pause of less than one second
    (1.0) = Pause of one second
    Sts = Students
    S = Student
(6) The CET stands for the College English Test and has two proficiency levels (Band 4 and Band 6) that students take in order to demonstrate their abilities in English when seeking jobs.

References

Adamson, B. (2004) *China's English: A History of English in Chinese Education*. Hong Kong: Hong Kong University Press.
Anderson, B. (1983/2006) *Imagined Communities: Reflections on the Origins and Spread of Nationalism* (new edn). New York, NY: Verso.

Blommaert, J. (2013) Citizenship, language, and superdiversity: Towards complexity. *Journal of Language, Identity, and Education* 12 (3), 193–196.
Blommaert, J. and Backus, A. (2012) Superdiverse repertoires and the individual. *Tilburg Papers in Culture Studies* Paper 24.
Charmaz, K. (2006) *Constructing Grounded Theory: A Practical Guide Through Qualitative Analysis*. Thousand Oaks, CA: Sage.
Creswell, J. (2013) *Qualitative Inquiry and Research Design: Choosing Among Five Approaches* (3rd edn). Thousand Oaks, CA: Sage.
Ellis, R. (2003) *Task-Based Language Learning and Teaching*. Oxford: Oxford University Press.
Feng, A. (2009) English in China: Convergence and divergence in policy and practice. *AILA Review* 22, 85–102.
Gil, J. and Adamson, B. (2011) The English language in mainland China: A sociolinguistic profile. In A. Feng (ed.) *English Language Education Across Greater China* (pp. 23–45). Bristol: Multilingual Matters.
Grimshaw, T. (2010) Styling the occidental other: Interculturality in Chinese university performances. *Language and Intercultural Communication* 10 (3), 243–258.
Heigham, J. and Croker, R. (2009) *Qualitative Research in Applied Linguistics: A Practical Introduction*. New York: Palgrave McMillan.
Hu, G. (2005) Contextual influences on instructional practices: A Chinese case for an ecological approach to ELT. *TESOL Quarterly* 39, 635–660.
Hu, G. and McKay, S.L. (2012) English language education in East Asia: Some recent developments. *Journal of Multilingual and Multicultural Development* 33 (4), 345–362.
Internationalization Committee (2007) Report on the status quo of the pedagogical practice at Shantou University (unpublished internal report). China Southern University, Shantou, China.
Jin, L. and Cortazzi, M. (2002) English language teaching in China: A bridge to the future. *Asia-Pacific Journal of Education* 22 (2), 53–64.
Liu, J. and Xiao, P. (2011) A new model in English language teaching in China: The case of Shantou University. *Chinese Journal of Applied Linguistics* 34 (3), 39–53.
Mao, L. and Min, Y. (2004) Foreign language education in the PRC. In M. Zhou (ed.) *Language Policy in the People's Republic of China: Theory and Practice Since 1949* (pp. 319–329). Norwell, MA: Kluwer Academic.
McPherron, P. (2008) Internationalizing teaching, localizing English: Language Teaching reforms through a south Chinese university. Unpublished dissertation, University of California, Davis.
McPherron, P. (2009) 'My name is Money': Name choices and global identifications at a south Chinese university. *Asia Pacific Journal of Education* 29 (4), 521–536.
McPherron, P. (2011) 'I pain, I gain': Self-assessment in a Chinese university academic writing course. In L.H. Phan and B. Baurain (eds) *Voices, Identities, Negotiations, and Conflicts: Writing Academic English Across Cultures* (pp. 99–119). Bradford: Emerald.
Menard-Warwick, J. (2013) 'The world doesn't end at the corner of their street': Language ideologies of Chilean English teachers. In V. Ramanathan (ed.) *Language Policies and (Dis)citizenship: Rights, Access, Pedagogies* (pp. 73–91). Bristol: Multilingual Matters.
Ministry of Education (2007) *College English Curriculum Requirements*. Beijing: Ministry of Education Press. [In Chinese and English.]
Nunan, D. (2005) *Task-Based Language Teaching*. Oxford: Oxford University Press.
Osnos, E. (2008) Crazy English: The national scramble to learn a new language before the Olympics. *New Yorker*, April 28.
Phan, L.H. (2008) *Teaching English as an International Language: Identity, Resistance and Negotiation*. Clevedon: Multilingual Matters.

Ramanathan, V. (ed.) (2013a) *Language Policies and (Dis)citizenship: Rights, Access, Pedagogies*. Bristol: Multilingual Matters.
Ramanathan, V. (2013b) Language policies and (dis)citizenship: Who belongs? Who is a guest? Who is deported? *Journal of Language, Identity, and Education* 12 (3), 162–166.
Richards, K. (2003) *Qualitative Inquiry in TESOL*. London: Palgrave.
Savignon, S. (2001) Communicative language teaching. In M. Celce-Murcia (ed.) *Teaching English as a Second or Foreign Language* (3rd edn, pp. 13–28). Boston, MA: Heinle & Heinle.
Watson-Gegeo, K. (1988) Ethnography in ESL: Defining the essentials. *TESOL Quarterly* 22, 575–592. doi:10.2307/3587257.
Wen, Q.F. and Hu, W.Z. (2007) History and policy of English education in Mainland China. In Y.H. Choi and B. Spolsky (eds) *English Education in Asia* (pp. 1–32). Seoul: Asia TEFL.

6 Language and Body in Concert: A Multimodal Analysis of Teacher Feedback in an Adult Citizenship Classroom

Olga Griswold

Knowledge is both a practice and a product of human interaction. What we know, how we come to know it and how we display what we know is shaped moment-by-moment as we engage in interaction with others. Classroom discourse, by its very nature, is a major locus of such knowledge construction, and teacher feedback on students' displays of knowledge is assumed to play a significant role in the shaping of learning. The effects of teacher feedback on knowledge formation have long attracted the attention of educational scholars (e.g. Brookhart, 2008; Hattie & Timperly, 2007; McHoul, 1978, 1990; Sadler, 2010). Researchers have investigated the informational content of feedback (e.g. Brookhart, 2008; Lyster & Ranta, 1997), its motivational power (Brookhart, 2008; Brophy, 1981) and its potential to spur the acquisition of the target structures in second language (L2) classrooms (e.g. Long et al., 1998; Mackey, 2006; Mackey et al., 2000; Yamamoto, 2005). Little investigation, however, has been made into which components of feedback students specifically orient to when they answer teachers' questions. The present chapter contributes to this still nascent area of inquiry by analyzing interaction in an adult English as a second language (ESL)/citizenship classroom and exploring the following questions:

(1) How does an instructor in such a classroom organize his or her feedback to students' displays of content knowledge?
(2) What role, if any, does the combination of gestural and linguistic components of feedback play in the students' ability to reshape their answers as deemed appropriate for the classroom and, eventually, the citizenship exam?
(3) What kind of knowledge is constructed as acceptable and necessary for future US citizens in the course of these feedback sequences?

Based on this analysis, I argue that the gestural and linguistic components of the teacher's feedback act in concert in providing students – i.e. US citizenship applicants attending the class – with the information that helps them answer questions about US civics not only in a factually accurate manner, but also in a linguistic format expected of them, as future US citizens, during the naturalization interview.

In order to gain US citizenship, immigrants must, among other requirements, demonstrate that they possess the basic knowledge of US history and government structure. This demonstration takes place during a formal one-on-one interview conducted in English with an immigration officer. Qualifying immigrants can prepare for this civics test through community-based, often free or very low-cost, adult citizenship classes. Attending such classes is not a requisite for naturalization. Many naturalization applicants, however, find them extremely helpful because on their own, they often find the process of applying for citizenship daunting. As Young (1991) points out, even long-term green-card holders frequently fear contact with immigration agencies, and when it comes to taking the naturalization test, a large number of applicants do not feel confident either in their English skills or in their knowledge of US civics.[1] Therefore, helping immigrants gain the knowledge and skills for passing the naturalization interview is the primary goal of citizenship classes.

But what knowledge and which skills in particular? Ostensibly, citizenship students learn concrete answers to the standard 100 questions constituting the civics test for naturalization.[2] The classes, however, also serve as powerful vehicles of educating immigrants about their rights and responsibilities, and also of turning them into 'real Americans' – a notion imbued with controversial and complex ideologies.

The idea that immigrants need to be turned into 'real Americans' is not new in US history. The junction of the 19th and 20th centuries – a peak time in US immigration – gave birth to the Americanization movement (Hartman, 1943). The purpose of this movement was to promote the naturalization of new arrivals, but also – most importantly – to foster their cultural assimilation. The idea permeating both the movement and American society in general at the time was that a 'real American' only spoke English (Dixon, 1916), was uncritically loyal to the US (Gavit, 1922) and held fast to the American democratic principles (Gavit, 1922). The movement gave rise to naturalization classes, which immigrants could attend for free in their communities and workplaces, and in which they were expected to absorb the knowledge of what it means to be a true American (Roberts, 1920).

The Americanization movement of the early 20th century with its radical assimilationist views has been largely abandoned today. The contemporary discourses on immigrant inclusion appear to promote a path to citizenship for immigrants accompanied by political and social integration while maintaining cultural and linguistic diversity (e.g. Chavez, 1992; Salinas, 1997; White et al., 1993; Young, 1991).[3] Despite the gradually changing views on naturalization, the primary aim of citizenship classes remains the same: to prepare applicants to prove their worthiness for American citizenship by demonstrating a basic knowledge of US civics and the ability to speak English. As the analysis presented in this chapter will show, the naturalization teacher promotes the following types of knowledge viewed as important for becoming a US citizen:

(1) An American citizen knows and understands his or her rights (see Excerpt 1).
(2) An American citizen knows the basic facts about the political establishments and major elected offices in the nation (see Excerpts 2 and 3).
(3) An American citizen is aware of the current events and political developments in the country and can talk about them in politically neutral language (see Excerpt 4).
(4) An American citizen uses common idiomatic phraseology when speaking English (see Excerpt 5).

This knowledge is not merely imparted from the teacher to the students, but is constructed jointly by all parties through classroom talk. Research over several decades has established that the initiation-response-feedback (IRF) sequence (Mehan, 1979a, 1979b; Sinclair & Coulthard, 1975) and its variations (e.g. Macbeth, 2004) are the primary format of teacher–student interaction and, thus, can act as a major vehicle for knowledge construction. In what follows, I analyze the format, the content and the bodily movement accompanying IRF sequences occurring during citizenship lessons and examine the role that the linguistic and embodied elements of feedback – particularly, corrective feedback – play in the shaping of the students' displays of civics knowledge.

Research on Classroom Feedback

Previous studies of IRF sequences (e.g. Drew, 1981; Macbeth, 2004; McHoul, 1978, 1990; Weeks, 1985) have shown that teacher correction is organized in ways fundamentally similar to the organization of repair in ordinary conversation.[4] Both types of sequences arise in response to interactional trouble that requires resolution before participants can produce further contextually relevant talk. Both can be initiated and completed either by the speaker who first produced the trouble source (in the classroom context, an erring student) or by another speaker (e.g. the teacher).

Nevertheless, there also exist significant differences between conversational repair and classroom correction. While ordinary conversation need not involve ostensible errors in the troublesome turn or any assessment thereof, but rather a difficulty in hearing, formulating or understanding the turn's content (Schegloff et al., 1977), classroom correction is explicitly aimed at evaluating student turns and replacing talk judged to be inaccurate (Friedman, 2010; Koole, 2012; Macbeth, 2004). Furthermore, when it comes to ordinary conversation, research evidence suggests a clear preponderance of self-repair (Schegloff et al., 1977), whereas in the classroom, teachers, i.e. 'Others,' tend to initiate and often complete the corrective sequence (McHoul, 1978, 1990).

Not only is other-repair prevalent in the classroom, it is generally expected and perceived as an inherent part of the educational process. Both instructors and students view corrections as a medium through which some of the teaching is accomplished and as a learning opportunity that teachers are professionally obligated to provide (Lyster et al., 1999; Macbeth, 2004; Panova & Lyster, 2002). In fact, with respect to L2 classrooms, multiple scholars (e.g. Chaudron, 1977, 1988; Doughty & Varela, 1998; Long et al., 1998; Lyster, 1998, 2001; Lyster & Ranta, 1997) have argued that corrections as a form of negative evidence about the target language[5] are essential for adult learners to acquire the structural and discursive components of this language. As a result, many classroom studies have attempted to investigate which linguistic elements teachers tend to correct (e.g. Friedman, 2010; Griswold, 2011; Lyster, 2001; Panova & Lyster, 2002), how teachers organize their corrective turns (Ellis et al., 2006; Lyster & Ranta, 1997) and whether students' uptake of corrections is indicative of learning (Mackey et al., 2000; Mackey & Philp, 1998; Panova & Lyster, 2002; Philp, 2003).

Until recently, however, one all-pervading and rather mundane component of teacher feedback – that of the teacher's bodily movement and gesture – has been conspicuously absent from the analysis. It will hardly come as a surprize to the reader that instructors frequently rely on gesture, bodily movement and realia in teaching beginning L2 users. In fact, Moscowitz (1976) found that one aspect that distinguished outstanding L2 teachers from the 'typical' ones was that the former used significantly more non-verbal means of communication than the latter.

A number of scholars have also examined the pedagogical value of L2 teachers' gestures in non-feedback episodes. Allen (1995), for example, looked at whether the use of emblematic gestures typical of the French culture aided L2 French learners' comprehension and recall of sentences. She found that students who were given stimulus sentences accompanied by emblematic gestures had both the highest level of immediate recall and the lowest level of attrition in a subsequent recall. In a later study, Allen (2000) also found that emblematic, pictographic and kinetographic gestures were used extensively by L2 teachers, and that students found them helpful in understanding meaning. Lazaraton (2004) similarly determined that gestures were a frequent and important component of classroom input, and although her methodology did not allow for drawing conclusions regarding their usefulness to the learners, it did allow for ascertaining the teacher's belief that gestures made the meaning more comprehensible.

Sime (2006, 2008) investigated the effectiveness of teacher's gestures from the students' perspective. Using the stimulated recall methodology, she found that learners saw their instructors' gesticulations as a means of enhancing comprehension, facilitating learning and providing feedback or orchestrating classroom interaction. Faraco and Kida (2008) also looked at the impact of teachers' gestures on learners. They determined that the teacher's non-verbal behavior could both facilitate learning, as in contributing meaning to explanations, and hamper it, when, for example, the teacher's gestures indicated acceptance of a student's output while the verbal feedback contained a correction of linguistic form. Faraco and Kida's (2008) second conclusion provided an impetus for the present study. The data below demonstrate that, in fact, the presumed confusion does not take place. Rather, by examining how students behaviorally display orientation to the gestural and verbal components of the teacher's feedback, I demonstrate that even low-proficiency ESL users perceive speech and gesture as a single, integrated feedback system, where one element can help disambiguate other potentially confusing elements, thereby allowing the students to perceive the feedback as clearly positive or negative. In turn, understanding the positive or negative essence of feedback allows them to reshape their displays of content knowledge as deemed appropriate for the citizenship class and, eventually, the naturalization interview. The students' experience and cultural knowledge gained as long-term US residents assist them in reformulating their answers.

Methods

The data for this study come from a corpus collected during an 11-month ethnographic project focusing on L2 socialization in citizenship classes. Two adult schools in a large urban center in Southern California, USA, served as research sites. The data, collected in 2004–2005, consist of 28 hours of videotaped classroom interaction supplemented by field notes on over 100 hours of participant observation as well as by formal and informal interviews with study participants.

The students in both classes were multilingual, with approximately 58% of students claiming Spanish as their native language.[6] The students' English skills varied from almost non-existent to native. Their socioeconomic and educational backgrounds also varied significantly. Because the classes operated on an open-enrollment basis,[7] a formal survey of the students' socioeconomic statuses and educational levels was not feasible. My informal conversations with them, however, revealed that their occupations varied from working-class jobs, such as maids, landscapers and restaurant workers, to positions considered to be middle class in the US, such as managers, college students, small business owners, an IT specialist, a filmmaker, etc. Similarly, the students' educational levels ranged from having only elementary education (i.e. six years or less) to possessing advanced degrees. Most class participants were educated outside the US, and while no formal language assessment was administered during the study, no noticeable correspondence between the level of formal education and the level of English proficiency was observed.[8]

The videotaped data were transcribed using the conventions of conversation analysis (Sacks *et al.*, 1974). IRF sequences were identified and analyzed with respect to their sequential organization, linguistic content and the gaze and bodily movement that accompanied the verbal feedback.

The analysis shows that positive and negative evaluations of student responses by the teacher had distinct and consistent compositions; that the components of feedback were linguistic, paralinguistic and bodily in nature; and that students oriented to all components (i.e. words, intonation, sequential organization, gaze, and bodily movement) in interpreting the teacher's feedback.

Features of Positive Feedback

Positive feedback had the most consistent features throughout the data. When a student's response to a question was deemed correct, the feedback – i.e. the F element of the IRF sequence – consisted of three clear turn components:

(1) The repetition of the keyword or phrase in the student's answer, produced with a falling intonation.
(2) A positive assessment, also produced with a falling intonation.
(3) An elaboration of the student's answer, usually through at least one complete sentence or more.

Little or no bodily movement, with the exception of short nods, accompanied this verbal feedback. The following excerpt, which occurred during the teacher's explanation of the Fourth Amendment to the US Constitution,[9] exemplifies this pattern:

Excerpt 1

```
01    Teacher: The government cannot come ba̲rging i̲nto o̲ur ho:̲mes,
02             witho̲ut our permi̲ssion.
03             (1.0) ((T. looks down at her notes))
04             Unle̲:s, (0.5) they ge̲t, wha̲t.
05             (1.1) ((gaze sweep across the classroom))
06    Luz[10]:  °They need a wa̲rrant.°
07  → Teacher: Kghm. Hm? A wa̲rrant.
               ((one short nod; gaze at the center of the class))
08  →          'T's corre̲ct. A se̲arch, (0.3) ((one short nod)) wa̲rrant.
09             (1.5) ((gaze sweep across the classroom to the left and back))
10  →          If th- poli̲ce wanna come i̲nto your apa̲rtment, and
11  →          take a lo̲ok,(0.9) they ha̲ve to ge̲t a se̲arch wa̲rrant,
12  →          fro̲m a ju̲dge.
```

The teacher begins the segment by stating a key provision of the amendment (Lines 01–02). At Line 04, she attempts to elicit an exception to this provision from the students, thereby providing an opening for them to display their understanding of their constitutional rights. One student, Luz, volunteers an answer (Line 06). The teacher evaluates her contribution as accurate. The evaluation is produced in the format described above: the teacher repeats the keyword 'warrant' (Line 07), positively assesses the answer with "T's correct' (Line 08) and finally elaborates on it by first inserting the specification of the warrant's type ('a search warrant') and then embedding the phrase in a complete sentence (Lines 10–12).

The non-verbal feedback during the sequence is limited to the teacher making two very short nods and sweeping her gaze across the classroom twice,[11] thus addressing all students together and none in particular. The nods complement the positive verbal assessment. The feedback as a whole validates the student's knowledge.

Moreover, throughout the sequence, the knowledge about legal rights is constructed not only as something the students need to know for the naturalization interview (as, indeed, they do), but also something that is relevant to being an American. Note the use of the possessive determiner in the phrases 'our homes' and 'our permission' in Lines 01–02. This determiner invokes the teacher's and the students' membership in the category 'Americans,' and the use of the possessive 'your' in 'your apartment' (Line 10) casts the information about the Fourth Amendment as relevant to the students as current residents and prospective citizens. It subtly reinforces the notion that Americans should know and exercise their constitutional rights.

Features of Negative Feedback

Negative feedback, on the other hand, was not uniform in nature. Two distinct but sometimes co-occurring forms of negative feedback were observed in the data. The first format was linguistically unambiguous. If the teacher deemed an answer incorrect, she often rejected it on the record (e.g. with a 'no'), which prompted an immediate self-correction on the students' part. Like positive feedback, the linguistically unambiguous negative feedback was accompanied by little or no bodily and gaze movement, as the following segment demonstrates:

Excerpt 2

```
01   Teacher:   Where is the United Nations' headquarters.
                ((gaze sweep across the classroom))
02   Rafael:    Washington?=
03 →Teacher:    =No [::, ((slight head tilt to the left; gaze on student))
04   Rafael:         [uh New [Y o: [rk.
05   Albert:                 [N'Yo: [hk.
06   Veronica:                     [New [York.
                ((gaze sweeps begin in overlap with Rafael's self-correction in 04
                and continue throughout the rest of the sequence))
07 →Teacher:                            [New York. That's
08 →            right. Building, the headquarters building, of the
09 →            United Nations, is in New, York, City.
```

In response to the teacher's question in Line 01, Rafael produces the tentative answer 'Washington?' The tentativeness is indicated by the try-marked upward final intonation (Schegloff, 2007). The teacher rejects the answer immediately, with no transition space after Rafael's turn. A slight head tilt accompanies the rejection. Her gaze momentarily locks on Rafael. Before the teacher's stretched 'no' in Line 03 is complete, multiple students, including Rafael, produce a more accurate answer in overlap with each other (Lines 04–06). The teacher evaluates the new contribution as correct in the same format as for Excerpt 1: the repetition of the key phrase ('New York'), a positive assessment ('That's right') and a complete sentence elaboration (Lines 07–09). Throughout the sequence, the teacher remains seated, continually sweeping her gaze across the class, pausing on Rafael only briefly when she rejects his first answer. The manner and speed of her gaze sweep remain unchanged throughout the sequence. Since a head tilt (not pivot) does not necessarily constitute a culturally recognized gesture of rejection, it appears that the students orient mainly to the linguistic component of the feedback by producing self-correction (on Rafael's part) and peer correction (on the parts of Albert and Veronica).

The second type of negative feedback was less transparent in its linguistic form. In rejecting some student answers, the teacher did not employ a clear negative term, such as 'no,' or a negative assessment, such as 'wrong' or 'incorrect.' Rather, she repeated the student's answer or a portion of it with a rising (questioning) intonation, turned away from the erring student and re-addressed the question to the other class participants, thus sequentially deleting the first answer.

Repetitions of student answers or portions thereof are typical of both implicit negative feedback, such as recasts or indirect prompts for self-correction (Lyster & Ranta, 1997; Panova & Lyster, 2002) and positive feedback, such as answer acceptances. As a result, the feedback consisting solely of repetitions may be linguistically and pragmatically ambiguous and confusing to the students (Mackey et al., 2000; Mackey & Philp, 1998; Panova & Lyster, 2002). The data in the present corpus, however, suggest that the nature of the feedback may be disambiguated through the teacher's bodily movement and paralinguistic features such as intonation.

Excerpt 3

01	**Teacher**:	Oka:y. Number fifte:en. Will you re:ad number fifteen.
02		Rafael? *((gazes and points to Rafael))*
03	**Rafael**:	How many times, may a representative, be r-elected.= *((The teacher lowers her gaze towards the worksheet she is holding))*
04	**Teacher**:	=How many times. *((steadily gazes at Rafael))*
05	**Rafael**:	(--) two? *((Teacher's gaze is on Rafael))*
06	**Teacher**:	Two:? *((Teacher shifts gaze from Rafael to the opposite side of the classroom in an exaggerated motion))*
07		(0.5) *((continues to look away from Rafael, no gaze sweep))*
08	**Students**:	There is no limit. No limit. *((Teacher's gaze moves to the back-center of the classroom))*
09	**Teacher**:	No there is no, limit. As lo:::ng as you keep getting
10		reelected you can run again, and again, and again, and
11		again, and again. So. The correct answer is A.
12		There's no limit.

The teacher first calls on Rafael to read a question from a worksheet. She selects him as the next speaker by calling his name (Line 02), gazing at him and pointing to him. As Rafael reads, the teacher moves her gaze to the worksheet she is holding, but upon completion of the reading, lifts her eyes back at Rafael, thus selecting him as the answerer, and restates the question (Line 04). Rafael hesitantly produces an incorrect answer (Line 05). The teacher, however, does not reject it explicitly. Instead, she repeats the answer, marking it as a question with a rising tone, and as she does so, she turns away from Rafael and gazes to the opposite side of the classroom. This head movement is quite exaggerated, with a noticeable chin dip in the middle and chin thrust up at the end.

The students' difficulty in interpreting this repetition as a rejection of Rafael's answer is signaled by a 0.5 second gap after the teacher's turn in Line 06. Despite this difficulty, however, the next turn produced by multiple students (Line 08) indicates that they do understand the repetition as negative feedback. Several aspects of the teacher's turn contribute to this understanding. First, her talk in Line 06, although it contains a repetition of the key portion of the answer, lacks other elements of positive feedback – namely, a positive assessment and an elaboration of the answer. Second, the repetition itself is produced with interrogative, rather than affirmative, intonation. Third, the teacher deselects Rafael as the speaker and redirects the question to his classmates. The new answer in Line 08 suggests that students orient to the absence of the components of positive feedback as well as to the teacher's bodily movement and gaze direction in interpreting her feedback as negative.

Superficially, Excerpts 1, 2 and 3 address the same type of material – civics test questions for naturalization. However, there are also subtle differences in how the information is treated in these sequences. In Excerpt 1, not only does the teacher, through the use of possessives, cast the knowledge as relevant to the students' daily lives as Americans, but she also formulates the initial question as a statement, inviting the students to co-construct the answer with her, possibly drawing on their knowledge gained outside the classroom (from TV, print media, etc.). Excerpts 2 and 3 are structured as display question sequences much more typical of a traditional classroom, with no indication that this knowledge can have a direct impact on the students' lives beyond passing the test.

Mixed Feedback: The Positive with the Negative

In addition to instances of feedback that were unambiguously positive or negative, the data also contain instances of feedback that, at first glance, may be construed as conflicting. Specifically, in many IRF sequences, the linguistic and sequential structure of the feedback appeared to clash with the gestures and bodily movement that accompanied it. Further examination, however, suggests that such ostensibly contradictory feedback was aimed at assessing the students' culturally relevant knowledge separately from its verbal display, and that students oriented to this 'separateness' in reformulating their answers. Excerpt 4 illustrates the phenomenon:

Excerpt 4:

```
01    Teacher:    Probably some day we will have another amendment, to
02                the Constitution, President Bu::sh, (0.8) wants: us to
                  ha:ve,
03 →              another amendment to the Constitution.= And what does
04 →              he want to amend the Constitution [to sa:y.
05    Rafael:                                       [Only the [(peo-
06 → Lani:                                                    ['buh:t gay?
07 →              (0.8) ((The teacher gazes at Lani in a sustained manner))
08 →              buht gay- marriage?
09 →              (1.5) ((The teacher vigorously nods four times))
10 →              because deh people don' li:(k)e. it. ((T. continues to nod, but
                  less vigorously, three times.))
11 →              (1.1) ((T. slowly turns away from Lani and sweeps her gaze
                  across the class))
12 → Teacher:    What does he want- What does he want the Constitution
13 →              to say. ((T. sweeps gaze across the class again))
14 →              (0.7) ((Gaze sweep continues))
15    Fasila:    That same [(
16 → Amaro:                [°Marriage is ( )° between the man, and the
17 →              woman. ((T. settles gaze on Amaro at the beginning of turn 16))
18 → Teacher:    That's right. He: wants to a::dd, something. To the
19 →              Constitution, that says, that marriage::, (0.6) marriage::,
20 →              (0.3) is, a contract between (.) one man, [and one woman.
21 → Lani:                                                  [one woman.
22    Teacher:   That's what he wants to put in the Constitution.
```

In this segment, after talking about the existing amendments to the Constitution, the teacher extends the discussion by probing the students' possible knowledge of current political issues (Lines 01–04). At the time the data were recorded in 2004, the viability of two potential amendments was being discussed in the press: the modification of the place of birth requirement for presidential candidates and the definition of marriage. As long-term US residents, students were exposed to the ongoing coverage of the issues in both English and non-English-language media and, as Excerpt 4 indicates, had formed opinions about them.

When the teacher introduces the topic of same-sex marriage into the discussion of constitutional amendments, she phrases her question in terms of the potential wording of the amendment, as indicated by the use of the word 'say' (Line 04). One of the students, Lani, begins to propose that the amendment will concern 'gay people' (Line 06). As she begins to speak, the teacher turns to Lani and continues to gaze at her in a sustained manner throughout the 0.8-second gap that follows the student's initial response, producing, however, no verbal feedback. The fact that in Line 08, Lani elaborates her initial response serves as evidence that she recognizes being selected as the next speaker, but also orients to the possibility that her first response may have been insufficient. She, thus, provides a self-repair by adding the word 'marriage' to her original formulation.

Lani's second attempt at the response is also followed by a considerable silent gap of 1.5 seconds (Line 09). Despite the lack of verbal feedback in that gap, the teacher positively evaluates Lani's follow-up answer in a rather unambiguous manner: she energetically nods in assent four times. Encouraged by this apparent approval, Lani proceeds to provide the reason for the proposed amendment (Line 10), which is accompanied by three further nods on the teacher's part, albeit less vigorous ones. In other words, the teacher clearly evaluates Lani's display of current political knowledge as correct through her bodily movements.

The sequential organization and content of the teacher's talk, nevertheless, fall in line with those accompanying negative feedback as described in Excerpt 3. At the completion of Lani's turn in Line 10, the teacher produces no verbal feedback but turns away from her and sweeps her gaze across the classroom. By the time she initiates her turn in Lines 12–13, the teacher no longer gazes at Lani, thus deselecting her as the next speaker. In this turn, the teacher almost verbatim repeats her question from Lines 03–04, thus sequentially deleting Lani's first response. This move constitutes the rejection of Lani's answer as correct and opens the possibility for other students to provide their own answers. Two students promptly do so (Lines 15–17). Amaro's answer, focusing on the definition of marriage and avoiding any mention of sexual orientation, receives a more canonical positive evaluation from the teacher, including a positive assessment term ('that's right') and an elaboration of the student's turn content (Lines 18–20). Lani orients to the need to reformulate her own answer as well. In Line 21, she completes the teacher's elaboration of Amaro's answer in recognitional overlap (Jefferson, 1987) with the teacher.

The teacher's feedback provided to Lani through bodily movement (nodding) is highly positive. The feedback encoded in words and accompanied by a shift in gaze direction, conversely, is negative. While gesture on the one hand and language and gaze movement on the other appear to be in conflict, these two types of feedback are designed to evaluate two separate parts of the knowledge display and therefore complement rather than contradict each other. Lani, in getting to the meat of the proposed amendment, has displayed accurate and culturally relevant knowledge. While she is not an American by legal status, her cultural knowledge marks her as a *de facto* member of American society. She understands the political and ideological issues underlying the definition of marriage like any other ordinary American does. The teacher positively evaluates this 'American' knowledge through multiple vigorous nods.

The class's goal, however, is to prepare students for the naturalization interview, where they are expected to display supposedly objective, neutral knowledge devoid of moral attitudes or politically charged views. In order to do so, the students might be expected to demonstrate that they can talk about the Constitution in neutral terms, as a legal document rather than a reflection of the current mores or, in other words, in terms of what the Constitution says, rather than how it reflects what, according to Lani (Line 10), people do and do not like. From this point of view, Amaro's answer is evaluated as more appropriate. Therefore, the teacher's ostensibly conflicting feedback validates the knowledge that the students possess as long-term residents in the US while at the same time allowing them to reshape the displays of this knowledge in a way more suitable for the citizenship classroom and, potentially, for the naturalization interview.

Excerpt 5 similarly demonstrates that negative feedback is not always aimed at correcting the accuracy of knowledge displays, but rather their form. In this sequence, the class is practicing the standard 100 civics questions. The teacher calls on a student, Abrienda, to name the colors of the American flag:

Excerpt 5

```
01 → Teacher:    Aw:, right.=Here we go.=Abrienda,
02               (1.1) ↑What are the colors of our fla:g.
03 → Abrienda:   U::h is thu::h ((looks to the side of the classroom))
04   Teacher:    Don't look. ((smiling voice))
05   Students:   Hah-hah- [hah-hah ((laughter continues))
06   Mei-Feng:            [(What./Why.) I don' kno:w,
07               (1.0) ((gradually abating laughter))
08 → Abrienda:   Blue, a:nd uh red- ↑white, the: u:h star, (0.6) blue,
09 → Teacher:    ↑°Mm↓hm.°
10 → Abrienda:   and white, [ a n d  re d.]
11 → Teacher:               [↑°Mm↓hm.] ↑ Mm↓hm, ↑usually, we s:ay the
                 colors in one way. >We say< red, white,
12 →             [and blue.]
13 → Students:   [and blue.]
14               (0.5)
15 → Teacher:    Red, [white, and blue.]
16 → Mei-Feng:        [white, and blue.]
17               (0.3)
18 → Teacher:    As a matter of fact, tha[t is the na::me of our flag.
19 → Mei-Feng:                           [Red, white, and blue. Red, white,
                                          and blue.
```

134 Part 2: Pedagogies

```
20 → Teacher:    [We ca::ll that (0.6) the o:ld red, [white and blue.
21 → Mei-Feng: [Red, white, and blue.
22 → Hua:                                            [white, and blue
23    Teacher:   So it's probably easier to remember, red, white, and [blue.
24    Hua:                                                             [blue.
```

At first, Abrienda has trouble answering the question, as indicated by sound stretches and delay markers in Line 03,[12] but eventually she names the three colors of the US flag in Lines 08 and 10, albeit in a different order from the formulaic one used by most adult English speakers in the US. The teacher positively acknowledges the response in Lines 09 and 11 with three 'mmhm' tokens produced with noticeable pitch rises and falls.[13] No other features of positive feedback, as described in Excerpt 1, however, are evident in this example. Instead, the teacher immediately reformulates Abrienda's response, drawing attention to the more culturally established order of the colors in Lines 11 and 12. The referent of 'we' in these two lines may be initially ambiguous, but the reference to 'our flag' in Line 18 suggests that by 'we' and 'our' (Lines 11, 12, 18 and 20), the teacher implies Americans. Indeed, the fact that Americans use a particular order of colors as the name of the flag[14] (line 18) is used as the rationale for treating this order as the more accurate (i.e. more 'American'), more memorable (Line 23) and, therefore, useful for the naturalization interview. Thus, the teacher provides feedback not on the accuracy of content knowledge, but on the appropriateness of the cultural knowledge, i.e. the use of standard idiomatic phrasing to talk about an American patriotic symbol.

Indeed, as Baptiste (this volume) notes, the ability to speak and write accurately about the colors of the American flag may potentially be the make-or-break of the citizenship test for some of the applicants: 7 out of 64 questions dictated to applicants during the writing portion of the test were about the colors of the flag (Winn, 2000, as cited in Baptiste, this volume), and the first 7 questions of the civics test (7%) administered at the time the present data were collected focused on the flag as well.

After the initial correction, Abrienda drops out of the sequence. Other students – and, notably, Mei-Feng, who indicated not knowing the answer to the question at the beginning of the sequence (Line 06) – engage in extensive practice of the 'correct' order of the colors (Lines 13, 16, 19, 21, 22 and 24), displaying their understanding that from the teacher's point of view, the form in which the knowledge of the course material is displayed is as important as the accuracy of the knowledge itself. The students are, thus, expected not only to know what Americans know (e.g. the colors of the flag), but also to speak about this knowledge in a very American way.

Discussion and Conclusion

The IRF sequences discussed above demonstrate that the teacher's feedback on students' displays of knowledge contained three distinct components. The first component is the linguistic content of the teacher's turn, including acknowledgments, assessments, rejection terms, repetitions and elaborations of the students' responses. The second component included paralinguistic features, such as the intonation of the teacher's talk and its sequential organization. The third component was physical in nature and included gestures, bodily orientation and gaze direction. I have argued that students orient to all three components simultaneously in order to interpret the teacher's feedback either as positive or as negative and, if necessary, to reshape their displays of knowledge in the form more acceptable in the classroom.

Earlier research (e.g. Mackey & Philp, 1998; Mackey et al., 2000) indicated that implicit feedback, such as recasts and clarification requests, both of which can take the form of repetitions of students' answers or portions thereof, tend to be ambiguous for learners, especially those with lower levels of L2 proficiency. The data presented in this chapter, however, suggest that the teacher's intonation, bodily movement, gaze direction and the inclusion of other elements in the feedback turn (e.g. acknowledgments, assessments and elaborations) play a significant role in disambiguating the nature of the feedback for the students. In other words, even learners with limited L2 proficiency take into consideration where the teacher is looking, how she moves her body, how she gestures and what tone of voice she uses when she is evaluating their answers.

Furthermore, I have argued that classroom feedback may be organizationally quite complex, with its different components aimed at evaluating different aspects of knowledge displays. The data contain sequences in which the language of feedback and the bodily movement accompanying it appear to be in conflict. Potentially, such feedback could send conflicting messages to the students. Student responses, however, indicate that they did not find such feedback confusing, but rather oriented to the fact that the teacher was assessing their culturally relevant knowledge separately from the form in which they verbalized it. The positive feedback provided through the body validated the students' vernacular knowledge as long-term US residents and *de facto* members of American society. The verbal feedback spurred the students to reshape public displays of this knowledge in a neutral, classroom-appropriate and, to a degree, more 'American' way as it is viewed from the citizenship classroom perspective. Such complex feedback contributes to the construction of a particular kind of knowledge – the pragmatic knowledge of discursive and linguistic strategies appropriate for the classroom and, potentially, other institutional environments, such as naturalization interviews, where the students are expected to prove their suitability for the status of an American citizen.

Moreover, preparation for the naturalization test was not the only goal of developing the knowledge about US civics. As the data demonstrate, the class also served as a vehicle for educating participants about the kinds of knowledge that would be useful to them beyond the naturalization ceremony: the knowledge about their rights as individuals and about civic and political developments that may affect them in their daily lives. For example, Excerpt 1 addresses the protections that students in this class – as people residing in the US – have under the 4th Amendment, but the content of this amendment is not included in the 100 official naturalization test questions, so students do not, technically speaking, need to know about such protections to pass the interview. Similarly, the issues of general civic awareness such as discussed in Excerpt 4 (same-sex marriage)[15] are not part of the citizenship test, yet having such awareness may mark an individual as an involved and civically minded citizen. By using possessives such as 'our' and 'your,' and the first-person pronoun 'we,' the teacher invited students to bring their existing knowledge to co-constructing notions studied in the citizenship classroom. She also cast students as members of American society, who, as good citizens, should be engaged and aware of their civil rights and of the political developments around them.

While the findings presented in this chapter are based on only two classrooms with the same instructor and, thus, cannot be unequivocally generalized to all citizenship courses, let alone all educational environments, they suggest the usefulness of investigating aspects of classroom interaction other than language in more detail. Outside the study of classroom discourse, gesture and gaze direction have been demonstrated as important elements in the construction of meaning in discourse (e.g. Fox, 1999; Goodwin, 1984, 1986, 1994; McNeill & Levy, 1993). In the classroom, however, only a few scholars have examined how teachers use gestures in explaining vocabulary and clarifying meaning. The majority of second language acquisition and L2 classroom discourse research continues to prioritize linguistic structures, assigning gesture and gaze an ancillary role in the teaching thereof. In order to better understand the role of teacher talk in the classroom, future research will need to look at more than the talk itself, but also at how the teacher's conscious or subconscious gesturing and gaze direction contribute to the organization of instructional sequences and, thus, to the construction of student knowledge.

Another important implication of this study relates to teacher education. Pre-service teachers in TESL programs often learn about verbal forms of feedback, including the potential efficacy of particular feedback types, such as recasts or metalinguistic comments, in helping students acquire the appropriate linguistic forms. Verbal feedback tends to be classified as positive or negative, with no gray areas of ambiguity. This chapter suggests that such gray areas do exist. It may be useful to increase the future teachers' awareness of the importance of their non-verbal behavior as it contributes to the students' understanding of verbal feedback. This is especially important for content-based classrooms, such as ESL/citizenship instruction, where the students' language skills may not allow them to express their much more sophisticated real-life knowledge, and where the teachers need to be able to evaluate what the students know differently from how the students are able to verbalize this knowledge in their L2.

Acknowledgments

I am deeply grateful to the students and the teacher who participated in this project. This study would not have been possible without their welcoming me to the class and allowing me to be part of their learning and teaching process for an extended period of time.

Notes

(1) Apropos of this issue, Baptiste (this volume) points out that immigration officers conducting naturalization interviews frequently recommend to failing applicants that they need to study more or attend school to prepare for the naturalization test. Having studied hard for the test is viewed as proving one's worthiness of US citizenship.
(2) See www.uscis.gov/citizenship for details.
(3) See, however, the English-Only movement and the work of such organizations as English First or US English for opposing views.
(4) For a comprehensive analysis of conversational repair, see Schegloff et al. (1977).
(5) Negative evidence is evidence about what is not possible in the target language.
(6) Some study participants, in fact, had been raised speaking a Native American language, but considered Spanish their 'main' language, had been educated in it and used it in their daily lives. For the purposes of this study, the students' self-identification as native speakers of a particular language (Spanish, Mandarin, Russian, etc.) was taken at face value.
(7) This means that students could join the class at any time during the term, and attendance was not consistent from one class session to another.
(8) This, in part, can be accounted for by different lengths of residence in the US, different ages of arrival, different levels of engaging with English speakers in the students' daily lives, etc.
(9) Among other protections, this amendment guarantees persons residing in the US freedom from unreasonable search and seizure.
(10) All participants' names have been replaced by pseudonyms to preserve their privacy.
(11) The teacher's talk in Line 07 appears to be delayed, ostensibly suggesting that she is about to produce a dispreferred turn. Space limitations prohibit me from discussing this delay in detail. For the present, suffice it to say that the throat clearing appears to be a simple biological function. The repair initiator 'hm?' following the throat clearing is triggered by the quietness of the student's answer in the previous turn, and the fact that the teacher does not pursue the repair further suggests that while she may have had initial trouble hearing Luz, this problem quickly resolved itself without the need for Luz to produce self-repair.

(12) The fact that the American flag is displayed in the classroom, and Abrienda could easily look at it and name the colors appears both to prompt the teacher's 'Don't look' in Line 04 and Abrienda's classmates' mirth in Lines 05–07.
(13) No references to the teacher's bodily movements or gaze are made in the discussion of this sequence because the teacher remained out of the camera shot throughout the interaction and, thus, her movements were not available for subsequent analysis.
(14) In fact, 'the Old Red, White, and Blue' is not a typical nickname for the American flag. 'The Old Glory,' 'Stars and Stripes' or 'the Star-Spangled Banner' tend to be used more commonly as nicknames. Thus, the teacher is not quite correct herself in this sequence.
(15) The question discussed in Excerpt 2 (UN Headquarters) is not currently on the naturalization test, but it was one of the questions when the data were recorded in 2004–2005.

References

Allen, L.Q. (1995) The effects of emblematic gestures on the development and access of mental representations of French expressions. *Modern Language Journal* 79, 521–529.
Allen, L.Q. (2000) Nonverbal accommodations in foreign language teacher talk. *Applied Language Learning* 11 (1), 155–176.
Brookhart, S.M. (2008) *How to Give Effective Feedback to Your Students*. Alexandria, VA: Association for Supervision and Curriculum Development.
Brophy, J. (1981) Teacher praise: A functional analysis. *Review of Educational Research* 51 (1), 5–32.
Chaudron, C. (1977) A descriptive model of discourse in the corrective treatment of learners' errors. *Language Learning* 27, 29–46.
Chaudron, C. (1988) *Second Language Classrooms: Research on Teaching and Learning*. New York: Cambridge University.
Chavez, L. (1992) *Out of the Barrio: Toward a New Politics of Hispanic Assimilation*. New York: Basic Books.
Dixon, R. (1916) *Americanization*. New York: McMillan.
Drew, P. (1981) Adults' corrections of children's mistakes. In P. French and M. Maclure (eds) *Adult–Child Conversation* (pp. 244–267). New York: St. Martins.
Doughty, C. and Varela, E. (1998) Communicative focus on form. In C. Doughty and J. Williams (eds) *Focus on Form in Classroom Second Language Acquisition* (pp. 114–138). Cambridge: Cambridge University Press.
Ellis, R., Loewen, S. and Erlam, R. (2006) Implicit and explicit corrective feedback and the acquisition of L2 grammar. *Studies in Second Language Acquisition* 28, 339–368.
Faraco, M. and Kida, T. (2008) Gesture and the negotiation of meaning in a second language classroom. In S.G. McCafferty and G. Stam (eds) *Gesture: Second Language Acquisition and Classroom Research* (pp. 280–298). New York: Routledge.
Fox, B. (1999) Directions in research: Language and the body. *Research on Language and Social Interaction* 32 (1), 51–59.
Friedman, D. (2010) Speaking correctly: Error correction as a language socialization practice in a Ukrainian classroom. *Applied Linguistics* 31, 346–347.
Gavit, J.P. (1922) *Americans by Choice*. New York: Harper & Brothers.
Goodwin, C. (1984) Notes on story structure and the organization of participation. In J.M. Atkinson and J. Heritage (eds) *Structures of Social Action: Studies in Conversation Analysis* (pp. 225–246). Cambridge: Cambridge University Press.
Goodwin, C. (1986) Gesture as a resource for the organization of mutual orientation. *Semiotica* 62 (1–2), 29–49.

Goodwin, C. (1994) Professional vision. *American Anthropologist* 96 (3), 606–633.
Griswold, O.V. (2011) The English you need to know: Language ideology in a citizenship classroom. *Linguistics and Education* 22 (4), 406–418.
Hartman, E.D. (1943) *The Movement to Americanize the Immigrant.* New York: Columbia University Press.
Hattie, J. and Timperley, H. (2007) The power of feedback. *Review of Educational Research* 77 (1), 81–112.
Jefferson, G. (1987) On exposed and embedded correction in conversation. In G. Button and J.R.E. Lee (eds) *Talk and Social Organization* (pp. 86–100). Clevedon: Multilingual Matters.
Koole, T. (2012) Teacher evaluations: Assessing 'knowing', 'understanding' and 'doing'. In G. Rasmussen, C.E. Brouwer and D. Day (eds) *Evaluating Cognitive Competences in Interaction* (pp. 43–66). Amsterdam: Benjamins.
Lazaraton, A. (2004) Gesture and speech in the vocabulary explanations of one ESL teacher: A microanalytic inquiry. *Language Learning* 54 (1), 79–117.
Long, M.H., Inagaki, S. and Ortega, L. (1998) The role of implicit negative feedback in SLA: Models and recasts in Japanese and Spanish. *The Modern Language Journal* 83 (3), 357–371.
Lyster, R. (1998) Recasts, repetition, and ambiguity in L2 classroom discourse. *Studies in Second Language Acquisition* 20, 51–81.
Lyster, R. (2001) Negotiation of form, recasts, and explicit correction in relation to error types and learner repair in immersion classrooms. *Language Learning* 51 (Suppl. 1), 265–301.
Lyster, R. and Ranta, L. (1997) Corrective feedback and learner uptake: Negotiation of form in communicative classrooms. *Studies in Second Language Acquisition* 20, 37–66.
Lyster, R., Lightbown, P. and Spada, N. (1999) A response to Truscott's 'What's wrong with oral grammar correction.' *The Canadian Modern Language Review* 55 (4), 457–467.
Macbeth, D. (2004) The relevance of repair for classroom correction. *Language in Society* 33 (5), 703–736.
Mackey, A. (2006) Feedback, noticing, and instructed second language learning. *Applied Linguistics* 27 (3), 405–430.
Mackey, A. and Philp, J. (1998) Recasts, interaction and interlanguage development: Are responses red herrings? *Modern Language Journal* 82 (3), 338–356.
Mackey, A., Gass, S. and McDonough, K. (2000) How do learners perceive interactional feedback? *Studies in Second Language Acquisition* 22 (2), 471–497.
McHoul, A. (1978) The organization of turns at formal talk in the classroom. *Language in Society* 7 (2), 183–213.
McHoul, A. (1990) The organization of repair in classroom talk. *Language in Society* 19 (3), 349–377.
McNeill, D. and Levy, E.T. (1993) Cohesion and gesture. *Discourse Processes* 16 (4), 363–368.
Mehan, H. (1979a) 'What time is it, Denise?': Asking known information questions in classroom discourse. *Theory into Practice* 18 (4), 285–294.
Mehan, H. (1979b) *Learning Lessons: Social Organization in the Classroom.* Cambridge, MA: Harvard University Press.
Moscowitz, G. (1976) The classroom interaction of outstanding foreign language teachers. *Foreign Language Annals* 9 (2), 135–143.
Panova, I. and Lyster, R. (2002) Patterns of corrective feedback and uptake in an adult ESL classroom. *TESOL Quarterly* 36 (4), 573–595.
Philp, J. (2003) Constraints on 'noticing the gap'. Nonnative speakers' noticing of recasts in NS–NNS interaction. *Studies in Second Language Acquisition* 25 (1), 99–126.

Roberts, P. (1920) *The Problem of Americanization.* New York: McMillan.
Sacks, H., Schegloff, E.A. and Jefferson, G. (1974) A simplest systematics for the organization of turn-taking for conversation. *Language* 50 (4, Part I), 696–735.
Sadler, D.R. (2010) Beyond feedback: Developing student capability in complex appraisal. *Assessment & Evaluation in Higher Education* 35 (5), 535–550.
Salinas, P.D. (1997) *Assimilation, American Style.* New York: Basic Books.
Schegloff, E.A. (2007) *Sequence Organization in Interaction: A Primer on Conversation Analysis.* Volume 1. Cambridge: Cambridge University Press.
Schegloff, E.A., Jefferson, G. and Sacks, H. (1977) The preference for self-correction in the organization of repair in conversation. *Language* 53 (2), 361–382.
Sime, D. (2006) What do learners make of teachers' gestures in the language classroom. *International Review of Applied Linguistics* 44 (2), 211–230.
Sime, D. (2008) 'Because of her gesture, it's very easy to understand' – Learners' perceptions of teachers' gestures in the foreign language class. In S.G. McCafferty and G. Stam (eds) *Gesture: Second Language Acquisition and Classroom Research* (pp. 259–279). New York: Routledge.
Sinclair, J.M. and Coulthard, R.M. (1975) *Toward an Analysis of Discourse.* New York: Oxford University Press.
Weeks, P. (1985) Error-correction techniques and sequences in instructional settings: Toward a comparative framework. *Human Studies* 8, 195–233.
White, M.J., Biddlecom, A.E. and Guo, S. (1993) Immigration, naturalization, and residential assimilation among Asian Americans in 1980s. *Social Forces* 72, 93–118.
Winn, M. (2000) Negotiating borders and discourse: A study of interaction in the US naturalization interview. Unpublished manuscript. Department of Second Language Studies, University of Hawai'i at Manoa, Honolulu.
Yamamoto, S. (2005) Can corrective feedback bring about substantial changes in the learner interlanguage system? *Teachers College, Columbia University Working Papers in TESOL & Applied Linguistics* [Online], 3, (2).
Young, W.A. (1991) *Unlocking the Golden Door: Hispanics and the Citizenship Process.* Washington, DC: National Council of La Raza.

Appendix A Transcription conventions

Symbol used in the transcript	Description	Meaning
[York [New York	Square brackets	The beginning of overlapping talk
What does he want the Constitution to say.	Period	Falling intonation
-buht gay marriage?	Question mark	Rising (interrogative) intonation
Abrienda,	Comma	Slightly rising (continuation) intonation
↑ What are the colors of our fla:g	Upwards arrow	Sharply rising pitch
↑°Mm↓hm.°	Downwards arrow	Sharply falling pitch
↑°Mm↓hm.°	Degree signs	Beginning and end of quiet speech
(1.1)	Number in parentheses	Pause in seconds
(.)	Period in parentheses	Pause of 0.1 second or less
We ca::ll that	Colon	Prolonged sound
Aw:,right=Here we go.=Abrienda	Equal signs	Talk produced without transition-space silence
.>We say< red, white,	'Greater' and 'lesser' signs	Indicate the beginning and end of compressed (fast) speech
Number fifte:en	Underline	Prominent or stressed syllable
Only peo-	Dash	Abrupt cutoff
( )	Empty parentheses	Unintelligible talk
(white)	Text in parentheses	Approximate hearing
h(h)h(h)	A series of 'h' in with parentheses	Laughter
.hhh	A series of 'h' preceded with a period	Audible inbreath
((smiling voice))	Italicized text in double parentheses	Transcriber's comments; non-verbal behavior

Part 3
Discourses

7 'You Are Part of Where You're From and a Part of Where You're Born': Youths' Citizenship and Identity in America

Jasmina Josić

A sense of citizenship among immigrant youth in the United States is often ambiguous, not only due to the ongoing process of learning for citizenship present among all young people, but more so due to the complex nature of immigrant experiences. This chapter follows three urban high school students of immigrant backgrounds sharing their stories of navigating their experiences in the spaces of their neighborhoods and schools, as well as the larger though somewhat abstract space of a nation (Anderson, 1983; Appadurai, 1995, 2006). Questioning the youths' construction of citizenship through their lived experiences, this chapter offers additional ways of viewing the intricate and often invisible self-positioning of young immigrants and first-generation Americans in American society. Moreover, it addresses the process of self-positioning of these youth and their struggles with the imposed social positioning, the externally assigned descriptors of their identity or the assumptions about their capacities and engagements. In this process, this chapter problematizes the recognition of immigrant experiences within larger racial and poverty issues in the US.

Citizenship and Citizenship Identity in a Multicultural Society

The term 'citizenship' refers to two different descriptions of an individual's status in a society: legal citizenship (*de jure*) and social citizenship (*de facto*). This study is particularly interested in the concept of social citizenship, or one's meaning of or engagement with social movement-related citizenship, without disregarding the importance of legal citizenship. Therefore, in this context, citizenship is viewed as membership of a society that also produces a sense of belonging to it

(Lister, 2007) and 'helps situate an individual in a society' (Conover, 1995 in Lister, 2007: 700).

The concept of citizenship has been identified as 'complex and contested' by researchers (McLaughlin, 1992) even prior to larger discussions about the impact of globalization and immigration on the legal and social notions of citizenship (Banks, 2007; Stromquist, 2002). Although the United States has been viewed as a multicultural country since its inception, the last three decades have featured drastic changes in the population demographics more accurately reflecting the diversity of the population. The US Census has estimated that well over a quarter of the population in 2010 consisted of ethnic minorities, while only two decades prior, this group represented a fifth of the total (Hobbs & Stoops, 2002; Humes et al., 2011). The implications of the growing population diversity are multiple for building an understanding of the concept of citizenship.

With its primary role to prepare young citizens, citizenship education in the US has traditionally embraced an assimilationist ideology with the goal to 'eradicate the community cultures and languages of students from diverse ethnic, cultural, racial, and language groups' (Banks, 2007: 20). However, this goal of citizenship education has changed over time. With increasing migration, social diversity and a focus on basic human rights, the goal of citizenship education is slowly shifting to assist all members of society develop their citizen identities (Banks, 2007).

Nevertheless, it is important to note that citizenship identities may not be the same as individual identities. Individuals have multiple and, to a degree, changing identities (Ross, 2007). While they are generally members of particular social groups, individuals also develop a 'repertoire of identities' and can shift among them depending on the 'particular social setting in which they find themselves' (Ross, 2007: 287). Therefore, identities are socially constructed and developed in relation to others (Ross, 2007). Furthermore, individuals have 'multiple civic identities' and 'move ... across many identities' based on how society responds to them (Ladson-Billings, 2005: 73). This multiple nature of civic identity is particularly pronounced with minorities, whom the dominant social discourses might prompt to shift their citizenship identities based on their desired social status (Ladson-Billings, 2005).

Producing Citizenship within the Relations of Space and Individuals

Concerned with the immigrant youths' construction of citizenship through their lived experiences, this chapter delves into the concept of citizenship and the understanding of youth citizenship experiences and citizenship identity from a sociocultural perspective. In this context, it is important not only to discuss the visible environment (local communities or social institutions of the state or education) where the majority of youth experiences are positioned, but it is also relevant to look at citizenship through the lens of cultural identity produced in those spaces.

> Identity is not as transparent or unproblematic as we think. Perhaps instead of thinking of identity as an already accomplished fact ... we should think, instead, of identity as a 'production', which is never complete, always in process, and always constituted within, not outside, representation. (Hall, 1990: 222)

Similarly to the discussion of the production of cultural identity, there have been calls for understanding cultural production of citizenship through the spaces of experiences.

> Citizenship is a form of cultural production ... the making of citizens must be understood as an ideological process through which we experience ourselves as well as our relations to others and the world within a complex and often contradictory system of representations and images. (Giroux, 1998: 16, in Arnot, 1997: 286)

As cultural identity develops and reconstitutes over time, the relevant notions of citizenship also change and emerge over time.

The cultural production of citizenship can be further explored through the concept of 'cultural citizenship' or a 'dual process of self-making and being-made within webs of power linked to nation-state and civil society' (Ong, 1996: 738). This duality of one's citizenship can also be viewed in the perceived and the experienced citizenship of youth. Young people's constructions of citizenship are generally shaped in an environment where institutionalized political, economic and social forces shape the notion of a citizen as a member of a nation with rights and responsibilities. However, along with this prescribed identity of national citizens (or lacking that citizenship), young people negotiate their self-made complex citizenship identities through the interactions within their spaces of experiences. This process of youths' self-making is being positioned along the process of being-made as the 'same' or 'Other' within their nation(s) (DeJaeghere & McCleary, 2010; Willis, 2003).

The process of positioning immigrant youth in the US is complex, though, most commonly, these youth are positioned as being different, or 'Other' to 'being American.' The meaning of 'different' is relational, never constant and depends on how the sameness or the lack of it is translated within the context and in relation to other societal dynamics (Hall, 1990; St. Pierre, 2000). Different immigrant youth have different experiences of 'Othernesses.' The experiences of immigrant youth in large urban centers with strong immigration patterns are different from the experiences in areas with fewer immigrants. However, it is important to question how the experiences of self as 'Other' shape the production of citizenship for these youth.

Framework for understanding citizenship

This chapter is shaped around the conceptual framework concerned with how the social institutions and processes (i.e. the social institution of a state or the process of teaching in the formal education system) are shaping an individual's struggle for self-definition as a citizen within the spaces of experiences. This struggle of an individual for self-definition as a citizen within institutionalized spaces carries an important dimension of power relations, namely, that between the individual and the collective. 'In such a contested political arena, individuals (the "I") are expected to identify with particular concepts of citizenship as members of the collective "we," to position themselves in relation to them and gain a sense of moral and political belonging' (Arnot & Dillabough, 2000: 3). It is often assumed that the collective represents all individuals, regardless of the differences in their experience. Therefore, the collective 'we' of the nation or of the community is starkly placed against, rather than with, the individual and presumes the assimilation of the individuals within the nation. Through the dynamics of power of those who consider themselves to be in the majority within that space, a category of 'Other' – which is not the same as the majority – comes into existence (Painter & Philo, 1995). The positioning of 'Others' in those spaces becomes problematic, as they often feel or indeed are 'turned into less-than-full-and-equal citizens of the places and societies in which they find themselves' (Painter & Philo, 1995: 116).

Moreover, the variances in individual experiences have provided room for viewing the concept of citizenship in abstract ways, and this abstractness of the idea of citizenship has led some to view it as an 'empty space that in theoretical terms could be occupied by anyone, assuming that anyone and everyone has the power to occupy such a place' (Donald, 1996, in Arnot & Dillabough, 2000: 3); it implies equal position among and within groups in which all members 'could ascribe to' it (Arnot, 2006: 80). However, from historical narratives, it is clear that 'only particular and privileged identities can and have occupied the place of citizenship' (Arnot & Dillabough, 2000: 3), while the concept remains more fluid for other groups or identities (i.e. ethnic minorities, immigrants, women, youth, etc.). More recently, the multicultural education literature emphasizes dynamics of power and privileges between people deemed citizens by a society and those groups or individuals not sufficiently discussed within that societal category (Banks, 2007). Overall, researchers and practitioners argue that an individual's relationship with others, including dynamics of power and privilege among individuals, affects one's identity within the institutionalized concept of citizenship (DeJaeghere, 2009; Giroux, 1980; Rubin, 2007; Stromquist, 2006).

Recognizing the role of social institutions and processes in shaping youths' citizenship, this chapter takes a closer look at the relationships of immigrant youth with the places of their experiences – the imaginaries of intangible national space (DeJaeghere & McCleary, 2010) and a more relevant neighborhood community (Appadurai, 1995) – and translates their experiences as members of those communities into narratives depicting varying notions of citizenship belonging and identity.

Methodology

Design

Positioned in the urban US context and informed by poststructural feminism, this chapter relies on qualitative interpretive design with elements of critical ethnography. The interpretive nature of the work encourages the critical practices of working with the study participants in the spaces of their experiences to understand their perspectives (Madison, 2005). Furthermore, informed by poststructural theory, this chapter questions how the structures – not only the institution of the state and the formal education processes, but also the political and economic structures that create and sustain the inequality in experiences – impact citizenship (Anyon, 2009; Baxter, 2002; St. Pierre, 2000).

Data

Data collection

Data were collected at a high school in Brooklyn, New York, over a period of four months in the spring of 2009 through three methods: school and class observations and researcher's journaling, small group interviews and follow-up individual interviews. After three weeks of observation of juniors and seniors in two social studies classes and informal conversations with students, 11 students agreed to participate in the small group interviews. These groups met over a period of five weeks at various times; students were able to join at a time that best suited their schedule each week. The semi-structured protocol was used to initiate student conversations; the open format of the questions allowed for active discussions often led by students who engaged one another to expand on their responses, allowing for rich data. Upon completing the interviews, students were invited for individual follow-up interviews that served as member-checks and also assisted in clarifying some of their perspectives.

Data analysis

The data analysis process was guided by the adaptation of Carspecken's (1996) stages of critical ethnography, Kvale's (1996) suggested steps for analysis of interviews, Cook-Sather's (2007) process of translation recognizing the representation of the participants' voices and experiences, as well as Baxter's (2002) interpretation of the process of questioning the relation of the social structures and youths' experiences. Data were first analyzed across all participants, identifying the constructions of citizenship and translating the experiences into narratives. Finally, the data were analyzed for the small group of students who had similar backgrounds and experiences, focusing on their narratives that delved into citizenship identity.

Positionality

As Hall (1990: 222) reminds us '[w]e all write and speak from a particular place and time … [and] what we say is always "in context", positioned.' Therefore, I will position my translation of youths' experiences and the understanding of their identity as a citizen. I was born and raised in a low-income family in an industrial city in Bosnia and Herzegovina. After graduating high school during the war years, financial constraints led me to drop out of college and work for the US army peacekeeping mission. The resources available through the US army assisted me in obtaining a college scholarship. I received both undergraduate and graduate degrees in the US. After 14 years living in the US as an international student, I have obtained permanent residency. I am a white person, religious minority and I am raising a first-generation bilingual American. These experiences have prompted me to engage in the processes of understanding youths' constructions and experiences of citizenship, particularly the citizenship of immigrant youth or youth living in poverty.

Participants

The chapter follows three students from Franklin Heights High School (FHHS)[1] in Brooklyn, New York. FHHS is a part of the small school movement, and was co-developed with a nonprofit organization, Global Citizens. The school shares the building with three other schools and is located at the border of a gentrified section of Brooklyn and an area with deep poverty and gang presence. The gang activities spill into the school, warranting a metal detector and security at the school entrance.

The students – Nico, Amira and Dustin – participated in a larger study about youths' conceptualization of citizenship, and were selected for this chapter as the participants who have more openly shared information about their immigrant background and how the experiences related to their immigrant background shape their perspectives about their position in the community as well as in American society. All three students participated extensively in the group interviews; Nico and Amira appeared in almost all group interviews and participated in the individual interviews. However, Dustin called off a scheduled individual interview, sharing that his mom felt we talked a lot in the groups, and therefore, he did not need to do an individual interview.

Hearing the American Immigrant Youth

This section presents two main threads of the immigrant youth narratives, unveiling some of the visible but also hidden contours of their citizenship. These threads reveal youths' belonging or their relations with the communities where they live and youths' understanding of their position in American society affecting their national, racial/ethnic and linguistic identity. Through these two threads, the youth also uncover how they engage in navigating the process of self-positioning in society along with the socially created notions of citizenship of young immigrants in the US.

Different life experiences of immigrant youth

At first glance, Nico, Amira and Dustin look like any other student in their school, or any other student in Brooklyn. They are commonly categorized as Latino or African American students in an impoverished area where poverty is defined by the percentage of students enrolled in the free or reduced-price lunch program in school. However, these three students, just as many others in their school, borough and city, have immigrant backgrounds that shape their life experiences and their experiences as citizens.

Nico is a first-generation American; his mother is from the Dominican Republic and his father is from Nicaragua. Although from Brooklyn, he now lives in the Bronx, taking a subway that stops in front of The Museum, an area that has recently been gentrified; the next subway stop is already in the 'dangerous' block; the school is located in between these two stops. Nico describes himself predominantly through his work with Global Citizens, an organization providing an after-school program.

> I'm Nico. I'm in the 11th grade. I go to FHHS. I participate in couple of after-school programs; Global Citizens is probably the one I'm most connected with. I've been there for three years, ever since freshman year. ... I think Global Citizens is a big part of me.

He describes himself through his actions; he has a rather significant portfolio of engagement for a high school junior from a disadvantaged area. However, Nico does not bring his personal background into this picture of himself.

Amira is from Brooklyn and still lives there. She is a first-generation American, from a Trinidadian mother and a Guyanese father. Amira quite openly talks about her background, sharing many details. Her voice projects well and is well suited to a very tall, confident, teenage girl.

On the other hand, Dustin is a young man of few words. 'I'm 16 years old. I'm St. Lucian. And, I came up here five years ago, and I'm in the 11th grade,' was Dustin's description of himself with a mix of British and Creole accent. Dustin lives a block away from the school, does not hold US citizenship and rarely talks about himself – rather, he provides insights into his life through the discussions about issues in his communities – St. Lucia, which he always describes with a smile on his face, or Brooklyn, where he navigates tricky cliques in his unsafe gang-ridden neighborhood.

While all three students focus on their academic work with varying results, their after-school engagement is different. Nico and Amira are A-students, very active in school and engaged in after-school activities. Despite having average grades, Dustin did not get very engaged in the after-school program and mainly spends his after-school time assisting his family.

The belonging of immigrant youth: 'I'm different from ... my community'

During the interview discussions about their neighborhood communities, their schools or their nation(s), these three students reveal nuanced experiences shaping their complex identities. The complex nature starts with their relationships with the neighborhood communities where they live or attend school. They seem to distance themselves from their local communities due to a number of factors, the most important one being the level of safety or crime in the community, but also the lack of interest in that community. While from Brooklyn, Amira is not from the immediate school neighborhood: 'I live in Brooklyn...But like, my area is not too bad, like you don't really have any violence, I don't hang out there...' (Amira). She indicates that she does not hang out in her neighborhood or know her neighbors. She just lives there. While having had different life experiences in Brooklyn, Nico provides some insight into this disassociation with neighborhood communities:

> I used to live in Brooklyn and now I live in Bronx. ... It is a longer commute to me here, but even here, I never hang out with people in Brooklyn, or even in the Bronx. I have more friends that I hang out with in Manhattan. That's where I mostly hang out ... I feel I enjoy it more.
>
> It's also the school, I feel more connected to the school, and feel like it's also my community. So you see Brooklyn community, Brooklyn and

Bronx, some areas are very dangerous, and even unsafe. I can honestly tell [you] that I see people in my class, and you know they are not going to make it that far, and you know they're gonna stay in the same cycle, where, (speaks slower) I'm almost proud of myself of not being caught in the same way that these kids do, but I guess it depends where you hang out, where you grew up ...

While he disassociates himself from the physical communities and the people that live in them, he talks about his association with young people from those communities who have similar degrees of interest in engaging in particular after-school activities; his friends who 'live in different places, they don't come to the school in Brooklyn, most of them. Most of them stay in Manhattan ... some of them are friends from the middle school that I stayed in contact with, some are from Global Citizens.'

Discussing the level of safety and opportunities in his neighborhood communities, Dustin sees himself as different from others in his community; he wants to overcome the expectations about its residents and does not want to 'fall on the bad track.'

I mean, community is, my community is, (pauses, sad smile) bad. Something is always happening outside; police is always standing around the corner. It's destructive... I would say that I'm a part of my community because I live there, but I feel that I'm different from a lot of the people in my community. Like, because, my community is not a good community, honestly... I see myself as a member of my community, but I don't see myself as somebody that belongs to that community. I have friends in my community, but ... honestly, a lot of my friends don't go to school, that's where I feel different from them, 'cause I go to school. They'd be the ones to say 'let's go here,' and I'd be the one to say 'I just have to make sure to do my homework for tomorrow, for school.' They're my friends and everything, but I just feel like, there's difference between us.

Instead, he often refers to St. Lucia as the community he enjoyed.

I'd say St. Lucia is nice, fun, it's sunny, has a lot of resources, I can go to the beach with my family on certain sunny days when nobody has anything to do; friends go around by bike. Since it's an island, country side, I can ride my bike, with my friends, go to the beach, and we're just there for the day, come home, and just nice breeze at night.

Perhaps it is not only the community that he misses, but also the safety he does not enjoy in his current community.

None of these students has a sense of belonging to their neighborhood communities. Instead, they navigate their educational experiences in and after school, or their imaginaries of a nation (their lived experiences in the US or abroad, and the memories of the nation shared by other family members) to develop a sense of belonging, a sense of membership.

Youths' citizenship identity

'Where you're from?': National identity

While discussing their perspectives about and relations with the nation, these students shed more complex details of who they are (or not) in American society. Nico identifies himself as an American, along with the identities related to his 'other nations.'

> My parents are from two different places, my mother is from Dominican Republic and my father is from Nicaragua. Now, I don't know anything about Nicaragua as I never been there, and DR[2], I used to go there every summer, which I know very well, my family members live there. But America … um, I *also*[3] identify myself as an American. I know Spanish, and I speak it fluently … And places I know here, are different here in America than [in] my other nations, it is obvious, but it also feels more like home in America than it does anywhere else. So America, I think is my nation, I was born in America, so yeah.

All three students have reservations about their American identity. Dustin, who moved to the US five years ago, does not wish to discuss his status in the country and often says, 'I consider St. Lucia my nation,' not America. Amira is the most vocal about her American identity. She does not say that she is American, as her heritage is complex.

> So, both my parents, like, were legal immigrants when I was born, [they had] whatever papers, required visas. So I was legal when I was born here. But, … on paper, you are an American citizen, but like as a person, you have this, not identity-crisis, but sometimes you identify with different parts of your culture …

Amira speaks about the multiple components of her identity, and even questions 'what is an American[?]' noting that 'everyone came from somewhere. Everyone, um, everybody from here is from somewhere.' She then continues,

> I can never say, I'm not offended if someone else says it, but like as of right now, it is difficult for me to say 'I'm an American,' because once you say you're an American they just categorize you with *what an American*

is supposed to be.[4] So, if everyone comes from a different country, it kind of makes it difficult, because you are proud of where [your parents] are from, and then you're proud of where you're born, so it is a weird thing, you are part of where you're from and a part of where you're born, and it doesn't really affect your citizenship or becoming a part of that society, so you just don't think about it, like [until] right now. Like I don't wake up every day and say, 'hey, my father is from Guyana, and my mom is from Trinidad, and I'm from here, let me go out and let me think about how it affects my day.' I don't do that, but it kind of does [affect me]. Because, [you get] *'Oh, where you're from?'* 'Um, *I was born here.* (laughs) ... My parents are from Trinidad, or.' And then they'd say, 'You're an American,' but ... I can't say it ... It would sound so perfect if I could say 'I love being an American,' but *I love being a person who lives in America as a citizen enjoying all the rights.* That kind of goes with the ideology of being an American. But I can't say it. I mean, I love America, don't take me wrong, like, I take pride in my country but, I can't. It doesn't spur something in me, I feel like I'm entitled to it, but I can't say it.

Having complex identities is normal for these youth. However, due to the dominant narratives of a unique and rather uniform national identity that they are facing in their everyday experiences in the US, these youth start questioning such multiple identities. Amira raises several important issues, including the question of 'where you're from?' often heard by racial minorities or individuals not speaking standard American English – though, she counters this dynamic by noting that 'everybody [in the U.S.] is from somewhere.' She was born in the US, and even though she has been to Trinidad only once when she was five years old and has never visited Guyana, she seems to consider herself from all three places, the US, Trinidad and Guyana. Additionally, she touches upon the dynamic of what an 'American is supposed to be' – the societal image of an individual claiming legal US citizenship – an image that often excludes non-white individuals. Finally, she lays the ground for discussing citizenship as a status, offering access to certain rights and opportunities.

Despite some critique of their nation, these young people like America. Nico and Amira acknowledge some of the opportunities only offered in America; their parents and many other people immigrated to the US for these additional life chances.

> I guess, America has been always caught up as a free nation, but it does have this ... it does have everything. It's not as great as people think it is. (short pause) I like it. ... It offers a lot of opportunities. It's not perfect but does offer opportunities. (Nico)

However, while discussing the meaning of that opportunity for different groups of people, they acknowledge the value of having 'American papers' to access the opportunities in America.

> People are born in America. But, like, you don't have to be a middle class, and you can afford to do a lot of things, and you can afford to visit other country, to come back.... but being born here, we have papers ... we have birth certificates; we have, like, documents ... (Amira)

Holding American 'papers' allows for enjoying certain rights, which are not accessible to all living in America. These students certainly accept the privilege of holding those rights regardless of the lack of a sense of belonging to the American nation.

Invisible immigrants, visible minorities: Racial and/or ethnic identity

Young immigrants are often assigned certain identifiers based on their visual characteristics, which affect their experiences or perceptions of self. Amira is not comfortable with how she is being categorized in American society as an 'African American' solely based on her physical appearance as a black minority.

> [T]he first day [in school], I didn't know how to call myself, because, it is difficult, because every single day I keep hearing, African American, African American, and there is no space for like 'Other'. And if someone says like 'define other,' I'll be like, 'I don't know what "other" is to me' because I'm *not*[5] an American. Ok, believe me or not, I love being here, living in America... the freedom that we have here. But I don't know, I just, I feel, like, when I call myself an American, it feels kind of weird because. ... Like technically, if there was a big deportation game, whatever, like, my mom would have to go back to Trinidad, and I think I'd have to go, I'm not so sure of details, but I don't know what to call myself. ... [I'm] nationality confused teenage girl, who thinks she's like an African American, but she's not so confirmed.

Amira shows the struggle with the identity assigned to her and questions the American portion of the African American categorization that does not recognize her full heritage or the legal status of all family members.

Nico and Dustin talk about their struggle in an indirect way. This absence of engagement in this discussion is also telling of their internal effort to understand the meaning of their background for their identity in America or perhaps their discomfort to openly share information about themselves. Nevertheless, Nico and Dustin provide insight into their self-identification through other discussions. For example, describing the differences between his middle school and high school climate, Nico positions himself as Hispanic, a larger racial category used in the US and a category he is slotted into for the purposes of statistics in his school. However, this is the only time he uses a racial description of himself, relying on the larger category of Hispanic. Moreover, Nico and Dustin address their understanding of being viewed as 'Other' in America through racial categorization as a factor that affects their experiences. They weave their experiences of being 'Other' with the importance of having strong role models for minority youth. They note that the overall expectations of minority youth have changed since the election of Barack Obama as president of the US. Nico describes an experience in the mall when he was 'goofing around' with his friends shortly after the 2008 election. A woman approached them, asked them if they knew who the president is and said that they should stop playing around and be more responsible. Nico ended by saying:

> Wow! Couple of months ago, people wouldn't even care. But, now, we have a different president, and they expect more of us, because we can't make anymore that excuse that we cannot do it, because of, you know, the system won't let us do it. But now, ... here's an African American president, so, almost they're saying there's no excuse for you [not] to do what you want.

He also notes that 'what people expect of you, I guess, also depends on your community, how you're viewed...how people expect you to act.' From his experience, he finds that people notice one's racial background and approach youth based on their assumptions about the individuals of such background.

> I have couple of White friends, we go out, and fool around all the time, and no one never, ever says anything. Never, ever say anything! We don't do crazy stuff, but you know, we make noise sometimes, like normal teenagers do. And I noticed one time when I'm with friends from this school, who're like, you know, I easily get more attention than I'm used to get[ting] when I'm with my White friends. ... Like what they see over here is like four African Americans. Blacks get pounded harder for the bad behavior than Whites do. (Nico)

Similarly, Dustin's experiences in his community seem to be affected by his racial categorization. He describes himself as Black St. Lucian, but the societal categories place him as Black or African American, and hence that is how some of the official 'representatives' of the system approach him. He shared that he very much dislikes his daily experiences of waiting in line to enter the school through the security checkpoint with a metal detector, as he sees it as 'putting us into that mindset' of waiting in jail lines. On another occasion, Dustin was ticketed by a police officer for being on the boardwalk with his bike (while passing the parked school bus), without an opportunity to explain. 'So ... I went onto sidewalk to cross over, and the police stopped me, they made me lay on the street, everything, they put my nose on the road, all kinds of stuff like that.' In light of these experiences, these young people acknowledge the importance of Barack Obama becoming the first African American president, and its meaning for minority youths' notion of the potential for achievement within a racialized society.

> I always kind of felt like I can do something. But now it's, like, around that ethnicity and nationality, I can actually do something now, because Obama just came; he stood up and like he was, like ... shining light for everybody. So now, now I think that I can actually get somewhere, before I guess, I thought so, but I didn't think that it could be possible. I never thought that a black person would ever reach that high, honestly. Never. (Dustin)

'I speak properly': Linguistic identity

Discussing the perceptions that others have of them, as immigrant minority youth, Nico and Amira touch not only on their appearance, but also on their language. Amira speaks only English, but Nico is bilingual. He shares,

> I've always been the same; I always carry myself with some maturity. Even the way I dress... I always speak correctly, I try to speak proper English... I used to spend my summers in DR, and when I get back to New York, you would notice, all I talk is Spanish. I speak [English] fluently now, but I speak way better and faster in Spanish.

Amira continues,

> I want to talk about that language thing, like what Nico said 'I speak properly.' People tell me I talk 'white,' and I don't understand what that means. They're like 'you talk white,' I'm like, 'what?' I was talking to my dad and he was saying that because I speak proper [English], he didn't say that I talk white, but he said that people think that when I talk with them they think I'm talking 'white.' And ... that language thing, I mean even like Barack Obama, [he] speaks 'white,' and that's ok, but for me, oh, no! I am supposed to speak 'black'; supposedly I can't speak 'white.'

Whether these young individuals try hard to speak 'proper [English]' in an effort to distance themselves from the immigrant descriptors, or simply as the only way they know how to speak English while growing up in a predominantly English-speaking country and trying to do well in school, is not clear. Though it seems that standards of how young immigrants are evaluated on their language skills are different from standards for people of influence. Nico commented on Obama's speeches: 'I love hearing Obama speak, he speaks so well, so strong, such a change from Bush. He always said he's not that good with words. (smiles) That was our president!' They acknowledge that expectations are either to speak standard American English and in essence assimilate within the majority white population, or to speak 'black.' However, language is not only viewed as a means of communication, but also an indicator of the potential of an individual and how far he or she might advance in life.

Negotiating Citizenship Identity

Through the experiences at their school and neighborhoods, these youth negotiate membership of their communities and American society, where the notion of citizenship is shaped not only through a legal lens, but also through their relationship or engagement within a community or society. Day-to-day experiences shape these youth into being an American, first. They are also members of their neighborhood communities, regardless of how they feel about belonging to those communities. As they delve into a discussion about citizenship, a reference to their immigrant background or the status they hold in society because of that background always emerges. It is a part of who they are, without them necessarily acknowledging or even recognizing it.

The experiences of how these youth are being viewed in American society through racial rather than their ethnic background – in essence, through what is visible, rather than less visible nuances of their ethnicities – affect their citizenship. Societal positioning of students is based on their appearance or reported background – racial or linguistic. Society views them as Latino or African American, living in a poverty-stricken metropolitan area. The young immigrants are in essence produced into racial minorities, even though they are not embracing the societal 'allotment' of belonging through those racial categorizations. Instead, these youth see themselves as interesting young people who have rich backgrounds; they see good students who are working toward getting into a good college; they see engaged citizens who either support their families or engage in their communities.

While these students are engaged in their communities in various forms, their association with national identity is still being shaped and contested. '[W]here you're from and where you're born' (Amira) is not static and changes depending on the context – regardless of where they were born, they are from America and at times from other parts of the world.

However, the recognition of who they are is not always clear and is affected by how they are viewed in school or their community and how their ethnic group is perceived within their nation. The sense of residency of all family members in the US also affects their self-identification in America.

Levinson and Holland (1996) argue that modern schools have complex roles in the formation of young people. On the one hand, education can provide certain levels of freedom and opportunities due to obtained knowledge. However, education can also reinforce the social position of individuals due to their backgrounds. This chapter followed three students of immigrant background who are not placing that background at the forefront of their existence; their life circumstances are not requiring them to do so, and they focus on being youth in New York City, rather than being an immigrant. The categorizations placed on them and many other youth in the formal education system encourage either their assimilation within the larger racial or societal categories, or self-definition through the lenses of immigrant experiences. This constant negotiation of the assumed position assigned by the larger social structures with the self-made complex identity is ongoing, and often invisible.

Fostering Citizenship in a Multicultural Society

In lieu of a conclusion, I would like to question the possibility of fostering multiple citizenship identities within multicultural societies, such as the US, where the politics of race and the politics of power that are built on the latter continue to complicate the efforts to shape citizenship education programs encouraging fluid identities. In an effort to contribute to the understanding of the process of immigrant population identity-making in the US, Nagel and Staehali (2005) propose that,

> while immigrants often do assert a politics of identity – a politics in which the rights to maintain markers of culture and to assert an identity as different than the host society are reserved – they also enact a politics of sameness – of blending with the host society in some ways or in some circumstances. These two politics are not contradictory or orthoganally positioned, but rather form the basis of an identity politics that is fluid rather than fixed and that is multiple rather than singular. (Nagel & Staehali, 2005: 490)

However, Deaux (2011) notes that 'modern' immigrants in the US are not always accepted as Americans, even when they receive legal citizenship, or were citizens by birth. Most common is an example of Arab Americans, who are often perceived as 'Other' even when they are first- or second-generation Americans (Nagel & Staehali, 2004). Additional research indicates that minorities in the US, such as African Americans, Asian

Americans and Latinos, are still often seen as 'less American' by White Americans (Deaux, 2011).

A recent development across many states and regions is the move toward educational policies that warn of ethnic associations of certain immigrant groups or minorities, such as the Arizona state legislature targeting ethnic studies classes in high schools (Lillie, this volume). In this climate, within the social studies curriculum and as a part of civic education across the country, the emphases are placed on understanding the individual rights and responsibilities and the engagement of individuals, rather than the collective that includes an individual. In essence, this represents a return to the assimilationist model of citizenship education that dismisses possible variations in the national identity through silencing the experiences of minority immigrant groups.

However, with the increasing diversity of the US population, it is important to envision building a balanced national identity inclusive of all of its citizens. The research shows that ethnic identities are not 'incompatible with the development of a strong national identity as an American' (Deaux, 2011: 72). Moreover, the groups who feel more respected by the American majority could build relationships with and contribute to the nation 'that has always been a nation of immigrants' (Deaux, 2011: 72). Therefore, a multicultural state can recognize the variety of types of youth citizenship identity and engagement, occurring in multiple arenas and intensities.

Notes

(1) The names of the school, the students and the nonprofit organization were changed for the purpose of this study.
(2) Dominican Republic.
(3) Emphasis added by the author.
(4) Emphasis added by the author.
(5) Emphasis made by the student.

References

Anderson, B. (1983) *Imagined Communities: Reflections on the Origin and Spread of Nationalism*. London: Verso.
Anyon, J. (2009) Introduction: Critical social theory, educational research, and intellectual agency. In J. Anyon (ed.) *Theoretical and Educational Research: Towards Critical Social Explanations* (pp. 1–24). New York, NY: Routledge.
Appadurai, A. (1995) The production of locality. In R. Fulton (ed.) *Counterworks: Managing the Diversity of Knowledge* (pp. 208–229). London: Routledge.
Appadurai, A. (2006) Disjuncture and difference in the global cultural economy. In M.G. Durham and D.M. Kellner (eds) *Media and Cultural Studies: KeyWorks* (pp. 584–603). Malden, MA: Blackwell Publishing.
Arnot, M. (1997) 'Gendered citizenry': New feminist perspectives on education and citizenship. *British Educational Research Journal* 23 (3), 275–295.

Arnot, M. (2006) Freedom's children: A gender perspective on the education of the learner-citizen. *International Review of Education* 52 (1), 67–87.

Arnot, M. and Dillabough, J.A. (eds) (2000) *Challenging Democracy: International Perspectives on Gender, Education and Citizenship*. New York: RoutledgeFalmer.

Banks, J. (2007) *Educating Citizens in a Multicultural Society* (2nd edn). New York: Teachers College Press.

Baxter, J. (2002) A juggling act: A feminist poststructural analysis of girls' and boys' talk in the secondary classroom. *Gender and Education* 14 (1), 5–19.

Carspecken, P.F. (1996) *Critical Ethnography in Educational Research: A Theoretical and Practical Guide*. New York: Routledge.

Cook-Sather, A. (2007) Resisting the impositional potential of student voice work: Lessons for liberatory educational research from poststructuralist feminist critiques of critical pedagogy. *Discourse: Studies in the Cultural Politics of Education* 28 (3), 389–403.

Deaux, K. (2011) An immigrant frame for American identity. *Applied Developmental Science* 15 (2), 70–72.

DeJaeghere, J. (2009) Critical citizenship education for multicultural societies. *Interamerican Journal of Education for Democracy* 2 (2), 223–236.

DeJaeghere, J. and McCleary, K. (2010) The making of Mexican migrant youth civic identities: Transnational spaces and imaginaries. *Anthropology and Education Quarterly* 21 (3), 228–244.

Giroux, H. (1980) Critical theory and rationality in citizenship education. *Curriculum Inquiry* 10 (4), 329–366.

Hall, S. (1990) Cultural identity and Diaspora. *Identity: Community, Culture, Difference* 2, 222–237.

Hobbs, F. and Stoops, N. (2002) *Demographic trends in the 20th Century: Census 2000 special report*. US Census Bureau. See http://www.census.gov/population/www/cen2000/briefs/index.html (accessed 19 August 2008).

Humes, K., Jones, N. and Ramirez, R. (2011) *Overview of race and Hispanic origin: 2010*. US Census Bureau. See http://www.census.gov/prod/cen2010/briefs/c2010br-02.pdf (accessed 2 May 2014).

Kvale, S. (1996) *InterViews: An Introduction to Qualitative Research Interviewing*. Thousand Oaks, CA: Sage.

Ladson-Billings, G. (2005) Differing concepts of citizenship: Schools and communities as sites of civic development. In N. Noddings (ed.) *Educating Citizens for Global Awareness* (pp. 69–80). New York: Teachers College Press.

Levinson, B. and Holland, D. (1996) The cultural production of the educated person: An introduction. In B. Levinson, D. Foley and D. Holland (eds) *The Cultural Production of the Educated Person: Critical Ethnographies of Schooling and Local Practice* (pp. 1–56). Albany, NY: SUNY Press.

Lister, R. (2007) Why citizenship: Where, when and how children? *Theoretical Inquiries in Law* 8 (2), 693–718.

Madison, D.S. (2005) *Critical Ethnography: Method, Ethics, and Performance*. Thousand Oaks, CA: Sage.

McLaughlin, T.H. (1992) Citizenship, diversity and education: A philosophical perspective. *Journal of Moral Education* 21 (3), 235–250.

Nagel, C. and Staehali, L. (2004) Citizenship, identity and transnational migration: Arab immigrants to the United States. *Space and Polity* 8 (1), 3–23.

Nagel, C. and Staehali, L. (2005) 'We're just like the Irish': Narratives of assimilation, belonging, and citizenship among Arab American activists. *Citizenship Studies* 9 (5), 485–498.

Ong, A. (1996) Cultural citizenship as subject-making: Immigrants negotiate racial and cultural boundaries in the United States. *Current Anthropology* 37 (5), 737–762.

Painter, J. and Philo, C. (1995) Spaces of citizenship: An introduction. *Political Geography* 14 (2), 107–120.

Ross, A. (2007) Multiple identities and education for active citizenship. *British Journal of Educational Studies* 55 (3), 286–303.

Rubin, B. (2007) 'There's still not justice': Youth civic identity development amid distinct school and community context. *Teachers College Record* 109 (2), 449–481.

St. Pierre, E.A. (2000) Poststructural feminism in education: An overview. *International Journal of Qualitative Studies in Education* 13 (5), 477–515.

Stromquist, N.P. (2002) *Education in a Globalized World: The Connectivity of Economic Power, Technology, and Knowledge*. Lanham, MD: Rowman and Littlefield Publishers.

Stromquist, N.P. (2006) Women's rights to adult education as a means to citizenship. *International Journal of Educational Development* 26 (2), 140–152.

Willis, P. (2003) Foot soldiers of modernity: The dialectics of cultural consumption and the 21st-century school. *Harvard Educational Review* 73 (3), 390–415.

8 Reinforcing Belonging and Difference Through Neighborhood Gentrification Projects in Rotterdam, the Netherlands

Jennifer Long

This chapter diverges from other chapters in this volume due to its geographic location and its focus on the perceptions and experiences of individuals from the host community (rather than immigrants) in relation to language, immigration and naturalization. There has been much scholarly attention dedicated to immigrant experiences of citizenship processes in the Netherlands (e.g. see van den Berg & Schinkle, 2009; Yanow & van der Haar, 2013); however, much can be gleaned from the practices of 'minor figures' as actors and purveyors of social authority (Miller & Rose, 2008), in relation to their role in the dynamic process of contemporary citizenship. In particular, this chapter examines discourses of belonging through the use of autochthony language[1] and the prioritization of the national language in public spaces in order to understand what it means to be a 'citizen' in the Netherlands today. This chapter also deviates from those typical, formal citizenship locations such as language-learning classrooms and naturalization ceremonies in order to investigate everyday situations of citizenship making, seen here through the practices and perspectives of local inhabitants involved in an urban gentrification project in Rotterdam, the Netherlands.

As discussed in further detail below, the Netherlands presents quite a different case study from that of the United States. The Netherlands came late to the understanding that it was an immigrant-receiving nation and it was not until the late 1970s that they began to provide official integration and settlement services for immigrants (Vink, 2007). Furthermore, although the Netherlands has been categorized as taking a multicultural approach to integration, scholars have refuted this claim, stating that multiculturalism was instead used as a way to describe the diversification of the population rather than providing any real equitable approach to pluralism (see Vink, 2007; also Duyvendak & Scholten, 2012). Today, federal integration policies in the Netherlands have taken a decidedly assimilative turn toward immigrant integration. What becomes apparent through my own investigation is that citizenship is indeed a dynamic, context-dependent process whereby local actors, such as the average native Dutch citizen, play a role in creating and identifying practices of citizenship that tend to exclude the immigrant 'Other.' In the case of the Netherlands, non-Western Turkish and Moroccan Muslim immigrants are the target of these local (and national) level discourses of non-belonging and dis-citizenship (see below). This chapter sheds light on the power of local inhabitants to contribute to discourses of national identity and investigates their role as gatekeepers in the process of citizenship in the Netherlands today.

The Dutch Context

Following the deaths of right-wing politician Pim Fortuyn in 2002 and film director Theo van Gogh in 2004, the Netherlands generated its own brand of Islamophobia that dominated the European landscape, especially when it was led by anti-immigrant and anti-Muslim politician, Geert Wilders. Wilders' Party for Freedom (PVV) received significant popular support and became one of three ruling political parties in a Dutch coalition government between 2010 and 2012. Although this coalition dissolved, the PVV remains a popular contender in national-level politics (Bolt, 2013). Wilders' most recent platform included breaking ties with the European Union and securing social supports for older generations, in addition to his long-standing platform concerning the decrease in non-Western migration and a renewed interest in Dutch national identity (Party for Freedom, 2012). Yet, it is Wilders' warnings against what he calls the 'Islamification of Western Culture' that have garnered him both national and international attention.

In the Netherlands, Muslim immigrants are known as *allochtonen*, which translates literally to 'foreigners.' Autochthony language became popular in the Netherlands around the turn of the millennium and replaced other labels such as ethnic minorities (*etnische minderhiden*) (Yanow & van der Haar, 2013: 228). Yanow and van der Haar (2013: 228) argue that autochthony language has found its way into many spheres in the Netherlands, from parliamentary debates, in workplace conversations, to 'the street' and that these terms have taken on a pejorative meaning. The term *allochtonen* is broken up into two categories: Western and non-Western *allochtonen*; however, it is only the non-Western *allochtonen* category that is associated with negative stereotypes. Officially, this term describes someone who was born, or has one parent who was born, in Turkey, Africa, Latin America or Asia (with the exception of immigrants from Indonesia or Japan) (Centraal Bureau voor de Statistiek, 2015). Non-Western immigrants are often derided in the media and by polemical politicians as being disassociated from Dutch culture, uninterested in the future of the Netherlands and a drain on the national economy and social welfare. Furthermore, this category carries a Muslim connotation, as those who are most often identified as *allochtonen* were originally guest workers from Turkey and Morocco, and their children, are Muslims (Roggeband & Verloo, 2007). Perceptions of Islamic values and culture are often thought not to mix well with the self-proclaimed tolerant and liberal societal values of the Netherlands. It is through this autochthony language that native Dutch residents create an understanding of an 'imagined community' where allochthonous residents are excluded (Anderson, 1983).

To understand the manner in which ordinary citizens create discourses of exclusionary belonging at the local level, this chapter asks: How do local residents construct discourses of belonging in everyday life? Through ethnographic investigation, it becomes apparent that native conceptions of national belonging mimic the contemporary national discourse concerning the non-belonging of Muslim immigrants due to their perceived difference and lack of interest in Dutch society. Using data collected from participant observation, in-depth interviews and print materials, I discuss firsthand experiences of a local gentrification project and reflect on the implications of this process on one's sense of belonging in the local (and national) community. I begin with a discussion of the literature concerning citizenship and immigrant integration, followed by an overview of the theoretical framework supporting this argument.

Participation and Citizenship

Despite opening their internal borders to European citizens, countries (such as the Netherlands) within the European Union have intensified their citizenship and naturalization processes for non-European immigrants (Joppke, 2010). As mentioned in the introduction (this volume), Bloemraad *et al.* (2008) have developed a useful model for thinking about (contemporary) citizenship which has four dimensions: legal status, equal rights, (political) participation and a sense of belonging. The latter two dimensions are of particular importance to the discussion in this chapter. In their analysis of the participation and assimilation of immigrants into society, Bloemraad *et al.* (2008: 162) note that scholars need to consider not just immigrants' political participation but also their economic well-being and social inclusion, as these factors influence one's ability to act as a citizen. This aspect of social inclusion is also featured in the development of one's sense of belonging. Here, the authors argue that the process by which a sense of belonging is created will necessarily exclude all those participants who do not fit within the 'we' category that represents the national majority group. This occurs for the purpose of creating social cohesion among the 'we' (versus 'they') category. This chapter examines participants' sense of belonging and perceptions of social participation in order to understand how ideas of citizenship, integration and the promise of equality are articulated in the everyday lives of native Dutch participants in Rotterdam.

Increasingly over the last 10 years, political and social discourses concerning belonging to the imagined community of the Netherlands have been understood according to cultural standards and norms. Tonkens *et al.* (2010: 237) describe this phenomenon as the *culturalization of citizenship*, where 'meaning is attached to cultural participation (in terms of norms, values, practices and traditions), either as alternative or in addition to citizenship as rights and socioeconomic participation.' In their research, Tonkens *et al.* (2010) explored how native Dutch participants perceived belonging to the imagined community of the Netherlands and found that this belonging was related to perceptions of loyalty to the Dutch nation. Certain Dutch politicians, like Geert Wilders, have added fire to these claims, arguing that issues of societal cohesion can be blamed on the increasing diversity of newcomers who have competing loyalties, for example, to their 'real' home or religion, rather than the Dutch nation. However, de Vroome *et al.* (2014) have convincingly argued that national identification (belonging) is more complicated than just a longing for one's home.

In their research, de Vroome *et al.* (2014) argue that social inclusion, leading to community and national cohesion, is affected by having a sense of purpose, such as having a job, for immigrants and native Dutch alike. Important to this discussion, the authors found that non-Western immigrants also needed to be familiar and have knowledge about the host culture in order to feel a sense of belonging. Their findings indicate that 'perceived discrimination, Dutch language proficiency, and the (amount of) time spent in the Netherlands' correlated to whether or not non-Western immigrants would identify with and be seen as a member of the host nation (de Vroome *et al.*, 2014: 21). As mentioned by the authors, these findings align with past research where national belonging was influenced by proficiency in the Dutch language and perceived acceptance by the majority community (de Vroome *et al.*, 2014).

Wodak (2013: 175) has recently argued for the use of *dis-citizenship*, originally used in disability studies, as a means to understand how immigrants may be viewed as not being 'real or authentic citizens with full rights in a specific country.' Ramanathan (2013) expands on this concept, highlighting how citizenship should be understood as a dynamic and context-dependent process – the investigation of which can be used to explore what it means to *not* be able to fully participate due to one's perceived difference in relation to the average citizen. Thus, cultural factors such as the ability to speak Dutch and be familiar with Dutch values, history, etc. affect the process of dis-citizenship and how native Dutch residents understand the belonging of foreign-born residents, according to their imagined community of the Netherlands.

This chapter provides further evidence concerning the ways in which the Dutch language and autochthony discourse set the native Dutch majority apart from local non-Western immigrant residents in everyday life experiences. Such questions are important to ask as they speak to the diverse understandings of citizenship and reflect perceptions of participation and a local sense of national belonging. In order to accomplish this, I use Fairclough's critical interpretivist approach when analyzing my data so that I not only provide empirical evidence concerning the *culturalization of citizenship* but also raise questions concerning inclusivity during local projects (see Feuerherm [2013] for a similar approach).

Methodology

Site descriptions

The data for this chapter come from 12 months of ethnographic fieldwork conducted in 2009–2010 that included participant observation and semi-structured interviews with individuals living, working or involved in a gentrification process of a borough named Bergpolder South (*Bergpolder Zuid*) in Rotterdam North (Figure 8.1).

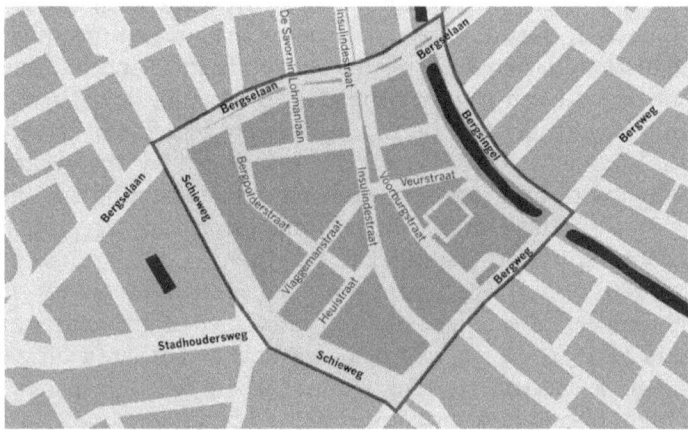

Figure 8.1 Map of Bergpolder South slated for gentrification (Deelgemeente Noord, 2010)

Bergpolder South is a section of the larger Bergpolder neighborhood and has received special attention from the local municipal government due to its designation as a neighborhood in need of close governmental oversight and support.

The Minister of Housing, Districts and Integration, Minister Vogelaar, established Bergpolder as one of the *Krachtwijken*[2] or 'empowerment neighborhoods' in 2007. *Krachtwijken* were a group of 40 neighborhoods that were set to receive additional funding from the government, with the goal of increasing livability and educational attainment levels, decreasing unemployment rates and ethnic tension, cracking down on safety concerns and monitoring how children were being raised through schools and integration programs (KEI, n.d.). These neighborhoods were also popularly known as *Vogelaarwijken* (after the minister), or more disturbingly, *achterstandswijken*, which can be translated as 'backward neighborhoods'; the latter term is associated with the residents who live there and who are seen as equally backward due to their religious beliefs or antisocial behavior (Martineau, 2006: 64). Bergpolder was added to the list of problematic neighborhoods because it had a high turnover rate of inhabitants (thought to be a result of the small housing units found in this neighborhood); moderate air quality (due to its location next to a major highway); small, cluttered streets that were thought to be dirty and often disturbed by nuisances such as car break-ins; as well as a limited supply of social facilities such as opportunities for sports, art and culture. Due to these issues and the fact that the federal government stopped financing World War II renewal schemes for Rotterdam (for which Bergpolder received funding) around the same time, the municipal and district government and other invested stakeholders decided to address the current state of Bergpolder South through urban renewal (*Deelgementee Noord*, 2011: 15).

The housing corporation[3] that owned much of the housing stock in this area, Vestia, released an urban renewal plan titled Master Plan for Bergpolder South (*Masterplan Bergpolder Zuid*, MPBZ) in May 2011. This plan provided an in-depth account of projects that were slated for completion in the year 2020. One example of these renovation projects involved converting many of the smaller two- and three-bedroom apartments that comprised 80% of the housing stock available in Bergpolder into larger single-family dwellings (*Deelgemeente Noord*, 2011: 29, 39). Urban planners thought that by providing bigger houses, students, entrepreneurs and young families would be able to stay in Bergpolder instead of moving out of the neighborhood. This approach was desirable so that the neighborhood would remain 'mixed' with regard to residents' socioeconomic classes. Mixed neighborhoods are desirable in *Krachtwijken* due to the perceived positive influence of the upper classes on the lower classes.

Kleinhans *et al.* (2007: 1058, 1069) found that individuals with higher incomes, higher education levels and residency in single-family dwellings had the highest level of social capital, which they define as having the 'benefit of cursory interactions, shared norms, trust and collective action of residents' in the neighborhood. According to the argument for developing mixed-income neighborhoods, middle- and upper-class residents are thought to be good role models for the lower classes in order to increase the overall social capital in the area and improve the social cohesion in the area (van Kempen *et al.*, 2009: 271).

Recent research, however, has pointed out that the vast majority of middle-class residents living in mixed neighborhoods tend to have closer relationships with those residents in the same economic class as themselves, regardless of other social or cultural attributes (e.g. Musterd & Pinkster, 2009; van der Graaf & Veldboer, 2009). Van Beckhoven and van Kempen (2003: 871) sum up this phenomenon succinctly: 'people in neighbourhoods seem to live alongside each other, not together.' Despite this, the Dutch authorities continue to operate and create urban schemes based on the assumption that mixed neighborhoods will create bonds between middle- and upper-class residents that will ultimately benefit lower-class neighbors (van der Graaf & Veldboer, 2009: 63). Such an approach camouflages the structural inequalities found between native Dutch residents (called *autochtonen*) and *allochtonen* in the participation process during urban renewal projects. As will be demonstrated below, this approach also conceals the bias of the participation process toward autochthonous residents and the ways in which participants imagine their belonging to the larger majority (national) community.

Data Analysis

The qualitative data used in this chapter were collected from each of the meetings I attended regarding the gentrification of Bergpolder South (25 throughout my time in the Netherlands) and the associated interviews with participants involved in the gentrification project.[4] These materials include 25 field note entries, 8 interviews and over 50 handouts and information packages from those hosting the meetings. All interviews were digitally recorded and professionally transcribed, verbatim.

Using an inductive approach, in line with qualitative research design, I used a grounded theory approach in order to gain an in-depth understanding of participants' experiences of participating in the gentrification process of Bergpolder South. In so doing, I read through my field notes, the written documents from the organizers, as well as the interview transcripts in order to find themes, using both open and selective coding techniques (Bryant, 2014). When I reached the point of theoretical saturation, that is, where the continued collection and analysis of data revealed no new theoretical categories (Bryant, 2014: 131), I determined the following themes as being significant in the process of gentrification and the role they played in providing a sense of belonging to the imagined community of the Netherlands: issues with the design of the feedback process, issues with allochthonous interest in the feedback process and perceptions of creating 'real' change through these gentrification efforts. I discuss each of these themes in turn.

Findings

Perceptions of participation: Issues in feedback design

During my fieldwork, I observed ordinary citizens taking part in renewal projects for the public places of their neighborhood, for example, in the conservation of neighborhood gardens or in more large-scale development that sought to gentrify entire neighborhood areas. Residents participated in these events in order to provide their input and feedback to the planning authorities who included city planners, municipal government officials, the creative designers and architects.

Vestia and the district government, who were in charge of the Bergpolder South renovation project, determined that they had been successful in getting feedback from residents through an extensive participation process (*Deelgemeente Noord*, 2011: 117). According to the master plan, Vestia and the government ensured they had contact with local stakeholders who included business owners, neighborhood groups and residents (*Deelgemeente Noord*, 2011: 19). This participation process began with five 'resident evenings' (*bewoners avonden*) between February and April 2010, where planners laid out their initial drawings and requested feedback from attendees as new versions of the plan were developed (*Deelgemeente Noord*, 2011: 113).

These evening meetings typically began with an introductory speech or presentation and broke off into smaller groups where workers explained the maps and charts that were laid out on tables. Participants were asked to make notes that were then attached to the documents themselves or written on a page of chart paper so that all attendees could see them and comment on each other's feedback as well as the plan itself. Within a couple of weeks, summaries of the participants' feedback were sent out (via email) in preparation for the next event or meeting. These evenings were held in a couple of different locations, for example in the local government building or the defunct railway station of the Hofplein Line (*Deelgemeente Noord*, 2011: 115). In order to advertise these nights, letters, information papers and fliers were distributed to the addresses in the affected area and advertisements were sent out around the district and distributed on the public squares in the week leading up to the meetings. All communication and correspondence of these events were in Dutch (with no translation).

In addition to these information-gathering evenings, Vestia and the district government invited residents to join a consulting group (*klankbord groep*) that began in June 2010. Planners also held week-long debate sessions where residents could come by and discuss the current plan (first in June and then in October 2010). The stakeholders also held a 'Mirror Evening' in September where residents could answer the question: 'Have we heard you correctly?' This meeting was held in response to a growing dissatisfaction among community members who felt that their concerns were not being adequately addressed. There was also a closing presentation where residents were presented with the latest draft of the master plan before it was finalized (*Deelgemeente Noord*, 2011: 117).

However, despite these efforts, there was an understanding that the process of gathering feedback was flawed. This was evident because Bergpolder South has a demographically mixed population[5]; yet, aside from representatives from the local Turkish cultural center and mosque, there were few participants from this community. According to Heneke, a native Dutch resident who was very active in the Bergpolder South gentrification process, the location of these meetings was an important factor that affected this outcome: 'I think where you organize these meetings is a large factor. For example, if you organize something at the church, then you will only see the people who are familiar with that church attend those activities' (Heneke, personal communication, 2010). Heneke's observation demonstrates the importance of providing a welcoming space for feedback and the perception that allochthonous residents would be uncomfortable in a church setting, perhaps because of its contrary religious character when compared to their perceived Muslim identity. Typically, these meetings were held in local community spaces, such as the district government office building, a newly renovated defunct railway station or one of the churches in Bergpolder, and they were scheduled after 6pm in the evening.

Secondly, Geert, a native Dutch resident who was an active member of the local neighborhood organization as well as a regular attendee of the meetings associated with the gentrification of Bergpolder South, argued that there was an issue with how to communicate with residents, implying that the notices mailed out to residents and put in the newspaper were insufficient at bringing out participants when he stated,

> Because who are the residents? How do you reach them? There is a resident's organization, of which I am a full-time member with 4 other people. [...] But there are many more people in Bergpolder, and how do you reach them? There are the newspapers, there are meetings, but most people do not attend them. How do you communicate? (Geert, personal communication, 2010)

Van de Wijdeven and Hendriks (2009: 125) argue that the Dutch have a meeting-room culture which they describe as being 'biased toward white, highly educated, male participants.' This organization style was apparent throughout the Bergpolder South process. For example, the participatory events were formal, beginning with a presentation about the project after which participants raised questions and made comments in (fluent) Dutch. This finding is supported by Garritt, a native Dutch resident working for one of the municipally funded neighborhood organizations, who made the following comment about the evening meetings:

> Vestia thinks that meetings should be only in the evening but that is not right. When you are demolishing 150 houses and (only) 25 people attend the meeting then something is not right. Then it is not ok. You should arrange it in another way. (Garritt, personal communication, 2010)

During my participation in such meetings, it became apparent that attendees perceived the location, timing, method of advertising the event and the language of communication used as appealing predominantly to autochthonous residents. As confirmed by my participant observation, by and large, few, if any, allochthonous residents attended such meetings. Despite the issues identified in the design of feedback measures, for example allochthonous residents lacking Dutch language proficiency to know when the events were happening or having the proficiency to participate in the meetings, autochthonous residents identified the non-participation of allochthonous residents as an issue. This is further discussed in the next section.

Perceptions of participation: Issues with allochthonous interest

In a 2010 renter's magazine distributed by Vestia, there was an article about the Bergpolder South project. In it, Rien Tuk, an employee of the Vestia Corporation who worked with the focus group (*klankbord groep*), said that they 'regret the fact that residents (of Bergpolder South) are left out of participating in some of the (resident input) meetings' and commented further:

> Many people shrug their shoulders when they hear about future plans for the area, but later when they read that there is a possibility that their houses will be demolished, they protest. We make efforts to bring everyone out. I even call people because having local residents involved makes a difference. (Vestia, 2010: 4)

Importantly, this employee, who is native Dutch, signals that there is a lack of interest (shrug their shoulders) to participate from Bergpolder South residents. This comment takes on a deeper meaning when contextualized against the belief that Bergpolder South residents are predominantly allochthonous. This adds to the perception that *allochtonen* lack interest or willingness to participate in local events. Finally, the corporate and government officials participating in this process seek to portray their role in this process as having done as much as they could to listen to the residents' plans.

A direct connection between non-Western Muslim immigrants as non-participants was made when organizers decided to hold an additional meeting to encourage allochthonous participation specifically. Representatives from the local Turkish cultural center and mosque, located in Bergpolder South, had requested that the meetings take place outside Ramadan and a meeting was held at the center in late 2010. In hosting a meeting at the local cultural center and mosque, it was thought that a more diverse crowd would attend. Bergpolder's (government) director, Jacco Bakker, was quoted in a local publication as saying,

> It is too bad that the people who are participating in the meetings do not really reflect the residents (who live in the area). To involve everyone, we have had one of the meetings in the building where the mosque is located. At this event, more attendees had diverse backgrounds. (Vestia, 2010: 4)

The extra effort on behalf of the organizers to collect more representative feedback concerning neighborhood renovations is notable and speaks to the importance of diversity for district government employees; however, this approach also highlights the perceived difference between autochthonous and allochthonous residents through the use of *us* and *them* language. This *us* and *them* distinction further contributes to the understanding of the 'we' (vs. 'they') community within the imagined Dutch nation.

In addition to these events, local stakeholders in this project created a Sounding Board Group (*Klankbord Groep*) that met with officials from the government and from Vestia in order to give feedback on the various versions of the plan leading up to the master document. During the group's second meeting in June 2010, the majority of the attendees, who lived outside the neighborhood and who would be categorized as autochthonous, discussed the fact that the majority of participants who were present that evening were not actually from the affected area and debated whether or not this was an issue. As a participant observer at this meeting, responses included such remarks as, 'Well, we're here, why don't our opinions count?' (Personal communication, 2010). A regular attendee who lived in Bergpolder North even provided a reason during an interview as to why those affected by the events were not there when he said:

Individuals who do not have higher levels of education will not come to these meetings because they have other, more pressing problems to work on. For example, maybe they're working right now or making sure that their children are doing their homework! (Personal communication, 2010)

Another attendee, Maureen said, 'Look, if they're not going to show up to these meetings, then why do we have to accommodate them?' (Personal communication, 2010). There are many underlying assumptions in these quotes which include a differentiation between the attendees and those living in Bergpolder South, the valuation of their perspectives as they were willing to attend and take part in these meetings and those stereotypical narratives that follow along with the Dutch understanding of socioeconomic status; that is, those with lower economic status are trying to better the lives of their children (by making them do better in school than they did) and that they are not interested due to 'more pressing problems.'

A discussion at this event included an agreement among all participants that the opinions of those present, who had made the choice to participate and who felt that they too would be affected by these renovations because of their proximity to Bergpolder South, would also count toward the decision-making process. Overall, the attendees concurred that Bergpolder South was in desperate need of renovation regardless of the potential negative impact (having to relocate to more affordable housing) on local residents. This need for change in the area was confirmed by one of the attendees when he said,

Regardless, there is a need for some changes to happen in the area. Although it may affect some people negatively (as in forcing some to move away), overall, these renovations can be a good thing because really, it can get quite dirty around those stair-houses![6] (Personal communication, 2010)

After this meeting, I set up an interview with Maureen, an autochthonous resident of Bergpolder North, and asked her to elaborate on her comments at the meeting earlier in the week. She said,

I'm not a racist but I think that there are often *autochtonen* who want to do everything for the *allochtonen*. [...] But here in the Netherlands, there is a bit too much care taken for the *allochtonen*, at least in these second and third generations. [...] You see this also with the sounding board group. The man from the local mosque came to the first meeting but then he didn't come again. It is a fact that everyone can come to these meetings because everyone is welcome, but that is not what happens.

In my opinion, there is more done for the *allochtonen* now than the *autochtonen*, and by this I mean the older people. That frustrates me! I do not see them (allochthonous community) as a disadvantaged group (*achtergestelde groep*), seriously not. [...] In this sort of area (Bergpolder), there are probably more *allochtonen* than *autochtonen* residents and maybe that's why there is such a focus on including them in the planning process; but this (hand-holding) approach is taken throughout all the Netherlands – to provide and do a lot for these *allochtonen*. (Maureen, personal communication, 2010)

Maureen's use of autochthony language expresses the underlying belief in the difference between *us* (*autochtonen*) and *them* (*allochtonen*) in her experiences in everyday life. Maureen's act of differentiation can be understood as a *discourse of difference* where the 'Other' is understood as being different based on 'a selection of specific traits attributed to one group, traits which are seen, in some sense, as being significant' in this case, choosing to take part in local events as an active citizen (Wodak, 1996: 113). Further, it is pertinent to note that Maureen begins her discussion with the phrase 'I'm not a racist but...' Teun van Dijk (1984) has explored the semantic significance of this phrase and its use by individuals as a means to state racialized claims about the 'Other' while avoiding being labelled a racist (as cited in Bonilla-Silva & Forman, 2000: 76). In Maureen's discussion, her statement that 'too much is done for *allochtonen*' reveals her feeling that *allochtonen* are in fact getting more than they deserve at the expense of those deserving such support, that is, the older autochthonous generation. In sum, Maureen's comments connect the exclusionary discourses from national politicians, like Wilders, to the everyday (re) production of belonging by local residents.

Perceptions of the feedback process: Perceptions of creating 'real' change

From the beginning of my participant observation of the community meetings, it was apparent that the majority of neighborhood residents who took part in the feedback process were people who would be described as autochthonous (native Dutch) residents. For example, at one of my first meetings concerning the government-led renewal project of Bergpolder South (*Bergpolder Zuid*), I noticed that there were not many residents, and in particular allochthonous residents, from the neighborhood itself. I raised these concerns with Albert, a facilitator at this meeting who was in his early twenties and finishing his studies at the Erasmus University in Rotterdam. Albert did not live in Rotterdam North but instead worked as an intern for Vestia. In response to my observation about the mix of attendees, or lack thereof, he said, 'Now that is something you can do with your research. If you can figure out how to gather the opinions of the allochthonous residents, then everyone would be happy. That is what everyone wants to know!' (Albert, personal communication, 2010). According to Albert, the allochthonous residents of the area did not typically participate in the gatherings concerning the future construction of their own neighborhood, and he felt that housing corporations had little recourse when he stated:

> What are you going to do about it? If we say to them (the autochthonous residents), 'Oh sorry, while we appreciate you coming out tonight we'd rather have the opinions of the allochthonous residents,' then you're not being fair to them because they are here and they want to participate. And truthfully, you'd have no one left to get feedback from (if you asked them to leave), because you don't see a lot of *allochtonen* at these meetings. So, we take what we can get. (Albert, personal communication, 2010)

Important to this discussion, Albert, an *autochtoon* (a native Dutch person), compared autochthonous interest and participation in the feedback process to that of allochthonous residents. From his discussion, it appears that Albert questioned whether allochthonous residents would participate at all when he stated 'truthfully, you'd have no one left to get feedback from,' a phrase which expresses a sense of pessimism regarding the possibility for increased allochthonous participation.

Regarding the importance of connecting with local allochthonous residents, as was the *raison d'être* for this gentrification project, and, as one could argue, an important reason behind the whole feedback process, autochthonous residents such as Bernard did not believe 'mixing' was his role as a neighborhood resident. This is apparent when Bernard stated,

> Connecting with other people? I do not know. I do not have a connection with *them* (*allochtonen*). Even when I meet them in the local community centre (in general, outside these meetings), I have no connection. [...] It is not really my goal to do something with them. I just see them as people. We are all people living here. (Bernard, personal communication, 2010, emphasis my own)

Bernard's observation that 'it is not his goal to do something with them' provides a unique perspective with regard to civic participation as an identifier of belonging and social inclusion. From these comments, it becomes apparent that participation is applied differently between autochthonous and allochthonous residents. Therefore, while Bernard's role (or duty) is to only take part, it is the duty of *allochtonen* to demonstrate their willingness to belong through their performance of the Dutch language (their proficiency) in public. In this way, allochthonous belonging to the majority community is decided upon by the autochthonous residents who act as social actors and purveyors of belonging and social inclusion. Bernard's discussion also calls into question the perception that diversifying the housing will inherently influence residents' connections with one another.

Finally, during an interview with a local autochthonous resident from Bergpolder (North), Carla discussed whether or not the proposed gentrification of Bergpolder South would change the behaviors or attitudes of the inhabitants for the better. This perception is built on the understanding that this urban gentrification project will lead to greater social cohesion among neighborhood residents regardless of their differences in socioeconomic class, religious identity, citizenship status, etc. To this question, Carla responded, 'But will they succeed? Looking at *Crooswijk* (a demographically similar neighborhood that underwent gentrification), regardless of what changes you make, its reputation remains bad. Even if you built villas there, (the) people who could afford them would never want to live there' (Carla, personal communication, 2010). In this statement, Carla is alluding to the continuance of *Crooswijk*'s negative reputation of having a majority of allochthonous and antisocial residents despite government intervention to gentrify and entice more middle- and upper-class residents to move there. In so doing, Carla questions, as Albert did above, whether or not there will be any 'real' change to come from this process.

Earlier in this interview, Carla's perception of the ingrained difference between allochthonous and autochthonous residents was apparent when she stated:

> I went to the city hall some years ago and there was something (going on) about integration. The *allochtonen* who attended were people that spoke Dutch well and had a job; (they are) not the problem. The problem is with people who do not want, or can't, speak Dutch. [...] I think if you provide very good education to young people, and they learn Dutch, they (will) have more opportunities to find a good job and then the problems will disappear. There is so much attention being given for so many years to this problem. In the past, it was about Turkish people who came here as guest workers, but nowadays you hardly hear anything about them. Then you had the Moroccans or Antilleans causing problems. I think they should tackle criminality and preferably they should export those people; they are not welcome here. (Carla, personal communication, 2010)

Carla's description of *allochtonen* differentiates between those who are willing and able to speak Dutch and integrate into Dutch society and those who are not. Furthermore, according to Carla, it is a matter of choice for *allochtonen* to integrate – a perspective which does not include any reflection on the existence of systemic racism or structural inequalities in Dutch society. Her description also highlights the importance for *allocthonen* to be gainfully employed, or, to be 'exported.' This description mimics much of the exclusionary discourses sounded at the national level and demonstrates how these larger discourses are reproduced at the local level.

Discussion

Autochthonous residents and workers involved in the gentrification of Bergpolder South perceived allochthonous residents, and *allochtonen* in general, as neither willing nor able to participate in this feedback-gathering process. This lack of participation led to the creation of a physical environment by autochthonous neighborhood residents that excluded allochthonous feedback. Through an investigation of the participation process itself, it became apparent that participation was thought to be a significant factor when describing and aligning oneself to particular communities in the neighborhood and the Dutch nation. As outlined above, belonging and participation are factors affecting perceptions of Dutch citizenship by ordinary residents.

In a similar vein, Talja Blokland's (2008) ethnographic study looked at how middle-class residents living outside a neighborhood (with higher levels of social capital than the residents living within the neighborhood) facilitated gardening projects in ghettoized neighborhoods in New Haven, Connecticut. These gardening projects were facilitated using the contacts and resources (social and economic capital) of the middle-class project leaders; however, they ended up having little input from the local residents.[7] Blokland (2008: 167) concludes that instead of challenging understandings of differences within the neighborhood, boundaries were reproduced between the two communities.

Like Blokland's work, this gentrification project reinforced the idea of difference along the *autochtonen/allochtonen* narrative divide. This was evident when looking at the usual participants in these events, who were largely autochthonous residents living outside of Bergpolder South. The structure of the participation process exacerbated this phenomenon as it only appealed to a particular group within the community, that is, those with the ability and means to meet at night, speak fluent Dutch (to gain knowledge of the event and effectively take part) and feel comfortable engaging in debate and discussion at community or government venues. Through ethnographic research, it became apparent that this form of participation typically works for government bureaucrats, urban designers and predominantly white, upper- and middle-class residents. With such a process, those living outside the affected area of the gentrification had more input and control over the future plans of the neighborhood than the neighborhood's residents themselves.

From my experiences in the field in general, there was a sense that the integration approach by the government was flawed, expensive, inefficient and, to a point, unnecessary. In everyday discussions, integration appeared to hinge on the idea of (active) participation in a manner that was very public and in a way showing one's allegiance to the community. The need to demonstrate one's allegiance was a selective requirement as it was only allochthonous residents, and not autochthonous residents, who needed to (publicly) take part.

From the above discussion, it is apparent that my interlocutors defined *us* and *them* categories differently; for example, in their everyday conversation, Maureen differentiated allochthonous individuals according to generation while Carla's definition included a nuanced understanding of Turkish versus Moroccan and Antillean residents. In practice, this differentiation was more often used to identify and categorize a larger imagined 'Other' community, rather than speak about specific local allochthonous residents. In reflection on the data presented above, my interlocutors drew on national-level political and media narratives, such as Dutch Turkish and Moroccans marrying and bringing spouses back from 'the home country'[8] when situating their ideology of belonging. Thus, it was the perceived reluctance to integrate or lack of participation in Dutch society that most often prompted individuals' need to differentiate between *us* and *them* and which influenced this process of context-dependent citizenship-making practices.

Conclusion

Throughout this chapter, it became apparent that native Dutch participants believed there to be issues in the feedback process, with the level of interest of allochthonous residents to participate in such a process and in the perception that mixed neighborhoods would create 'real' change among their diverse residents. Instead, as is apparent from the above discussion, native Dutch participants reinforced an understanding that allochthonous residents were not active participants in local events. This lack of participation was connected to their willingness to be active members in Dutch society and therefore represented their perceived (lack of) loyalty to the Dutch nation. These events also led native Dutch residents to play the role of actors and purveyors of their imagined community, in so doing, demonstrating their role as 'minor figures' in the process of citizenship.

In all, although diversity of participants remained an important theme within government-led neighborhood projects, representative participation from allochthonous residents was not achieved in this feedback process. Furthermore, while the integration of residents was an important rhetoric for government officials, it was not always a priority from the perspective of local residents. This unequal participation contributes to the view that allochthonous individuals do not participate enough in the community and are inactive citizens. Such initiatives demonstrate how active citizenship is an important attribute of Dutch cultural identity that fosters social acceptance and belonging (see also van Bochove *et al.*, 2009; Schinkel & van Houdt, 2010).

Notes

(1) Autochthony language references ideas of self, soil, and indigeneity (Ceuppens and Geschiere, 2005). In the Dutch sense, this language has been used to signal a need to define and/or protect a native Dutch identity and culture.
(2) *Krachtwijken* denotes more than one problem neighborhood, while *Krachtwijk* is the singular form of the noun.
(3) Housing corporations are large private organizations that receive government subsidies to provide affordable housing for low-income individuals.
(4) All participants' names are pseudonyms to protect the identities of the participants.
(5) There are no statistics outlining the exact numbers of allochthonous vs. autochthonous residents in Bergpolder South. Instead, Bergpolder has an above national average of residents who are categorized as non-Western allochthonous individuals that is 36% (as opposed to the national average of 11%) (Bergpolder & Liskwartier, 2011). From my own observations, the majority of allochthonous residents live in Bergpolder South.
(6) Stair-houses or *trap huizen* are colloquially known as social housing that is cheap to rent and overcrowded. These three- to four-story buildings have one single stairway, hence, their name.
(7) Lower-income residents joined the project with the hope of taking advantage of the middle-class resident's resources (e.g. her social networks). Blokland (2008) found that the lower-income residents stopped their involvement with the project once it became apparent that the interest of the middle-class facilitator only went as far as the provision of gardening space.
(8) This practice is seen as problematic because the spouses, mainly women, do not speak Dutch and are thought to be unfit to raise the next generation of children in the Netherlands, in ways that facilitate their integration (see Kamerman's [2009] newspaper article 'Putting "import brides" to the Dutchness Test').

References

Anderson, B.R.O. (1983) *Imagined Communities: Reflections on the Origin and Spread of Nationalism*. London: Verso Editions and NLB.
Bergpolder and Liskwartier (2011) *Everything about krachtwijk Bergpolder* [Web blog post]. See http://www.bergpolder-liskwartier.nl/read/krachtwijk_bergpolder?submenu#.VAZZzmNNSlI (accessed 13 July 2015).
Bloemraad, I., Korteweg, A. and Yurkdakul, G. (2008) Citizenship and immigration: Multiculturalism, assimilation, and challenges to the nation-state. *Annual Review of Sociology* 34, 153–179.
Blokland, T. (2008) Gardening with a little help from your (middle class) friends: Bridging social capital across race and class in a mixed neighbourhood. In T. Blokland

and M. Savage (eds) *Networked Urbanism: Social Capital in the City* (pp. 147–170). Aldershot/Burlington, VT: Ashgate.

Bolt, A. (2013) Wilders' party now Netherlands' most popular. *Herald Sun*, March 29. See http://blogs.news.com.au/heraldsun/andrewbolt/index.php/heraldsun/comments/wilders_party_now_netherlands_most_popular/ (accessed 13 July 2015).

Bonilla-Silva, E. and Forman, T.A. (2000) 'I am not a racist but...': Mapping White college students' racial ideology in the USA. *Discourse & Society* 11 (1), 50–85. doi:10.1177/0957926500011001003

Bryant, A. (2014) The grounded theory method. In P. Leavy (ed.) *The Oxford Handbook of Qualitative Research* (pp. 116–136). Oxford/New York: Oxford University Press.

Centraal Bureau voor de Statistiek (CBS) (2015) Niet-Westerse Allochtoon (Non-Western foreigner) [web report]. See http://www.cbs.nl/nl-NL/menu/methoden/begrippen/default.htm?ConceptID=1013 (accessed 2 July 2015).

Ceuppens, B. and Geschiere, P. (2005) Autochthony: Local or global? New modes in the struggle over citizenship and belonging in Africa and Europe. *Annual Review of Anthropology* 34, 385-407. doi: 10.1146/annurev.anthro.34.081804.120354

De Vroome, T., Verkuyten, M. and Martinovic, B. (2014) Host national identification of immigrants in the Netherlands. *International Migration Review* 48 (1), 76–102. doi:10.1111/imre.12063

Deelgemeente Noord (2010) *BP3738?* [Information Package]. See http://bergpolderkrachtwijk.blogspot.ca/2010/06/bp3738-ontwikkeling-bergpolder-zuid.html (accessed 13 July 2015).

Deelgemeente Noord (2011) *Master Plan Bergpolder South* [public meeting documentation].

Duyvendak, J.W. and Scholten, P. (2012) Deconstructing the Dutch multicultural model: A frame perspective on Dutch immigrant integration policymaking. *Comparative European Politics* 10, 266–282. doi:10.1057/cep.2012.9

Feuerherm, E. (2013) Keywords in refugee accounts: Implications for language policies. In V. Ramanathan (ed.) *Language Policies and (Dis)citizenship: Rights, Access, Pedagogies* (pp. 52–72). Bristol: Multilingual Matters.

Joppke, C. (2010) *Citizenship and Immigration*. Cambridge: Polity Press.

Kamerman, S. (2009) Putting 'import brides' to the Dutchness Test. *NRC*, December 6. See http://vorige.nrc.nl/article2270070.ece (accessed 2 July 2015).

KEI, the Dutch Centre for Expertise and Innovation in Urban Renewal (n.d.). The policy. (Encyclopedic website.) See http://kennisbank.platform31.nl/pages/28250/The-policy (accessed 2 July 2015).

Kleinhans, R., Priemus, H. and Engbersen, G. (2007) Understanding social capital in recently restructured urban neighbourhoods: Two case studies in Rotterdam. *Urban Studies* 44 (5/6), 1069–1091. doi: 10.1080/00420980701256047

Martineau, E. (2006) 'Too much tolerance': Hang-around youth, public space, and the problem of freedom in the Netherlands. Unpublished doctoral dissertation. The City University of New York, New York.

Miller, P. and Rose, N. (2008) *Governing the Present: Administering Economic, Social and Personal Life*. Cambridge/Malden, MA: Polity Press.

Musterd, S. and Pinkster, F.M. (2009) Unraveling neighborhood effects: Evidence from two European welfare states. In J.W. Duyvendak, F. Hendriks and M. van Niekerk (eds) *City in Sight: Dutch Dealings with Urban Change* (pp. 41–60). Amsterdam: Amsterdam University Press.

Party for Freedom (2012) Their Brussels, our Netherlands: Elections platform for the PVV 2012–2017. See http://www.pvv.nl/images/stories/verkiezingen2012/VerkiezingsProgramma-PVV-2012-final-web.pdf (accessed 31 July 2015).

Ramanathan, V. (2013) Language policies and (dis)citizenship: Access, rights, pedagogies. In V. Ramanathan (ed.) *Language Policies and (Dis)citizenship: Rights, Access, Pedagogies* (pp. 1–18). Bristol: Multilingual Matters.

Roggeband, C. and Verloo, M. (2007) Dutch women are liberated, Migrant women are a problem: The evolution of policy frames on gender and migration in the Netherlands, 1995–2005. *Social Policy & Administration* 41(3), 271–288. doi:10.1111/j.1467-9515.2007.00552.x

Schinkel, W. and van Houdt, F. (2010) The double helix of cultural assimilationism and neo-liberalism: Citizenship in contemporary governmentality. *The British Journal of Sociology* 61 (4), 696–715. doi: 10.1111/j.1468-4446.2010.01337.x

Tonkens, E., Hurenkamp, M. and Duyvendak, J.W. (2010) Culturalization of citizenship in the Netherlands. In A.C. d'Appollonia and S. Reich (eds) *Managing Ethnic Diversity after 9/11: Integration, Security, and Civil Liberties in Transatlantic Perspective* (pp. 233–252). London: Rutgers University Press.

Van Beckhoven, E. and van Kempen, R. (2003) Social effects of urban restructuring: A case study in Amsterdam and Utrecht, the Netherlands. *Housing Studies* 18, 853–875. doi: 10.1080/0267303032000135474

Van Bochove, M., Rušinović, K. and Engbersen, G. (2009) Local and transnational aspects of citizenship political practices and identifications of middle-class migrants in Rotterdam. In J.W. Duyvendak, F. Hendriks and M. van Niekerk (eds) *City in Sight: Dutch Dealings with Urban Change* (pp. 103–120). Amsterdam: Amsterdam University Press.

Van de Wijdeven, T. and Hendriks, F. (2009) A little less conversation, a little more action: Real-life expressions of vital citizenship in city neighbourhoods. In J.W. Duyvendak, F. Hendriks and M. van Niekerk (eds) *City in Sight: Dutch Dealings with Urban Change* (pp. 121–140). Amsterdam: Amsterdam University Press.

Van den Berg, M. and Schinkle, W. (2009) 'Women from the catacombs of the city': Gender notions in Dutch culturist discourse. *Innovation: The European Journal of Social Science Research* 22 (4), 393–410. doi: 10.1080/13511610903108877

Van der Graaf, P. and Veldboer, L. (2009) The effects of state-led gentrification in the Netherlands. In J.W. Duyvendak, F. Hendriks and M. van Niekerk (eds) *City in Sight: Dutch Dealings with Urban Change* (pp. 61–80). Amsterdam: Amsterdam University Press.

Van Kempen, R., Musterd, S. and Rowlands, R. (2009) Deepening crisis or homes for the future? Some reflections and implications for policies in large housing estates. In R. Rowlands, S. Musterd and R. van Kempen (eds) *Mass Housing in Europe: Multiple Faces of Development, Change and Response* (pp. 265–278). Basingstoke: Palgrave MacMillan.

Vestia (2010) *Via Vestia* 4 (4), 34. See http://www.vestia.nl/Vestia%20brede%20brochures/Via%20Vestia/Via%20Vestia%20winter%202010%20Rotterdam.pdf (accessed 2 July 2015).

Vink, M.P. (2007) Dutch 'multiculturalism': Beyond the pillarization myth. *Political Studies Review* 5 (3), 337–350.

Wodak, R. (1996) The genesis of racist discourse in Austria since 1989. In C.R. Caldas-Coulthard and M. Coulthard (eds) *Texts and Practices: Readings in Critical Discourse Analysis* (pp. 107–128). London: Routledge.

Wodak, R. (2013) Dis-citizenship and migration: A critical discourse-analytical perspective. *Journal of Language, Identity, and Education* 12, 173–178. doi: 10.1080/15348458.2013.797258

Yanow, D. and van der Haar, M. (2013) People out of place: Allochthony and autochthony in the Netherlands' identity – metaphors and categories in action. *Journal of International Relations and Development* 16, 227–261. doi:10.1057/jird.2012.13

9 Ideologies and Collocations of 'Citizenship' in Media Discourse: A Corpus-Based Critical Discourse Analysis

Ariel Loring

The word *citizenship* is multifaceted and dynamic, often adopting different interpretations in various contexts (Loring, 2013).[1] This chapter focuses on the framing of citizenship in a national newspaper, as this medium has the power to reiterate nationalist ideologies of membership and position individuals as belonging to or excluded from their fellow citizenry. When citizenship is discussed in the media, it is commonly in reference to its legal dimension in the context of immigration. However, ideals of citizenship are also part of media discourse; the word *citizenship* is often used as a substitute for desirable ethics, values and principles, as in 'good citizenship' and 'citizenship award.' Thus, the media both produces and reproduces dominant discourses about citizenship in various settings and through multiple genres while highlighting different interpretations of the word *citizenship*.

While an analysis of news media can be a daunting task, this chapter delimits a segment of media discourse and analyzes the language used to discuss citizenship, the images evoked and the ideologies present. In particular, the research questions guiding the analysis are: (1) How is citizenship portrayed in American media? and (2) What are the societal ramifications of these depictions of citizenship? It is important to ask these questions because the news media impacts how individuals perceive, interpret and rationalize events around them (Duffy & Rowden, 2005).

Media Research

Why media research is important

Citizenship is discussed in the media quite regularly as it is a topic with wide-reaching scope and timely importance. In its depiction of citizenship, the news media reiterates attitudes and common expressions which can influence public opinion (though its ability to *change* readers' minds is in doubt) (Duffy & Rowden, 2005). In particular, and what will be the focus in this chapter's methodological approach to news analysis, are the strategies (implicit or not) that the media uses to present and affect opinions, namely, repetitions, concordances and collocations. These are subtle techniques that portray an author's perspectives and biases.

Through frequent repetition of keywords, the media emphasizes a particular stance on an issue and encourages a particular reaction by its readers. For example, from a corpus analysis of the Bank of English, Stubbs (1996) noticed the noun *unemployment* appeared more regularly than the adjective *unemployed*. This was interpreted as an inclination for British public discourse to highlight the abstract, general nature of *unemployment*, thus focusing on societal problems as a whole, rather than the personal situation of people *being unemployed* (as cited in Hunston, 2002).

Concordances and collocations reveal the media's tendency to link particular words together. When two or more words co-occur, they are portrayed as natural associations and their presence can be accepted without critical evaluation. This is the case with the words *falling* and *standards*, which are often collocated together. When this compound enters the lexicon as a fixed expression, the description, accurate or not, is accepted as reality. As stated by Stubbs (1996: 195), 'If collocations and fixed phrases are repeatedly used as unanalyzed units in media discussion and elsewhere, then it is very plausible that people will come to think about things in such terms.' Media analysis is important research because it pinpoints precise discursive strategies and evaluates their underlying ideological stances. Unless questioned, the media's depiction of 'truth' can perpetuate social ideologies.

The media as a data source

The media is a fitting source of data for an analysis of linguistic patterns, societal ideologies and dominant discourses. Practically speaking, media language is readily accessible, and theoretically speaking, evaluating media language avoids the pitfalls of Labov's (1972) Observer Paradox, where self-monitoring changes the style of language produced. Since all media language is knowingly manufactured for an audience, the awareness of an observer's presence does not alter the delivery of the message. In reporting on political events, media discourse transmits political rhetoric to its constituents, who then translate it to everyday conversations (van Leeuwen & Wodak, 1999). News media also offers a window on the language attitudes of the general population, because not only does the media affect public opinion (Bell, 1991; Gabrielatos & Baker, 2008; Garrett & Bell, 1998), but it also reflects the sentiments of its readers who often subscribe to newspapers that share their own worldviews (Crawley & Sriskandarajah, 2005).

A first step in media analysis is to identify the various genres present, which in this chapter will be exclusively comprised of the written daily newspaper. Allan Bell, a sociolinguist and journalist, identifies a distinction between the genres of news and advertising. Under the banner of 'news,' which he also calls 'editorial copy,' is service information (lists of weather forecasts, sports results), opinion (editorials) and the press news itself (Bell, 1991). The fact that newspapers perceive and present opinions as separate from news (Bell, 1991) reveals a journalistic ideology of not only portraying opinion-free news stories, but also that this endeavor is feasible.

Van Dijk (1998) is notable for classifying various grammatical features that distinguish news stories from other styles of language. Some of these features include nominalization, formal jargon, relevance structuring (moving important information to the front of a sentence) and passivization. Above the syntactic level, van Dijk (1988) further analyzes news reports at the discourse level. Under his cognitive theory of discourse processing, readers are able to summarize what a news story 'is about' from their ability to derive semantic macrostructures from the article's cohesion and coherence. To convey a cohesive and coherent news account, reporters rely on socially shared scripts that readers understand through their collective knowledge and attitudes. Readers must also be familiar with the media's news schemata of composing a story in a hierarchy of relevance, which is preferable to a chronological organization.

Additionally, the media has the ability to influence public opinions through the framing of its news stories. Frames (or schemata) encourage particular interpretations and discourage other interpretations of the same set of facts. Acknowledging that framing is a selection (conscious or not) of certain details that increases or decreases their saliency within a text (Entman, 1993) leads one to conclude that texts are always opinion-laden. While a news article may not attempt to propagate bias, the author's point of view is often expressed through quotes, quote placement, visuals, metaphors, caricatures and catchphrases, which give these ideas more weight when attitudes are formed (Nelson et al., 1997).

When analyzing the news media as a source of power, several qualities come to light. The newsroom adheres to its own *de facto* policies concerning which stories are told and from whose perspectives, often in accord with the value systems of majority societal groups (Breed, 1955). Often owned by large corporations, newspapers are impacted by many commercial and business interests. Because news reporters' investigations come into contact with police and government, the media is inherently tied to powerful institutions (van Dijk, 1989). Exemplified in Lambertus (2003), news accounts of ethnic groups and racial minorities can stereotype minorities and exaggerate conflict.

Approaches to analyzing news discourse

Researchers have employed various analytical strategies for investigating news discourse. Bell (1991, 1998) views news reports as stories, not articles, following a Labovian approach of narrative analysis (Labov, 1972). He explains his analytical method as asking, 'What does this story actually say happened?' (Bell, 1998: 65). This question leads to reconstructing the story's *event structure* by identifying events, news actors, place structures and time structures, and noting ambiguities and discrepancies throughout the report. This type of methodology is a fruitful starting point to explore ideological positionings.

Another important influence on news analysis research is the field of critical discourse analysis (CDA), which acknowledges that language use is intertwined within systems of power and ideology (Fairclough & Wodak, 1997). The media is a popular data source for CDA research due to its sphere of influence and its prolific production of discourse. Recently, scholars have preceded CDA research with corpus analysis, as is the case in this chapter. When merging these two approaches, the large-scale corpus analysis informs CDA by revealing keywords and clusters, collocations and concordances, which CDA can then investigate from a closer standpoint (Baker *et al.*, 2008; Gabrielatos & Baker, 2008; Mautner, 2007, 2009). Supplementing qualitative CDA, which is criticized for its subjective nature, with quantitative corpus analysis provides a deeper and more precise analysis (see Mautner [2009] for a more detailed account of the advantages and critiques of conjoining these two approaches).

Discrimination in news discourse

Relevant to this chapter is research specifically concerned with depictions of minorities and discrimination in the news. Wodak (2007) analyzes Austrian anti-Semitic post-war discourse to unearth instances of everyday racism, which she calls *syncretic racism*. This type of oblique racism occurs when the discourse of exclusion is dereferentialized so that the audience can *infer* discriminatory undertones through shared knowledge and collective memories. In other work on anti-Semitism in post-war Austria, Wodak (2003) analyzes oral and written news accounts to explore stereotypes, labels, allusions, minimizations and quotations while demonstrating how racist rhetoric is coded in discourse. Austrian discourse is also investigated in van Leeuwen and Wodak's (1999) study of official rejection notices concerning immigrant families' reunion applications. The discursive strategies of legitimation and justification create rejection letters based on 'objective' reasons while simultaneously appearing sensitive to human rights issues. Legitimation is additionally analyzed in Martín Rojo and van Dijk's (1997) study of the political discourse of the

Spanish Secretary of the Interior, in a speech on the military expulsion of 'illegal' African migrants.

Specific to print media, Lambertus (2003) analyzes various newspapers' portrayal of a land-use protest between Native Canadians and Caucasian ranchers in 1995. She examines relevance structures, linguistic structures, thematic structures and rhetorical strategies in news stories, and conducts ethnographic interviews with journalists to demonstrate the media's tendency to broadcast only the views of the police while silencing minorities. In the UK, through a combination of CDA and corpus analysis, Gabrielatos and Baker (2008) report on a 10-year data sample of 19 UK newspaper articles concerning refugees, asylum seekers, immigrants and migrants (RASIM). Analysis reveals that the vast majority of themes commonly associated with RASIM are negative and include references to destinations, numbers, economic problems, residence, repatriation, legality and plight. The researchers conclude that in doing so, the British press creates and sustains what can be described as a moral panic (Hill, 2008) around RASIM (Baker *et al.*, 2008; Gabrielatos & Baker, 2008).

Methodology

This particular study is informed by the methodological approaches outlined above, but it most closely follows Baker *et al.* (2008) and Gabrielatos and Baker (2008) in that it analyzes media discourse of citizenship from a corpus-based CDA standpoint. The advantage of this approach is that both quantitative and qualitative techniques are utilized, lending triangulation to what is often seen as subjective qualitative research.

Corpus approach

The corpus created here is an effort to understand the various constructions and scenarios in which citizenship is discussed. A LexisNexis Academic search of the word *citizenship* was performed, retrieving all articles and blogs from *The New York Times* during the period from April 1, 2011 to June 30, 2011, which included Arab Spring protests, the death of Osama bin Laden and birther conspiracy theories regarding US President Obama's citizenship. *The New York Times* was selected as the basis for analysis because of its widespread presence and influence. Stories reported in *The New York Times* not only affect the national discourse, but are also syndicated in local newspapers. This three-month data sample consists of 171 articles and blogs and comprises over 150,000 words and 369 pages of text. The corpus was stored as an Excel spreadsheet and was created by reading through all articles and noting relevant observations such as discourse genre, keywords, key people, concordances, context and general notes. While the style of corpus assembly required a smaller sample, the degree of researcher involvement allowed for closer control of the data.

Since the objective of this study is to observe the myriad of ways that citizenship is discussed, all tokens of *citizenship* are important. While most commonly reported in foreign and national stories, the word *citizenship* appeared in numerous other genres, as illustrated in Figure 9.1.

For the most part, these named genres are the section labels used by *The New York Times* itself, but some categories are consolidated into a general heading; for instance, *Arts* consists of the following subdivisions: Arts & Leisure, Arts/Culture, Book Review, Dining In/Dining Out and Performing Arts. Likewise, *Opinion* consists of Editorials, Op-Eds and Letters to the Editor. Use of the word *citizenship* is affected by article genre.

As mentioned, also accounted for in the corpus is an inclusion of keywords and key people in stories referencing citizenship, as well as a note if key people are directly quoted or not, following van Dijk's (1991) analysis of quotes. For every occurrence of the word *citizenship*, a 10-word concordance span was compiled to analyze the words in its immediate vicinity. Researcher notes were used to record arising hypotheses and recurring themes.

Data collection ceased once the corpus size reached approximately 150 articles, which coincided with a three-month time period. The corpus was analyzed by extracting various themes and examining them in individual Excel documents. For example, a separate spreadsheet was created of the 216 collocations of the word *citizenship* to better visualize and sort the data by patterns.

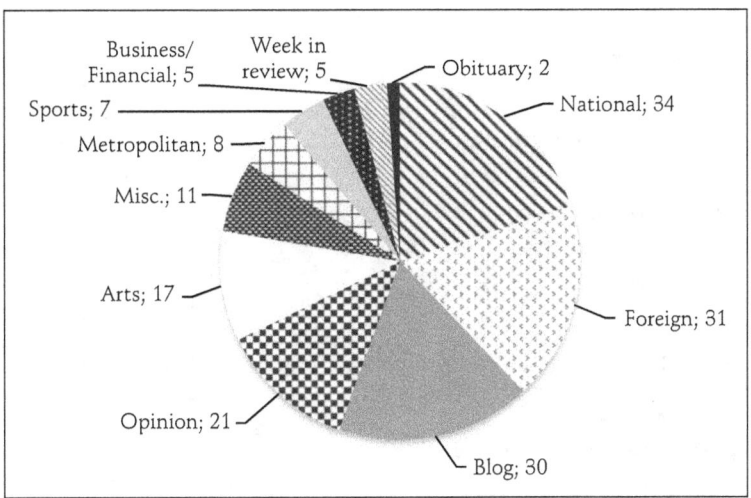

Figure 9.1 News genres of citizenship

CDA approach

While the corpus data can reveal large-scale trends and exemplify numerous uses of *citizenship*, CDA is also needed as a tool to analyze specific articles more closely. Thus, four articles from the three-month span were selected for an in-depth discourse analysis. Many of the articles in the data pool referenced citizenship peripherally, or as an aside that was not centrally related to the article's subject. For example, in the article 'City signs to help pedestrians (They aren't just for tourists)' (Grynbaum, 2011: A19), the word *citizenship* is mentioned just once in the 669-word article, as follows: 'Still, for many New Yorkers, self-guided navigation remains a sign of true city citizenship.' While the meaning of citizenship here is important, this is not an article centrally devoted to citizenship. Therefore, the four articles selected for a closer analysis were chosen from a smaller subgroup of articles that included more than one token of the word *citizenship*. Covering a wide spectrum of topics, the four articles are shown in Table 9.1.

The discursive features investigated in these four articles are repetitions, collocations, choice of references and people, quoted material and opinionated language, in order to ascertain which meanings of citizenship are depicted and in which light.

Findings

First presented is the analysis of the corpus data, specifically the topics of concordances, collocations and themes. This is followed by CDA of each of the four articles selected for in-depth analysis, concluding with notes about peripheral meanings of citizenship.

Corpus analysis

From the corpus, 216 tokens of *citizenship* arose, each with its 10-word concordance strand. Using a concordance program from

Table 9.1 Four articles for CDA

Title	Author	Genre	Date	Word count
Conspiracies are us	Kate Zernike	Week in Review	May 1, 2011	1193
Good citizenship: Assessing civics knowledge and education	Sarah Kavanagh and Holly Epstein Ojalvo	Blog (The Learning Network)	May 10, 2011	1943
More (wealthy) Americans are renouncing citizenship	Catherine Rampell	Blog (Economix)	June 16, 2011	557
Promise of Arab uprisings is threatened by divisions	Anthony Shadid and David D. Kirkpatrick	Foreign	May 22, 2011	1506

lextutor.ca/concordancers, the concordance lines for *citizenship* were examined to see how *citizenship* behaves syntactically. Table 9.2 exhibits the most common words that immediately precede and follow the word *citizenship*.

These concordances illustrate that *citizenship* is often used as part of a larger noun phrase with a preceding adjective providing nationality information or with a possessive determiner. When introduced with a preposition, most commonly *to* and *of*, we see either a *path to citizenship* or an abstract noun such as *notion, sense* or *definition of citizenship*. Following the word *citizenship* is either the word *and* or a prepositional phrase headed by *for* (*for immigrants, for illegal immigrants, for same sex spouses*), *in* (*in Switzerland, in a democratic Libya, in 2001*) or *to* (*to Arabic speakers, to young people, to stateless people*). *Citizenship* also commonly precedes a comma or a sentence boundary.

Moving beyond the words immediately adjacent to *citizenship*, words that co-occur with *citizenship* within its 10-word concordance strand were also examined in terms of their frequency counts. Figure 9.2 from wordle.net illustrates which content words most frequently appear with *citizenship*, with more prevalent words represented in larger text.[2]

As seen in this figure, the most common word that occurs within 10 words of *citizenship* is *American*, with 34 appearances.[3] In a similar realm, *United* and *States* each occur 13 times, and *US*, 8 times. This shows the predominance of associating citizenship with a specific nation(ality); there are 71 tokens of [nation], and, unsurprisingly, since the newspaper is New York based, to a large extent that nation is the United States. However, other countries, capitals and nationalities are included, most commonly *Canadian* (5) and *Canada* (3), *Switzerland* (4) and *Swiss* (4), *Iranian* (4), *Puerto Ricans* (3), *Israeli* (3), *French* (3) and *Damascus* (3). While not necessarily included in the immediate concordance, a wide variety of geographical places (other than the United States) and groups of people occur in the corpus keyword list, illustrated in Figure 9.3.

Table 9.2 *Citizenship* concordances

Preceding words		Following words
American/United States	citizenship	
(other country)	citizenship	
his/her/their	citizenship	
(abstract noun) + *of*	citizenship	
path to	citizenship	
	citizenship	*and*
	citizenship	*for* + (noun phrase)
	citizenship	*in* + (country; year)
	citizenship	*to* + (noun phrase)

192 Part 3: Discourses

Figure 9.2 *Wordle* of the most common *citizenship* collocations

Dispiriting content

The list of people and places in Figure 9.3 does more than merely reveal the scope of *The New York Times*'s coverage. When citizenship is referenced with respect to particular countries, the stories do not tend to be upbeat, uplifting stories; rather, themes of strife, turmoil, terrorism and political opposition are common. For example, the article about Yemen from Figure 9.3 describes the aftermath of rebellion:

> It will be difficult for Yemenis to repair what the Saleh regime has destroyed. But we will survive this ordeal, because the youth, political parties and many in the military realize that sacrifices will be necessary in the months to come, and that these sacrifices will be the basis for forging a modern Yemen built on the principles of citizenship and equal rights for all. (Al-Kokabany, 2011: A31)

In these concluding sentences of the article, citizenship is referred to in a legal, yet metaphorical sense. But crucially, it is referenced in light of past and present Yemeni struggles.

Another example of citizenship linked with political revolution in the Middle East is seen in the following: 'As the Arab world beyond the border struggles with the inspirations and traumas of its revolution – a new notion of citizenship colliding with the smaller claims of piety, sect and clan – something else is percolating along the old routes of that empire...'

• Al Qaeda	• France	• Israel	• Nigeria	• Syria
• Arab	• Gaza	• Kurds	• Puerto Rico	• Turkey
• Bahrain	• Germany	• Lebanon	• Russia	• Yemen
• Circassians	• Hamas	• Libya	• Rwanda	
• Damascus	• Honduras	• Muslim	• Spain	
• Egypt	• Iran	• Nazi	• Sudan	

Figure 9.3 Groups of people and places referencing *citizenship* in keyword list

(Shadid, 2011: WK1). From the approximately 50 articles that are included in Figure 9.3, many are concerned with the Arab Spring and conflict in the Middle East. However, even articles referencing citizenship with respect to European countries focus on controversial events, as evidenced from the following article titles: *Pugnacious advocate for gays in a hostile land* [Russia] (Schwirtz, 2011), *French legislation takes effect banning full-face coverings* (Erlanger, 2011), and *In reversal, German paper endorses Italy's top banker* (Ewing, 2011). This last article is a response to the German newspaper *Bild* stereotyping and denigrating the banker as 'a feckless Italian who can't be trusted with money,' which again, depicts a negative story.

The one genre of news story whose content does not adhere to this theme is the sports genre. Three articles from Figure 9.3 mention citizenship and a particular country in terms of team representation as it is aligned with nationality.

Mention of nationality

When stories include a reference to citizenship alongside a person's nationality or country of origin, it implies that this information is pertinent and necessary to character description. For example, in a 2000-word article about an art dealer's legal troubles, one sentence describes his citizenship: 'Mr. Wildenstein, who holds dual French and American citizenship, is enmeshed in at least a half-dozen lawsuits; some, provoked by the raid, are being brought by heirs who claim the artwork was stolen from their families' (Carvajal & Vogel, 2011: A1). The same day, another article references citizenship by addressing a subject's nationality: 'A ministry statement said that one of the hunted men, who had Jordanian citizenship, threw a grenade at the other two – both Palestinians – to prevent them from surrendering' (Akram, 2011: A6). A closer analysis reveals this to be an oft-repeated trend of providing supplemental information about citizenship in a non-restricted relative clause. Pointedly, this information is only provided when the individual is not solely a US citizen, because that is assumed to be the norm. Citizenship identification is included when people do not reside in their country of origin. It is similar to instances when someone's race, religion, gender or sexual orientation is depicted because it may be unexpected based on prior patterns. Newspapers reference nationality in this light in part because their audience expects to receive this information.

Immigration and President Obama

Returning to the *Wordle* in Figure 9.2, other common themes from the concordances are domestic immigration and the birther movement. *Immigration* occurs nine times, which is a logical association of citizenship, but what also frequently collocates together is *illegal* and *immigrants*. There are 10 tokens of the word *illegal*, and all but one collocate with *immigrant(s)*.[4] By specifically using this corpus to analyze the word *immigrant*, the expression *illegal immigrant* outnumbered the phrase *undocumented immigrant* more than 10-fold (Loring, 2016). When used with *citizenship*, the term *illegal immigrant* frequently appears in the construction 'a path to citizenship for illegal immigrants.' A consequence of this popular collocation is that *illegal* is seen as a fundamental characteristic of people; furthermore, it is sometimes the case that the *immigrant* half of the compound is omitted. This leads to the reduction of people to merely *illegals*, a form of linguistic discrimination.[5] Themes of illegal immigration are also linked to articles that reference the *Dream Act* (eight tokens), *maternity tourists* (the converse relationship to *anchor babies*),[6] *Latino voters* and *Mexploitation*.

Gaining traction in the years after Barack Obama became president in 2008, and reaching a peak in the spring of 2011, was the claim by some Republicans, and notably, Donald Trump, that President Obama was not a US citizen; alongside this claim were the demands that he release his long-form birth certificate. Seven of the eleven tokens of *Obama* in the *Wordle* (Figure 9.2) are in the possessive, and nine involve *doubts* and *questioning* (Figure 9.4).

It is significant that in a three-month news period, all but two associations of the President of the United States with *citizenship* question President Obama's own citizenship. This is an example of what Jane Hill (2008) would call *covert racial discourse*, where fixation on Obama's citizenship status is executed subtly through indexicality and erasure.

In fact, it is notable the extent to which a discussion of citizenship is kept at a minimalist level (Sim & Print, 2009). This is seen in the focus on citizenship in terms of legality: *right(s)* (7), *responsibilities* (1), *government* (3), *federal* (4), *democratic* (2), *eligible* (3), *verify* (2) and *passport* (4). This depiction goes hand-in-hand with the tangibility of citizenship. It is often referred to as something that can be *had* (13),[7] *proved* (4), *claimed* (3), *questioned* (4), *renounced* (9), *denied* (3), *given (up)* (2), *received* (2), *obtained* (4), *sought* (4) and *qualified* for (3). Thus, the range of citizenship is limited to a one-dimensional level, akin to the swearing-in ceremonies for naturalized minors

- '… as he challenged President Obama's citizenship.'
- 'Obama, who has had his citizenship questioned…'
- '… had not questioned Mr. Obama's citizenship.'
- '… among the Republicans questioning the citizenship of Mr. Obama…'
- 'public doubts about President Obama's citizenship…'
- 'doubt (about) Mr. Obama's citizenship…' (×3)
- 'new evidence of Mr. Obama's citizenship…'

Figure 9.4 Collocations of *citizenship* and *Obama*

that define citizenship solely in terms of the certificate document (Loring, 2013). The corpus analysis provides a solid foundation of trends from which to further investigate representative articles.

Critical discourse analysis

The following articles analyzed with CDA are discussed in terms of what meanings of citizenship are conveyed and are supported with textual evidence.

Article 1: 'Conspiracies are us'

This article discusses a prevalent news story at the time, already mentioned, concerning President Obama's citizenship status. The purpose of this article is to discuss conspiracy theories and why they occur and are sustained. Paragraphs alternate between discussing Obama's birth certificate in particular and conspiracies in general. This is supported through the repetition of keywords: *conspiracy(ies)* (23), *Obama('s)* (11), *president(al)* (12), *America(n)/(s)* (12), *believe/belief* (9), *argue(d)* (7), *doubt(er)/(ed)* (7), *birth* (4), *document(s)* (4) and *evidence* (4). When citizenship is discussed in terms of a legal document that can be publically released, doubted and authenticated, it is once again reduced to its official, tangible representation. This has consequences for citizenship applicants, teachers and government officials, who may be influenced by the ways that citizenship is discussed in national news.

The overarching message of the article is that the birther platform is a conspiracy because it is unfounded in facts and has a racist base:

> But the attacks on Mr. Obama, she [Professor Kathryn Olmsted] argued, are at essence about race. And because these theorists are fueled by partisan hatred, many won't be satisfied. 'They'll always question the authenticity of the documents they're given,' she said, 'because they're not driven by a quest for truth.' (Zernike, 2011, p. WK1)

In ending the article with a quote from an authoritative source, the lasting impression on the reader is one that supports President Obama and degrades the birthers. This impression is also generated through the use of cited references: five different authors or professors are quoted (four directly and one indirectly), while only a six-word quote is given from the 'doyenne' of the birther movement. President Obama himself is only quoted as using the word 'silliness' to describe the birther claims. This is a trend that exists in other articles from *The New York Times* about the birther debate: Obama is usually not quoted directly. The reader may infer that he is deliberately silenced or purposefully absent to avoid lending credibility to such claims.

Despite the author's intentions to dispel the birther controversy, the frequent collocations of the word *citizenship* with the words *doubt*, *evidence* and *Obama* undercut this goal. When these words are presented together (Figure 9.5), it signifies that they are not only plausible associations, but logical ones.[8]

Even though these statements lack the support of the author, when repeated they reveal dominant ideologies and beliefs often held by the American public: *it is logical that the president's citizenship status is in question, it is a common position to doubt the president's citizenship, the president is in a position where he must prove himself as legitimate.*

Article 2: 'Good citizenship'

As evident in the title, 'good citizenship' correlates to the knowledge and teaching of civics, though the phrase is not specifically defined. The authors' objective is to provide suggestions for citizenship curriculum in light of poor performance on standardized tests: 'Fewer than half of American eighth graders knew the purpose of the Bill of Rights on the most recent national civics examination and only one in ten demonstrated acceptable knowledge of the checks and balances among the legislative, executive, and judicial branches...' This message is supported by repeated keywords within the topics shown in Figure 9.6.

Based on the most commonly repeated words, citizenship is primarily discussed in terms of civics. In fact, the article concludes with a civics lesson plan which follows Common Core standards, in which civics is defined in terms of politics; government; law; rights; the 'common good'; diversity; (shared) values, beliefs and principles of democracy; conflict; social life; participation; public service; and knowledge. This list of civics characteristics is, for the most part, aligned with official discourse from the US Citizenship and Immigration Services (USCIS) and what is assessed on the naturalization test. However, aspects such as understanding 'American political and social conflict' is something addressed only briefly in the citizenship test, as it runs counter to the goal of portraying US history in a positive light. The same is true for participation and knowledge; while these facets are discussed in political discourse, they are not directly tested on the exam, creating a discrepancy between policy (speech) and practice (action) (Loring, 2013).

- 'evidence of Mr. Obama's citizenship'
- 'those who doubt Mr. Obama's citizenship' (x2)
- 'they doubt the president's citizenship'
- 'legitimate president'
- 'Obama doubters'

Figure 9.5 Tokens of *citizenship* in 'Conspiracies are us'

Civics	• civic(s) (54)	• government(s) (10)	• politic(s), political (8)
	• citizen(ry) (3)	• American(s) (12)	• constitution(al) (5)
	• history (4)	• national (7)	• right(s) (6)
School	• school(s) (22)	• student(s) (31)	• education(al) (25)
	• class(es) (10)	• group(s) (12)	• curriculum (5)
	• teachers (4)	• teen(agers) (6)	• lesson(s) (3)
	• course(s) (4)		
Knowledge	• know, knowledge, knowledgeable (12)	• learn(ing) (11)	• teach, taught (6)
Testing	• test (5)	• assess(ing) (3)	• standard(s), standardization (3)
	• exam(ination) (2)		
Motivation	• motivate(d), motivation (7)	• engage(d), engaging (6)	• effective(ly) (4)
	• entice (2)		• improve (3)

Figure 9.6 Repetitions in 'Good citizenship'

The close relationship between citizenship and civics is also seen in the collocations with the word *citizenship* in the article (Figure 9.7). Here, citizenship is associated with civics, government, rights and responsibilities, which represent the content areas from the naturalization test.

The authors primarily discuss civics using negative descriptors; it is something lacking, dull and in need of improvement. The low civics test scores are referred to as a 'crisis' by former Supreme Court Justice O'Connor, and are also called 'disappointing' and 'American students' worst subject.' The assertion that civics education is failing is ascertained by quantitative test scores.

The focus on standards, testing and assessment, illustrated in Figure 9.6, also demonstrates the view that citizenship can actually *be* assessed. This has implications for the naturalization exam itself because it promulgates the assumption that testing is reliable and valid. As scholars point out, the widespread ideology of fair and objective testing further strengthens the positions of power that the tests and test developers hold. Additionally, this requires test takers to conform to the tests' standards (McNamara & Shohamy, 2008; Shohamy, 2001). However, the authors of the article do

- 'Good citizenship: Assessing civics knowledge and education' [title]
- '... what students know about government and citizenship...'
- '... the rights and responsibilities associated with citizenship?'
- 'How can people be motivated to learn more about citizenship and government?'

Figure 9.7 Tokens of *citizenship* in 'Good citizenship'

propose moving beyond tests as a measure of civics knowledge in a lesson proposal: 'Would they [students] be most motivated by engaging in projects, by creating portfolios, by doing community service, by taking field trips, by taking a required test?' This quote again highlights the theme of lack of motivation, which is presented throughout as a barrier for teachers and students to overcome.

Article 3: 'Renouncing citizenship'

This article differs from the other three in content, length and style. It explores a recent increase in wealthy American expatriates who have renounced their US citizenship and explains this trend in terms of the US tax code. The US requires citizens to pay taxes even when living abroad if they report gains of over $636,000; this along with other filing complexities have prompted 'many individuals [to] conclude that their lives would improve by shedding their U.S. citizenship.'

The stylistic difference in this article is that it is reported in the first person ('I'm sure,' 'I believe') and is entirely based on the perspective of one individual, international tax attorney Andrew Mitchel. He is only indirectly quoted, affecting the presentation of the story. The author, Rampell, uses modals and tentative reporting verbs, italicized in Figure 9.8.

As a consequence of this reporting style, the language appears more circumspect and ambiguous, as Rampell restrains from implying a causative relationship between wealth and expatriation.

With eight tokens of the word *citizenship* in one short article, this example presents the most overt and consistent discussion of citizenship in the corpus. Key repeated words are: *expatriate, expatriation, expatriating* (14); *tax* (11); *individual(s)* (7); *file, filing* (5); *wealthy, wealthier* (4); *rules* (4); and *change(s), changed* (4). The frequent collocations of *citizenship* with *wealth* and *tax* depict citizenship as a financial (dis)advantage, which reduces its meaning and significance to the financial sector. Because citizenship is discussed in terms of *renouncing, giving up, shedding, stress* and *hassle*, it is treated as a tangible, official document for practical purposes. It is ironic that while many immigrants (either wealthy or not) are striving to become

---

- 'The increase *may* be due to recent changes in tax law.'
- 'The figures *appear* to refer primarily to those Americans wealthy enough...'
- 'Mr. Mitchel, however, *suggests* that two technical tax-related changes...'
- 'The second reason for the increase in expatriations, I *believe*, is the recent publicity...'

Figure 9.8 Mitigating language in 'Renouncing citizenship'

citizens in the United States, some wealthy Americans are revoking their status, although the article does not draw this explicit connection.

Article 4: 'Arab uprisings'

Of the four articles, this is the sole account of foreign news. Written in the midst of the Arab Spring, it reports on strife in North Africa and the Middle East, asking, 'Can the revolts forge alternative ways to cope with the Arab world's variety of clans, sects, ethnicities and religions?' Words that express differences across people and countries are often repeated, as are words pertaining to conflict (Figure 9.9).

The scope of the article is revealed by segmenting the most common words into the themes on the left-most column. Ten different countries or regions are mentioned, along with their residents. In particular, the repeated collocations of *Arab* and *world* (7) emphasize that similar issues and revolutions affect people cross-nationally, despite intranational divisions.

Examining who is quoted, there is a similar tendency as in the first article to reference the views of professors and intellectuals. Additionally, there are direct quotations from everyday people and activists. President Obama is quoted once from a recent speech, referring to many of the article's own common themes of *divisions, ethnicity, religious sect* and *repression*. Interestingly, Libyan Colonel Qaddafi, while mentioned by name

Diversity	• sect(s), sectarian, secular (11)	• religion(s), religious (7)	• divide, divisive, divisions (7)
	• identity, identities (7)	• diversity (4) • clan(s) (4)	• ethnicity, ethnicities (3)
Countries and People	• Syria(n) (12)	• Libya(n) (6)	• Tunisia(n) (5)
	• Lebanon (4)	• Egypt(ian)/(s) (4)	• Iraq (3)
	• Yemen (1)	• Bahrain (1)	• Persian Gulf (1)
	• Arab world (7)	• Beirut (4)	• Cairo (4)
	• Damascus (3)	• Tahrir Square (3)	• Alawite(s) (7)
	• Christian(s) (7)	• Muslim(s) (6)	• Coptic(s) (4)
Conflict	• revolution(s) (8)	• protests, protesters (5)	• repression, repressive (5)
	• revolt(s) (5)	• supporters (5)	• war (4)
	• activist(s) (4)	• tensions (3)	• violence (2)
	• uprisings (2)	• rebels (2)	

Figure 9.9 Repetitions in 'Arab Uprisings'

four times, is not quoted. This has the effect of silencing him, sustaining the story from the protestors' perspective.

The article is also the only one of the four to move beyond the tangibility of citizenship in terms of an actual document. This is seen in the concordances with the word *citizenship* (Figure 9.10), which for clarity are presented in a larger context than the 10-word span collected in Table 9.2 and Figure 9.2.

The collocations *idea of citizenship*, *broader citizenship* and *universal citizenship* are conceptualizations of citizenship as morals and identities beyond individual nations. The phrase 'citizenship that unites, not divides' intends to overlook differences between religions, sects and clans, and inspire a shared government uprising. It implies a transnational conception of citizenship (Glick Schiller *et al.*, 1995) where community ties extend beyond national borders. Whereas prior usages of the term *citizenship* are collocated with *government*, thus implying that the two go hand-in-hand in a reciprocal relationship, citizenship here is presented as an alternative to corrupt government. It is these alternative meanings of citizenship that are discussed below.

Peripheral meanings of citizenship

While concordances from the corpus data reveal common trends and phrases such as *broader citizenship*, and the CDA analysis closely investigated articles with a central focus on citizenship, as the previous section began to address, there are ways in which citizenship is discussed that extend its meaning beyond a legalistic status. Table 9.3 provides a list of such phrases within an extended context.

The first two examples, *democratic citizenship* and *second-class citizenship*, while important collocations, are not actual extensions of the traditional meaning of citizenship. These phrases refer to rights, which is a key aspect of citizenship as maintained by the *Oxford English Dictionary* and USCIS (Loring, 2013). *Democratic citizenship* here refers to the right to participate

- 'The revolutions and revolts in the Arab world... offer a new sense of national identity built on the *idea of citizenship*.'
- 'In an arc of revolts and revolutions, that idea of a *broader citizenship* is being tested as the enforced silence of repression gives way to the cacophony of diversity.'
- '... no matter what promises the rebels make about *universal citizenship* in a democratic Libya...'
- '... their [protestors'] demand is blunt: *Citizenship that unites, not divides*.'

Figure 9.10 Collocations of *citizenship* in 'Arab Uprisings'

Table 9.3 Peripheral uses of *citizenship*

Phrase	Context	Article title	Author	Genre	Date
Democratic citizenship	'Large numbers of Americans identified *democratic citizenship* as a privilege of whites alone – a position embraced by the Supreme Court in the Dred Scott decision of 1857.'	Reconcilable differences	Eric Foner	Arts (Book Review)	May 1, 2011
Second-class citizenship	'…the only principle he [Solicitor General Paul Clement] wishes to defend is discrimination and *second-class citizenship* for gay Americans.' (Richard Socarides, President of Equality Matters)	Law firm won't defend Marriage Act	Michael D. Shear & John Schwartz	National	April 26, 2011
	'Policies that instead create *second-class citizenship* are simply un-American.'	American citizenship	Karen K. Narasaki	Opinion (Letter to the Editor)	April 7, 2011
Universal citizenship	'… the large extended clans of the west … will never accept any revolution arising from the east, no matter what promises the rebels make about *universal citizenship* in a democratic Libya…'	Promise of Arab uprisings is threatened by divisions	Anthony Shadid & David D. Kirkpatrick	Foreign	May 22, 2011
Global citizenship	'… Google, YouTube, Wikipedia, Facebook, Twitter – whose sweep, programming and ideology of openness and *global citizenship* are the envy of the world.'	Television's curse was its blessing	Virginia Heffernan	Blog [Opinion-ator]	May 8, 2011

(Continued)

Table 9.3 (Continued)

Phrase	Context	Article title	Author	Genre	Date
	'His [Mr. Obama's] address, given in the twilight of George W. Bush's presidency, was most memorable for its citation of the "burdens of *global citizenship*."'	An odd-couple alliance	Mark Landler	Week in Review	April 10, 2011
Citizenship for the stateless	'Unpopular governors were sacked. Wages were raised. There will be *citizenship for the stateless*.' (Syrian Prof. Moubayed)	Syrians keep up protests amid doubts on reforms	Anthony Shadid	Foreign	April 21, 2011
Active citizenship	'Get off the couch and take responsibility for your community. [British Prime Minister] Cameron is trying to spark *active citizenship*.'	The big society	David Brooks	Opinion	May 20, 2011
Informed citizenship	'We cannot afford to continue to neglect the preparation of future generations for *active and informed citizenship*.' (Justice O'Conner)	Civics education called national crisis	Sam Dillon	National	May 5, 2011
Digital citizenship	'Now students start in sixth grade with a *digital citizenship* and ethics unit – dangers of cyberbullying included – followed by an introduction to blogging…'	At a private school, virtual learning and the rock	Jenny Anderson	Blog (City Room)	June 21, 2011
Citizenship award	'Artest, a Los Angeles Lakers forward, received the J. Walter Kennedy *Citizenship Award* from the Professional Basketball Writers Association.'	Rose shines as the Bulls eliminate the Pacers	N/A	Sports	April 27, 2011

in a democracy and receive equal treatment; the two tokens of *second-class citizenship* refer to a minority group (gay Americans and American children of undocumented immigrants) being treated as less than equal through the denial of basic human rights.

The subsequent three examples, *universal citizenship, global citizenship* and *citizenship for the stateless*, depict citizenship in a transnational light. Traditionally, citizenship is defined within the contexts of a particular country (Glick Schiller *et al.*, 1995), but these four articles broaden its scope by removing citizenship from this constraint. The phrase *citizenship for the stateless* would be a contradiction if citizenship could only exist as a relationship with the state. The expression therefore suggests that being a citizen involves rights, responsibilities and privileges, irrespective of how the government classifies its inhabitants. The two tokens of *global citizenship*, in discussing the varied topics of international politics and social media, adhere to the notion that commonalities and shared ties exist transnationally (see McPherron, this volume).

The next three phrases from Table 9.3, *active citizenship, informed citizenship* and *digital citizenship*, highlight participation and knowledge as components of citizenship. These articles point to a deficiency in these peripheral citizenship categories and advocate for active, informed, digital citizenship as a means to produce a more community-based, well-informed population. It is arguable that this type of citizenship should be taught, even though the US naturalization test doesn't measure these qualities (Loring, 2013).

The final example, *citizenship award*, is a well-known and oft-used phrase. It is the ultimate extension of the word *citizenship*, removing its meaning from the legal domain and using it instead to mean a *good person*. Indeed, in this article the citizenship award is given to 'honor a player or coach for outstanding service and dedication to the community.' Thus, the meaning of citizenship here relates to the prior three examples, in which character attributes and ties to the community are held up as facets of citizenship.

Implications

This chapter has analyzed various meanings of citizenship that arise in print media, specifically in *The New York Times* from a three-month period in 2011. It has determined that citizenship is usually referenced with regard to a particular country or nationality. A person's citizenship is mentioned when it is deemed important to the story, which often occurs when it is seen as an unexpected detail. Common themes in the spring of 2011 were the authenticity of President Obama's citizenship status and illegal immigration, which both treat *citizenship* as an official, tangible document used to confer and deny certain rights.

CDA of four newspaper articles shows *citizenship* presented in terms of the birther controversy and other conspiracy theories, the assessment of students' civics knowledge, expatriates renouncing American citizenship for tax purposes and revolutions in Arab countries during the Arab Spring of 2011. Using CDA as a tool for analysis reveals how language is used to establish truths and elicit particular perspectives. Readers possess or develop assumed knowledge in reading these articles, respectively: (1) that it is logical to question a president's citizenship even in the face of established evidence, (2) that standardized tests can demonstrate that middle and high school students do not have an understanding of citizenship, (3) that citizenship is a financial burden for wealthy Americans and (4) that citizenship can transcend national identity. While varied, what the first three stories share is a view of citizenship that is concrete, static, official and finite. This is seen in the verb choice and article content. The fourth article delves into peripheral meanings of citizenship, and as the final section further demonstrated, there are various extensions of the word *citizenship* that are not traditionally used. Identifying these meanings through an in-depth analysis of language and citizenship is significant; not only does the media have the power to influence the way society as a whole views and interprets citizenship, but it is also a reflection of current ideologies. Furthermore, the framing of citizenship issues raises questions about normative definitions of citizenship, underscores conflicting perspectives of who belongs and who should be excluded and re-emphasizes the connections between citizenship and geographic terrains.

Notes

(1) This paper is based on a dissertation chapter from Loring (2013).
(2) Function words and possessives have been omitted, verbs have been converted to their infinitival form, and all nouns have been made singular.
(3) Also of note are the 15 tokens of *Mr.* as a title, a third of the time collocating with *Obama* (see Figure 9.4).
(4) From the quantitative corpus literature, this is a common collocation that also has statistical significance (a high T-score which measures strength of collocation and a high MI-score which measure certainty of collocation) (Hunston, 2002).
(5) In April 2013, the Associated Press ceased using the phrase 'illegal immigrant' except in direct quotes. *The New York Times* did not eliminate its use, but recommended using alternative expressions (Haughney, 2013).
(6) *Anchor baby* is the more prevalent term, but both are offensive.
(7) *Had* is not included in the *Wordle* because it is not treated as a content word.
(8) The first two examples in Figure 9.5 are co-listed in Figure 9.4.

References

Akram, F. (2011) Hamas captures suspect in Italian's killing: 2 others dead. *The New York Times*, April 20, p. A6.
Al-Kokabany, N. (2011) Daring to hope in Yemen. *The New York Times*, June 7, p. A31.

Baker, P., Gabrielatos, C., Khosravinik, M., Krzyzanowski, M., McEnery, T. and Wodak, R. (2008) A useful methodological synergy? Combining critical discourse analysis and corpus linguistics to examine discourses of refugees and asylum seekers in the UK press. *Discourse & Society* 19 (3), 273–306.
Bell, A. (1991) *The Language of News Media*. Cambridge, MA: Blackwell.
Bell, A. (1998) The discourse structure of news stories. In A. Bell and P. Garrett (eds) *Approaches to Media Discourse* (pp. 64–104). Malden, MA: Blackwell.
Breed, W. (1955) Social control in the newsroom: A functional analysis. *Social Forces* 33 (4), 326–335.
Carvajal, D. and Vogel, C. (2011) Venerable art dealer is enmeshed in lawsuits. *The New York Times*, April 20, p. A1.
Crawley, H. and Sriskandarajah, D. (2005) Preface. In R. Greenslade (ed.) *Seeking Scapegoats: The Coverage of Asylum in the UK Press*. London: Institute for Public Policy Research.
Duffy, B. and Rowden, L. (2005) *You are What You Read? How Newspaper Readership is Related to Views*. London: MORI Social Research Institute.
Entman, R.M. (1993) Framing: Toward clarification of a fractured paradigm. *Journal of Communication* 43 (4), 51–58.
Erlanger, S. (2011) French legislation takes effect banning full-face coverings. *The New York Times*, April 12, p. A4.
Ewing, J. (2011) In reversal, German paper endorses Italy's top banker. *The New York Times*, April 30, p. B2.
Fairclough, N. and Wodak, R. (1997) Critical discourse analysis. In T.A. Van Dijk (ed.) *Discourse as Social Interaction* (pp. 258–284). Thousand Oaks, CA: Sage.
Gabrielatos, C. and Baker, P. (2008) Fleeing, sneaking, flooding: A corpus analysis of discursive constructions of refugees and asylum seekers in the UK press, 1996–2005. *Journal of English Linguistics* 36 (1), 5–38.
Garrett, P. and Bell, A. (1998) Media and discourse: A critical overview. In A. Bell and P. Garrett (eds) *Approaches to Media Discourse* (pp. 1–20). Malden, MA: Blackwell.
Glick Schiller, N., Basch, L. and Szanton Blanc, C. (1995) From immigrant to transmigrant: Theorizing transnational migration. *Anthropological Quarterly* 68 (1), 48–63.
Grynbaum, M.M. (2011) City signs to help pedestrians (They aren't just for tourists). *The New York Times*, June 28, p. A19.
Haughney, C. (2013) The Times shifts on 'illegal immigrant' but doesn't ban the use. *The New York Times*, April 23.
Hill, J.H. (2008) *The Everyday Language of White Racism*. Malden, MA: Wiley-Blackwell.
Hunston, S. (2002) *Corpora in Applied Linguistics*. Cambridge: Cambridge University Press.
Kavanagh, S. and Epstein Ojalvo, H. (2011) Good citizenship: Assessing civics knowledge and education. *The New York Times Blogs*, May 10.
Labov, W. (1972) *Language in the Inner City*. Philadelphia, PA: University of Philadelphia Press.
Lambertus, S. (2003) News discourse of Aboriginal resistance in Canada. In L. Thiesmeyer (ed.) *Discourse and Silencing* (pp. 233–272). Philadelphia, PA: John Benjamins.
Loring, A. (2013) Language and U.S. citizenship: Meanings, ideologies, and policies. Doctoral dissertation. Retrieved from ProQuest Dissertations and Theses. (UMI no. 3596915.)
Loring, A. (2016) Refugees, aliens, and immigrants: Positionings in naturalization classes and the media. In E. Feuerherm and V. Ramanathan (eds) *Refugee Resettlement: Language, Policies, Pedagogies*. Bristol: Multilingual Matters.
Martín Rojo, L. and van Dijk, T.A. (1997) 'There was a problem, and it was solved!': Legitimating the expulsion of 'illegal' migrants in Spanish parliamentary discourse. *Discourse & Society* 8 (4), 523–566.

Mautner, G. (2007) Mining large corpora for social information: The case of 'elderly.' *Language in Society* 36 (1), 51–72.
Mautner, G. (2009) Checks and balances: How corpus linguistics can contribute to CDA. In R. Wodak and M. Meyer (eds) *Methods of Critical Discourse Analysis* (pp. 122–143). Thousand Oaks, CA: Sage.
McNamara, T. and Shohamy, E. (2008) Viewpoint: Language tests and human rights. *International Journal of Applied Linguistics* 18 (1), 89–95.
Nelson, T.E., Clawson, R.A. and Oxley, Z.M. (1997) Media framing of a civil liberties conflict and its effect on tolerance. *American Political Science Review* 91 (3), 567–583.
Rampell, C. (2011) More (wealthy) Americans are renouncing citizenship. *The New York Times Blogs*, June 16.
Schwirtz, M. (2011) Pugnacious advocate for gays in a hostile land. *The New York Times*, June 18, p. A9.
Shadid, A. (2011) Can Turkey unify the Arabs? *The New York Times*, May 29, p. WK1.
Shadid, A. and Kirkpatrick, D.D. (2011) Promise of Arab uprisings is threatened by divisions. *The New York Times*, May 22, p. A1.
Shohamy, E. (2001) *The Power of Tests: A Critical Perspective on the Uses of Language Tests*. Harlow: Pearson Education Limited.
Sim, J. and Print, M. (2009) Citizenship education in Singapore: Controlling or empowering teacher understanding and practice? *Oxford Review of Education* 35 (6), 705–723.
Stubbs, M. (1996) *Text and Corpus Analysis*. Oxford: Blackwell.
van Dijk, T.A. (1988) *News Analysis: Case Studies of International and National News in the Press*. Hillsdale, NJ: Lawrence Erlbaum Associates.
van Dijk, T.A. (1989) Critical news analysis. *Critical Studies* 1 (1), 103–126.
van Dijk, T.A. (1991) *Racism and the Press*. New York: Routledge.
van Dijk, T.A. (1998) Opinions and ideologies in the press. In A. Bell and P. Garrett (eds) *Approaches to Media Discourse* (pp. 21–63). Malden, MA: Blackwell.
van Leeuwen, T. and Wodak, R. (1999) Legitimizing immigration control: A discourse-historical analysis. *Discourse Studies* 1 (1), 83–118.
Wodak, R. (2003) Discourse of silence: Anti-Semitic discourse in post-war Austria. In L. Thiesmeyer (ed.) *Discourse and Silencing* (pp. 179–210). Philadelphia, PA: John Benjamins.
Wodak, R. (2007) Pragmatics and critical discourse analysis: A cross-disciplinary inquiry. *Journal of Pragmatics and Cognition* 15 (1), 203–227.
Zernike, K. (2011) Conspiracies are us. *The New York Times*, May 1, p. WK1.

Afterword

Ariel Loring

Immigration and naturalization are vital topics that are becoming more prominent; one needs merely to look at the sheer magnitude of such news stories in the last decade for confirmation. Recent world events have triggered a steady discussion of im(migration) and citizenship in terms of national unity, political strife, economic problems, terrorism and civil war. The language used to discuss these issues exemplifies increased passion, fear and stridency.

As I write this from California, USA, in July 2015, a recent random murder in San Francisco committed by a Mexican undocumented immigrant has resulted in a national uproar regarding crime and deportation. Political debates have arisen regarding whether federal aid should be denied to San Francisco and the other 200 'sanctuary cities,' so named because their local law enforcement agencies do not assist federal immigration authorities in tracking or retaining immigrants without a court order or warrant. This issue has become political fodder for the 2016 presidential candidates on the campaign trail, who have used this story to support their stance on immigration, whatever that might be. One Republican presidential candidate continues to make headlines with his unsubstantiated claims that most Mexican immigrants are drug traffickers and rapists.

The desire to deport non-citizens in the US is one prevalent political topic; other worldwide events involve how to deter migration in the first place. In April and May of 2015, a succession of dangerously crowded human trafficking boats from North Africa to Europe capsized, resulting in the deaths of over 1000 migrants. Debates concerned the extent to which European countries should provide search-and-rescue support for the migrants' vessels, the responsibility to accept and resettle asylum seekers and whether stricter policies would discourage people from even attempting the journey. The US government also considered how to dissuade migrants from crossing its southern border after a sharp increase in border crossings by unaccompanied minors from Central America in 2013 and 2014.

Other recent debates have demonstrated the intersectionality between immigration and national and religious categories. This was highlighted in 2014 when the European Court of Human Rights upheld France's ban of the burqa and other full-face coverings in public. In the last several years, Belgium and cities within Spain, Italy, Denmark, Russia and Switzerland have issued complete or partial bans on Islamic face-veils. What these laws demonstrate is that after new immigrants have been admitted and 'dangerous' immigrants have been deported, national, religious, ethnic and linguistic differences within a country are still viewed as problematic. A lack of total assimilation and integration is considered an obstacle to national identity.

The consequence of these and other events is that im(migration) remains at the forefront of the global stage and further speaks to the need for critical evaluation. Applied linguistics and sociolinguistics illuminate these discussions because immigration, naturalization and citizenship are fundamentally interwoven with language issues. While not all of the contributors to this volume are linguists, we all recognize the prominence of language when analyzing this subject matter.

I am often asked by non-linguists how language is related to citizenship, so I will conclude by clarifying this nexus. The issue of citizenship tests, which are given in a country's official or symbolic language(s), function as a gatekeeping measure by denying naturalization to those who are illiterate, lack proficiency in the required language or fear their proficiency level is inadequate. For asylum seekers, language issues affect who is granted refugeehood. The assumption is that one's language abilities are an appropriate and reliable standard for assessing national identity (Blommaert, 2009; Eades, 2009), which, as sociolinguists know, is never a foregone conclusion.

The status of a language can factor into one's motivation to migrate and one's perception of the new destination. A language like English is seen as the means to unlock global opportunities and secure stable futures. Such ideologies about language are encoded in ideologies about speakers and their countries of origin. English has become strongly etched onto the notion of 'Americanism' through centuries of national identity induction (Pavlenko, 2002; Piller, 2011). Thus, becoming an American citizen implies becoming a member of the English-speaking group. Those who speak foreign languages are relegated to outsider status.

The details are far more complex than this, however. Just as language is a tool for unity (we are all English speakers), it is also a tool for division (we speak English differently). Not only are foreigners seen as outsiders, but so is anyone who speaks non-standard English. This includes people who have a trace of a non-native accent and native English speakers who come from a multilingual community (e.g. Chicano English speakers in the US [Bayley, 2008]). Even these groups of people – who *are* American citizens – can be treated as outsiders, by their schools, peer groups, strangers, government agencies and symbolic systems (Bourdieu, 1991). In part, this is due to the indexicality of language: what associations we make when hearing various languages and accents. Thus, this volume and other recent literature point to the need to disassociate 'citizenship' from 'legal status' since many of the identity issues that affect immigrants affect native-born citizens as well.

The last, but by no means final way that language is integrated with citizenship and immigration is through discourse. By this, I am referring to the language used to talk about citizenship and immigration. Too often the rhetoric dehumanizes immigrants, migrants and asylum seekers and characterizes immigration as a crisis. This is certainly demonstrated in the various news stories summarized above.

There is no denying the connection between language and immigration, and with it, belonging, identity and exclusion. Underlying this connection are fundamental questions to the field that are as important to ask in today's political climate as they were in the past. Why are differences (linguistic, religious, ethnic) negative? Why is exposure to and proficiency in many languages seen as a deficit rather than a benefit? Why are immigration and migration viewed as a threat to a nation's citizens? How can descendants of immigrants rationalize the exclusion of new immigrants? These were the questions that first motivated me to become an applied sociolinguist and are questions that I and other linguists continue to grapple with in our scholarly work.

References

Bayley, R. (2008) Latino varieties of English. In H. Momma and M. Matto (eds) *A Companion to the History of English Language* (pp. 521–530). Oxford: Wiley-Blackwell.

Blommaert, J. (2009) Language, asylum, and the national order. *Current Anthropology* 50 (4), 415–441.

Bourdieu, P. (1991) *Language and Symbolic Power.* Cambridge, MA: Harvard University Press.

Eades, D. (2009) Testing the claims of asylum seekers: The role of language analysis. *Language Assessment Quarterly* 6 (1), 30–40.

Pavlenko, A. (2002) 'We have room for but one language here': Language and national identity in the US at the turn of the 20th century. *Multilingua 21* 2 (3), 163–196.

Piller, I. (2011) *Intercultural Communication: A Critical Introduction.* Edinburgh: Edinburgh University Press.

Index

Allochtonen, 18, 165–166, 170–181, 181(5)
American Dream, 13, 17, 39–41, 46, 82, 84
Americanism (Americanization), 122, 208
Anderson, B., 4, 106, 145, 166
Aoki, K., 80–81
Appadurai, A., 68, 145, 149
Arias, M. B., 79, 82, 85, 86
Arnot, M., 147–148
Assimilation (assimilative), 2, 6, 8, 12, 37, 79, 81–83, 122, 146, 148, 159–161, 165–166, 208
Autochthonous language, see Autochtonen
Autochtonen, 18, 164–166, 168, 170, 173–180, 181(1)

Baker, P., 58, 185, 187–188
Banks, J., 6, 46, 146, 148
Bell, A., 185–187
Belonging (see also Discourse of belonging; Ideology of belonging), 2, 4, 7, 12–14, 16–18, 56–57, 63, 68–69, 80–81, 96, 116–117, 145, 148–149, 151–156, 159, 164–171, 176–181, 184, 204, 209
Bilingual education, 13, 83–84, 89–90, 95, 96(10)
Birther (movement), 188, 193, 195–196, 204
Bloemraad, I., 4, 7, 166
Blommaert, J., 58–59, 101, 109, 116, 208
Borders, 2, 4, 6, 8, 16, 67, 80–82, 94, 200, 207

Chang, R. S., 80–81
Citizenship
  –Active, 176, 180–181, 202–203
  –Birthright, 9, 14, 27, 58, 80
  –Classes and instruction, 66, 121–123, 125, 133, 135–137
  –Education, 146, 160–161
  –Global (orientation), 7, 13–17, 19(7), 101, 103, 106, 109–116, 201–203
  –Handbooks, 29, 33, 36–41, 47(5)
  –Historically, 3–4, 9–10, 14–15, 19(3), 20(18), 29–30
  –Identity, see Identity, citizenship
  –Interpretations of, 1–8, 14, 16, 29, 46, 56–58, 80, 95, 101, 116, 145–149, 166–168, 207–209
  –Policies in the Netherlands, 8, 164–166
  –Policies in the US, 8–11, 14–15, 122
  –Policies worldwide, 8–9, 15–16, 19(8)
  –Test, see Naturalization test in US
Civics, 58, 161, 177, 196–198, 202, 204
  –As assessed on naturalization test, 10, 13, 15, 17, 19(10), 19(15), 33–34, 40–43, 46, 48(9), 50–51, 54–55, 122–123, 130, 133–134, 136
Collocation, 185, 187, 189–190, 192, 194, 196–200, 204(4)
Communicative language teaching (CLT), 102–104, 106, 109, 116–117
  –And student-centered approaches, 104–106, 110
  –With Chinese characteristics, 109, 117
Community
  –As related to belonging (see also Belonging), 166, 170, 178, 180–181
  –As related to citizenship, 4, 6, 14, 29, 40, 46–47, 80, 148, 159, 167, 202–203
  –As related to teaching, 102, 110–111, 116–117
  –Research, 60–62, 64–66, 68–69
  –See also Neighborhood, community; Imagined, community
Concordance, 185, 187–191, 200
Conversation analysis, 126
Corpus analysis, 18, 85, 185, 187–190
Covert racial discourse, 194
Crawford, J. W., 82–84, 96(8)
Critical discourse analysis (CDA), 18, 187–188, 190, 195, 200, 204

Critical race theory, 81
Culture of learning, 105, 118(4)

Das Gupta, M., 56–57
Deaux, K., 160–161
De facto, 145
  –Membership, 13, 132, 135
  –Policies, 12, 19(13), 186
De jure, 145
De Vroome, T., 167
Dis-citizenship, 7, 17, 57–58, 61, 67–70, 82, 87–88, 95–96, 116–117, 165, 167–168
Discourse
  –And power, 28
  –And the media/news, 84–85, 184–185, 187–188
  –In the classroom, 121, 136
  –Nationalist vs. self-improvement, 105
  –Of anti-immigration, 17, 82, 85–86, 93, 95–96
  –Of belonging, 164–166
  –Of exclusion, 176, 179, 187
  –Of Islamophobia, 18
  –Of policy, 5–6, 11–12
  –Racial (see Covert racial discourse)
Discrimination, 1, 59–60, 93, 167, 187, 194, 201
Displays of knowledge, 121, 123, 125, 127, 130, 132–135

Engagement, 2, 61, 69, 145, 151–152, 156, 159, 161
English language teaching, 102–104
English learners (ELs), 11, 17, 79–96, 96(1), 97(14)
  –And RCs, 86, 89–90, 92–93
  –Marginalization and segregation of, 86–88, 93–96
English-Only
  –Ideologies of, 79, 82–83, 90
  –Language policies, 81, 83, 95–96
  –Movement, 17, 83–84, 96(8), 137(3)
English Writing Test, 27–29, 33–35, 38, 41–42, 44–47, 48(9), 50–55
Ethnography
  –Auto-ethnography, 103
  –Critical ethnography, 149–150
Exclusion, (see also Discourse of exclusion) 4, 7, 11, 14–16, 58, 67–68, 80, 96, 166, 176, 179, 187, 209

Fairclough, N., 28, 168, 187
Faltis, C., 79, 82, 85, 87
Feedback, 17–18, 121–122, 123, 135–137, 171–174, 176–177, 179–181
  –Gaze, see Gaze
  –Gestural, 121–122, 124–125, 128, 130, 132, 135–136
  –IRF, see Initiation-response-feedback sequence
  –Negative, 128–130, 132–133, 135
  –Non-verbal, 124–125, 127, 137
  –Positive, 126–127, 132, 135
Feuerherm, E., 2, 33, 58–60, 68, 70, 168
First generation, 12–13, 16, 18, 82, 85, 145, 151–152, 160
Foreigner talk, 31
Foreign/Local teachers, 11, 17, 102–103, 106–117, 118(1)
  –Definitions of, 101–102, 118(1)
  –Privileging of foreign over local, 106–107, 109–111, 115–117
Fox, B., 136
Framing, 12, 116, 184, 186, 204
Future selves, 17, 92–93, 95–96

Gabrielatos, C., 58, 185, 187–188
Gándara, P., 79, 82–84, 87, 94, 96(2)
Garrett, P., 185
Gatekeeping, 1, 11, 14–15, 27–28, 113, 115, 165, 208
Gaze, 126–132, 135–136, 138
Gentrification, (see also Neighborhood meetings) 18, 151, 164, 166, 168, 170–172, 177–179
Gesture, see Feedback, gestural
Glick Schiller, N., 7, 67, 200, 203
Global
  –Citizenship, see Citizenship, global
  –(vs. local) English-speaking community, 16–17, 101, 103, 110, 113–114, 118
Goodwin, C., 136
Grounded theory, 33, 103, 170

Heater, D., 3–4, 7, 19(3)
Hu, G., 101–102, 105

Identity
  –Citizenship, 47, 64–65, 68–69, 116, 145–146, 149–150, 159–161
  –Cultural, 147, 181
  –Linguistic, 94, 96, 158–159

–National, 1–2, 4, 15, 18, 154–155, 159–161, 165, 181(1), 200, 204, 208
–Racial, 156–158
–Theories of, 11–12, 62, 103, 209
Ideologies, 1–2, 59, 69, 79, 146–147, 184–187, 196–197, 204
–Of Americans, 13, 27, 47, 122, 155
–Of belonging, 18, 81, 180
–Of English language, 12–13, 82, 85–86, 117, 208
–Of English-only, see English-only ideologies
–Of freedom and opportunity, 17, 68
–Of majoritarianism, 81, 84, 96
–Of native speakers, 17, 106, 111
Imagined community, 4, 106, 166–168, 171, 174, 180
Immigrant/Immigration, 1–2, 15–16, 27, 30, 79–85, 96, 122–123, 164–166, 207–209
–Anti-, see Discourse, anti-immigrant
–Illegal, 6, 13–14, 19(6), 79, 85, 191, 193–194, 203
–Integration of (see also Integration), 4, 165–166
–Of Muslims/non-Westerners, 12, 16, 18, 165–168, 174
–Youth, 12, 18, 145–161
Immigration and Nationality Act (INA), 9–14
Immigration and Naturalization Service (INS), 27, 30, 32–34, 40–42, 48(7), 56–57, 70(1)
Inclusion, 7, 58, 80, 122, 166–167, 177–178
Initiation-response-feedback (IRF) sequence, 109, 123, 126, 130, 135
Integration, 4, 8, 18, 101, 110, 116, 123, 164–167, 169, 178–181, 181(8), 208
Interviews
–Co-construction of, 12, 17, 62–66, 69–70
–High-stakes, 12, 15, 45
–Methodology/theories of, 57, 61–62, 64–66, 68, 74, 149–150
–Naturalization, see Naturalization test/interview in US
Islamophobia, 18, 165

Joppke, C., 1, 166
Jus sanguinis, 8–9
Jus soli, 8
Knowledge construction, 61, 121, 123, 136

Language policies, 2, 7–8, 12, 16, 80–83, 95
–Of English-only, see English-only language policies
–Restrictive in Arizona, 17, 79–88, 94–96
Lillie, K. E., 83–88, 92, 94, 96(7)
Linguistic insecurity, 110
Local teachers, see Foreign/local teachers
Loring, A., 6, 13, 20(16), 20(17), 29, 37, 46, 66, 184, 194–196, 200, 203, 204(1)
Lukes, M., 82–83
Lyster, R., 121, 124, 129

Macbeth, D., 123–124
Marshall, T., 4, 6–7
McHoul, A., 121, 123–124
Member(ship), 4, 6–7, 11–14, 16, 18, 81–82, 84, 88, 95, 118, 127, 132, 135–136, 145–149, 153–154, 159, 167, 180, 184, 208
Meyer v. Nebraska, 83
Miller, P., 164
Minorities
–Ethnic/racial, 15, 146, 148, 155–161, 165, 186
–Omission of, 44
–Silencing of, 161, 188
Moore, S. C. K., 79, 82–87

N-400 naturalization application, 10, 20, 30–31, 34–35, 45
Nagel, C., 160
Nation-state, 4, 6–7, 12, 14, 68, 147
Naturalization, 2, 6, 9, 68
–Application, see N-400 naturalization application
–Policies, see Citizenship policies
Naturalization test/interview in US, 5, 9–10, 12–16, 20, 27–39, 42–47, 56–58, 60, 65, 68–69, 70(2), 122, 125, 127, 130, 133–136, 137(1), 138(15), 196–197, 203, 208
–Also see English Writing Test
–And literacy, 9–10, 14, 32, 42
–Standardization of, 9–10, 16, 29, 32–33, 44–45
Neighborhood, 16, 18
–Community, 149, 152–154, 157, 159, 179
–Gentrification meetings, 16, 18, 170–177
–Mixed, 169–170

Ong, A., 59, 67, 147
Orgad, L., 6, 9, 10, 13, 19(10), 29, 32–33, 36, 38–39, 41
Osnos, E., 117
Others (also Othering), 7, 12, 46, 79–81, 94, 124, 147–148, 156–157, 160, 165, 176, 180
Outsiders, 2, 14, 16–18, 208–209

Passports, 17, 31, 57–58, 63–69, 194
Participation (and full participation), 2–7, 13–14, 16–18, 33, 46–47, 57–58, 69, 80–81, 87–88, 95, 101, 103, 111, 117, 166–167, 170, 173–174, 177, 179–181, 196, 200, 203
Participatory action research (PAR), 60–62, 66, 70
Permanent resident, 2, 6, 8–9, 30, 47(1)
Plyer v. Doe, 80
Positionality, 12, 62–63, 69, 150
Positioning, 1–2, 11–12, 28, 62, 106, 147–148, 184
  –Ideological, 187
  –Self-, 12, 145, 151, 157
  –Social, 145, 159
Power, 12, 15, 28, 45, 47, 56–58, 61, 67, 121, 147–149, 160, 165, 184, 186–187, 197, 204

Ramanathan, V., 2, 7, 14, 46, 57–58, 67, 80, 82, 95, 96(3), 101, 167
Refugees, 2, 15, 17, 33, 57–60, 69–70, 70(3), 188, 208
  –Definition of, 58–59
  –Iraqi, 13, 57, 60–61, 66–68
Resettlement, 1–2, 15, 58–61, 65, 68–69
Responsibilities, see Rights and responsibilities
Ricento, T., 7, 58–59, 67, 69

Rights, 3–4, 6–8, 14, 27, 44, 47, 56–57, 61, 80, 83–84, 96(6), 96(7), 101, 123, 127, 136, 146, 155–156, 160, 166–167, 187, 192, 194, 196, 200, 203
  –And responsibilities, 2, 5–6, 19(4), 43, 122, 147, 161, 197
Rios-Aguilar, C., 79, 87–88, 96(2)
Rose, N., 164

Sadiq, K., 6, 8, 13–14, 19(6)
SB 1070, 79, 85–86, 96
Schegloff, E. A., 124, 128, 137(4)
Segregation, 87–88, 93–94
Staehali, L., 160
Standard American English, 155, 159
Structured English Immersion (SEI), see Language policies, restrictive in Arizona
Swearing-in ceremony, 5, 10, 13, 19(5), 194

Talmy, S., 57, 62, 66, 70
Transnational, 7, 13, 57, 67, 69, 200, 203

United Nations High Commissioner of Refugees (UNHCR), 58–59
United States Citizenship and Immigration Services (USCIS), 5–6, 9, 32, 34, 40, 42, 45–46, 48(7), 70(1), 137(2), 196, 200

Van Dijk, T. A., 176, 186–187, 189
Van Leeuwen, T., 185, 187

Wiley, T., 7, 13, 72, 80, 82–85, 96(6), 96(7)
Winn, M., 27–31, 33–42, 45–47, 47(5), 134
Wodak, R., 7, 58, 84, 167, 176, 185, 187

Young, W. A., 122–123

For Product Safety Concerns and Information please contact our EU Authorised Representative:

Easy Access System Europe

Mustamäe tee 50

10621 Tallinn

Estonia

gpsr.requests@easproject.com